A SONG FOR NAGASAKI

Dr. Takashi Nagai

PAUL GLYNN

A Song for Nagasaki

The Story of Takashi Nagai
Scientist, Convert and Survivor
of the Atomic Bomb

Foreword by Shusaku Endo

IGNATIUS PRESS   SAN FRANCISCO

Original editions:

©1988 by Paul Glynn
All rights reserved

Published in 1988 by the Catholic Book Club of Australia
Marist Fathers Books, Hunters Hill, N.S.W., Australia

First published in the United States of America
in 1990 by William B. Eerdmans Publishing Company

Cover photograph: Marist Fathers
Hunters Hill, N.S.W., Australia

Cover calligraphy: Kaligraf, istockphoto.com

Cover design by Riz Boncan Marsella

Published in 2025 by Ignatius Press, San Francisco
All rights reserved
ISBN 978-1-62164-812-3
Library of Congress Control Number Pending
Printed in the United States of America ∞

*With gratitude to
Toni and Jack Josephs, Sydney,
and to the Nagai family,
Tony Glynn and the people of Tomigaoka, Japan*

CONTENTS

FOREWORD

by Shusaku Endo

The suburb of Urakami became famous when the Nagasaki A-bomb burst above it. Long before that, it had held a place of extraordinary importance in the hearts of Japanese Christians. During the long centuries when an all-powerful Japanese government had totally proscribed the Christian religion, it was the farming community of Urakami that had faithfully preserved and lived the Christian faith.

In the early 1860s the central government learned of these secret Christians and had them arrested and jailed. News of this persecution reached America and the ears of President Ulysses Grant, who was at that time involved in discussions with a group of Japanese government diplomats. They had crossed the ocean to renegotiate a treaty between the two countries. The president's remarks that any nation that did not recognize freedom of religion could not be considered "enlightened" resulted in the Japanese government freeing the imprisoned Christian farmers. They celebrated this religious freedom by erecting with their own hands the magnificent cathedral of Urakami.

On that sad day when the American A-bomb exploded over Urakami, the cathedral was reduced to rubble and a great many Christian descendents of those who built it were killed. The dean of radiology at Nagasaki University, Dr. Takashi Nagai, found himself in the middle of this nuclear catastrophe. Even though he knew his involvement meant exposure to deadly radiation, Nagai threw himself and his medical skills into the

9

service of the victims in the stricken city. He fell ill with radiation disease and spent the short remainder of his life bedridden.

Nagai began to write. One of his books, *The Bells of Nagasaki*, evoked an extraordinarily deep response in the hearts of the Japanese people. This was at a time when most Japanese still regarded Christianity as something alien and shied away from anything concerning the Christian religion. *The Bells of Nagasaki* became a unique exception to this. It became a national best seller, despite its explicit Christian flavor. The Japanese people rediscovered in this book something that had long lain buried under war—love!

The citizens of Nagasaki came to venerate the bedridden doctor as a saint. Their veneration of the man continues to this day, long after his death. Paul Glynn has fittingly commemorated that legacy in this book. Christian and non-Christian alike were deeply moved by Nagai's faith in Christ that made him like Job of the Scriptures: in the midst of the nuclear wilderness he kept his heart in tranquillity and peace, neither bearing resentment against any man nor cursing God.

Southern section of Nagasaki University Hospital after the A-bomb explosion.

I

Calmness, the Number One Son

Takashi Nagai saw the light of day in ancient and unspoiled Shimane Prefecture. It is northeast by north of Hiroshima, and its long coastline is washed by the Sea of Japan. The winds that howl down across Siberia in the northwest fill its mountain valleys with snowdrifts in winter. Consult a map and you will see how natural a landing place it was for the ancient Chinese and Korean settlers who responded to the adventure and idealism of the call, "Go east, young man, go east." The newcomers were struck by the mountainous nature of the sparsely populated land and especially by its green beauty that gushes up like fountains from rich volcanic soil. Geologists surmise that sixty million years ago Japan lay like an improbable embryo on the bottom of the sea off the Asian mainland. When the tectonic plates beneath the Pacific Ocean and the East Asian mainland moved ponderously into each other, the seabed buckled and the islands of Japan emerged dripping from their dark womb.

Old geography books described Japan as being part of the "Ring of Fire"—the earthquake-volcano arc that stretches up the west coast of South America, through Mexico and California, across the Pacific through Hawaii and Japan, and south through Indonesia to New Zealand. After Japan emerged from the sea, volcanoes erupted everywhere and poured out masses of lava that cooled to basalt rock. The ice ages brought glaciers that moved slowly down mountains, crushing this basalt and gouging out new valleys. Wind, storm and especially the cyclones spawned in the tropics continued the slow process of creating Japan's fertile soil and rich valleys.

Historians pick up traces of human habitation in Japan from Neolithic times. About the time Caesar invaded Britain, the time when Christ's grandparents were born, there was a cultural leap forward in Japan culminating some centuries later in a single clan establishing effective authority and founding a capital in the south of what is now Nara Prefecture.

Long before writing came, the people had created a rich Shinto mythology. Shimane's Izumo Taisha shrine and its environs were the locale for many of the semidivine deeds of the heroes and heroines worshipped in Shinto. The stories are still favorites with little Japanese children. There is, for instance, the horrible eight-headed monster that terrorized this whole area until a valiant god engaged it in a furious battle and slew it. Shimane was venerated as holy ground by Nagai in his primary school: it was the birthplace of the *Nihon-teki* (purely Japanese) spirit.

Nagai's birthplace is south of the city of Izumo in Shimane Prefecture and about ten minutes' drive from the town of Mitoya. Completely hidden away between low mountains, it is a hamlet of a dozen houses, some of which are thatched with miscanthus reed. Such thatched houses were seen everywhere in the Japanese countryside thirty years ago and are examples of folk art at its best. The thick thatch makes houses cooler in summer and warmer in winter and blends in beautifully with the rice fields. But the days of leisurely folk crafts are gone, and the expense of renewing thatch has spelled the end of most thatched roofs. Saburo Yasuda, who is Takashi Nagai's cousin, has kept the house exactly as it was when Nagai spent his boyhood here.

Nagai's parents and grandparents are buried close by the home. Their Shinto tombstones, unlike the finely cut granite you see in Japan's predominantly Buddhist graveyards, are natural uncut stone. Nature is sacred to Shinto, and so everything is kept as natural as possible. Grandfather and father now lie peacefully side by side, but what explosive episodes lace the family annals! Grandfather Fumitaka Nagai, of samurai stock, was master of a profession of long-standing in Japan and China, *kampo yaku*, or Chinese herb medicine. He was accorded the title of doctor, practicing in a country place called Tai, which means "the well in the rice fields". The shrewd farmers came to look on the doctor's herbs and natural methods as wellsprings of healing, and Dr. Nagai prospered.

Grandfather Fumitaka's "Number One Son" (firstborn son) was Noboru, a name that means "calmness". He was anything but! His father tried him out in six different schools, but he was expelled from all of them for wild behavior. In desperation and at considerable expense, Dr. Nagai hired a private teacher. His son had succeeded in demoralizing teachers in six schools when they had headmasters, deputies and rigid systems as support. Now he was pitted against a single teacher, and with zest he set his not inconsequential talents to the task. The teacher soon lost heart and showed a clean pair of heels. Fumitaka, which means "elegant nobility", was a man of classical Eastern patience. Not losing his calm, he quietly accepted the strange situation, arranged for Number One Son Noboru to go to work on a farm and prayed for better fortune.

Was it the sheer daily grind, working alternately on paddy terraces and between the cedar and cypress rows up the steep mountainside, that tamed the hyperactive rebelliousness? As Noboru toiled alone in unaccustomed silence, he began to notice the dawn and evening skies, the good soil, the reliability of the mountains. He found contentment in sudden storms that drenched him and in one hundred other surprises of life in the open. His cynicism slowly diminished like snowdrifts before early spring breezes. A resolve gradually took deep root until, in his twentieth year, he packed his meager belongings and disappeared. Like the Bible's prodigal son, the Japanese youth had his father very much in mind when he set out. As the eldest son, he had an obligation to his father's name, house and profession. He now burned with shame and was determined to set things right.

He traveled far until he found a doctor practicing the new Western medicine and was employed as a general helper. He was at the doctor's beck and call all day, standing beside him as he treated patients or operated, mixing his prescriptions, meeting new patients, running messages. At night he would pore over the medical books the kindly doctor loaned him. There had never been anything wrong with his intelligence, and hard farm work in all weathers on nourishing country fare had given him a tough and robust body. He needed it now as he set out at a furious pace trying to make up for lost time. It helped him to remember samurai talk he had heard from his father. A true samurai was resourceful, calm and as steadfast as a mountain cedar.

Young Noboru consistently studied into the small hours and tied a rope from the rafters with the noose under his chin. If he nodded off, he woke with a jerk! The doctor gave his helper with the tight farmer's hands every opportunity to study books about medicine and assist with patients. Those rough hands gradually softened and became adept at copying medical diagrams and feeling stomachs for abnormalities. The boy who hated study became a man who could not read enough. He came to relish the prospect of pitting his hands and mind against our ancient enemies, sickness and death.

Finally, aged twenty-five, he felt ready to sit for the examinations set by the Ministry of Health in the Meiji government, and he passed with flying colors. The year was 1904. The parchment medical diploma was his passport to return to his father's house. The father was true to his name, Elegant Nobility, and welcomed his son back in. He had never despaired of Noboru, and each morning at sunrise he had gone into his garden and bowed to the East. After thanking the sun and all the gods for his blessings, he begged them to help Noboru become responsible. Each night he asked them to bring him home someday.

Filial piety has been a cornerstone of life in the Far East since the days of Confucius, five hundred years before Christ. In tradition-conscious Shimane, it was the paramount virtue. Now the father's cup was almost full. For three proud years he watched his son regain a reputation working hard and effectively in the local hospital. It was time to find Noboru a wife.

Some hold mistaken notions about Japan's arranged marriages. A go-between, asked to find a spouse for someone, uses common sense to discover a person who will make a suitable match from the point of view of family background, education, interests, age and personality. A meeting, the *miai*, is arranged between the couple. If both express the wish to meet again, they do, and eventually they decide whether to marry or not. Modern Japanese statistics show that such arranged marriages have a lower divorce rate than *renai*, or "love", marriages, where the couples arrange everything themselves.

The go-between who introduced Dr. Noboru to the eligible Tsune, meaning "constant", knew what he was about. Tsune came from an old samurai family, and her spirited temperament matched that of the self-made and dynamic Dr. Noboru. A robber once broke into her home and crept into the room where Tsune, still an unmarried teenager, slept alone. He clamped a hand over her mouth, waved a knife and told her what would happen if she screamed out. She nodded, and her composure reassured him. He told her to lead him to money. She stood up, bowed and said: "Yes, but first I just must go to the bathroom." Another bow, and she slipped out. Momentarily confused, he was after her in a flash, knife held close, whispering threats. She darted into the bathroom and shot home the wooden bolt. This was not the scenario he planned! She reemerged, bowed, slipped silently back to her room and led him to a box of money. She quickly counted it, said yes, that was all she had and handed it to him with a bow. The next day the police picked him up. Her description narrowed their field of suspects, and all they had to do was to find money with lipstick smeared on it. In the bathroom, she had rubbed this newfangled cosmetic from her lips onto her fingers.

The aging herbalist was a fervent believer and an officeholder in Taisha Shinto and felt great joy when his doctor-son and Tsune exchanged sake cups, "three times three", in solemn Shinto ritual before a *kannushi*, or Shinto priest, and the *Yaoyorozu*, the eight hundred million gods of Shinto. Shinto believers regard their gods in a way similar to how Christians view the saints in heaven.

In the following year, the young doctor was on a sick call when labor pains gripped Tsune. The spasms came to their climax, and suddenly the situation was critical. The baby's head would not come out, and the face of the expectant mother was bright with greasy sweat. Finally the attendant doctor said: "I'll have to crush the baby's head." The pain and anxiety made her voice dry and thin, but there was no mistaking her determination. "No. Don't kill my baby."

Some hours later Tsune's husband returned, and a red-faced bawling son greeted him. The first thing the doctor noticed was how big the head was. That large head, which was almost crushed, was later to occasion many a laugh in hatter's shops. The old herbalist grandfather was deeply touched when the young parents took one of the ideographs from his own name to call the boy Takashi, meaning "nobility". His cup was full when he joined the young couple in the thanksgiving ceremony at the Shinto shrine.

A man deeply imbued with Confucian filial piety, he saw himself not so much as an individual but as the recipient of the trust and hopes of countless ancestors whose courage and sacrifice had given him life and a name. He had suffered deeply when his own Number One Son Noboru had seemed insensitive to that trust. Now all was rectified. He died soon after the baby's thanksgiving ceremony, aged only sixty-one but a contented man. The year was 1910.

Noboru was grief-stricken at the sudden death of a father who had suffered so much on his account. The young doctor arranged the traditional obsequies he knew his father loved. The Shinto *kannushi* wore white linen kimonos, and their tall jet-black headgear was identical with that worn in the Emperor's court of the sixth century A.D. The plaintive notes of the ancient woodwinds spoke to Noboru's numb heart. Their melodies, he thought, were surely captured from the snow crane and the wild geese of the untamed moors and marshlands of those primitive times when Japan was still called Yamato.

2

Fireflies, Snow and a Lioness

About 1550, Europeans came to Japan, and brisk trade developed. Early in the 1600s, the Tokugawa shoguns enforced the famous Decree of Expulsion declaring Japan off-limits to Europeans. Henceforth any Europeans found in Japan would be executed, as would any Japanese who went to the West and returned home. Japan was closed to the West lest Europeans, with superior military weapons, turn Japan into a colony like India, the Philippines or Mexico.

In the Opium War of 1839–1842, the Japanese peered cautiously through their heavy shutters and were staggered to see how easily huge China was defeated by European firepower. Westerners flooded into China, the once-forbidden empire, and helped themselves to unequal trading concessions. In 1853 Commodore Perry of the U.S. Navy arrived in Japanese waters with a fearsome-looking squadron, demanding similar concessions. A cowed shogun accepted an unwelcome treaty that was signed in a small village called Yokohama. After initial resistance to Western modernization, Japan threw herself into studying and mastering every field of Western superiority, determined not to end up like China. Industrial cities sprang up, trains and steamships hastened travel and trade, compulsory universal schooling was established, and universities were founded to propel Japan into the scientific age. The samurai class lost the right to carry swords, but conscription came in and many samurai became the generals and admirals of the new army

and navy, while others became leading politicians, industrialists and business tycoons.

By 1894, just forty-one years after capitulating to Commodore Perry, Japan was ready to join in the Western game of colony grabbing. She fought and defeated China for hapless Korea.
Ten years after that, having "arrived" as a modern power by
signing an equal alliance treaty with Britain, Japan took on Russia and stunned the West by virtually destroying the czar's navy
and dictating peace terms. The Japanese people were euphoric
and gave themselves single-mindedly to the task the Meiji government set them—to bring Japan up to the standards of the
enlightened, scientific West.

Dr. Noboru Nagai and his wife Tsune, with little thought
of personal remuneration, answered the national call and labored
might and main to bring Western medicine into the valleys
around Mitoya. It was less than ten years after Japan defeated
Russia. After Number One Son Takashi was born, four children followed in as many years. The pioneer country practice did not bring in much money. Japan's peasants were mostly
tenant farmers who received precious little from the land-
owners. The Nagais did not press for payment if a patient
was impoverished.

The doctor's life was particularly hard during Shimane's gru-
eling winters, when snowdrifts piled high against the house.
On nights like this, when a sick call came, Tsune would help
her husband into his thickest clothing and sit him on the porch
step while she wound straw rope around his Wellington boots.
She would bow him off and then busy herself somewhat distractedly until he was in sight of home on the way back. When his
"Hoo-waah" came floating down on the crisp night air, she
would rush out with a lantern and trudge through the snow
to greet him and take his bag. Inside, she brushed him clean
of snow and sat him on the step, untied the straw rope and
pulled off the boots. When he had emerged from the piping

hot *o-furo*, the Japanese deep bath, she led him to the kitchen and poured him hot sake with egg broken into it.

Tsune was a quick learner and became her husband's ablest assistant. From an early age, eldest son Takashi was impressed by seeing his mother and father poring happily together over medical books. He remembers his father teaching her anatomy from sketches in a German medical book. The sight of his parents happily engrossed in books convinced young Takashi that study was as natural and pleasurable as eating. Later, writing as a research scholar in Nagasaki Medical University, he paid tribute to the "thatched-roof university" of his childhood.

Takashi's mother and father taught their small children spartan axioms of the samurai. There was, for instance, the famous Kei Setsu Ko. This sentence consists of just three ideographs, "firefly", "snow" and "success", and is an example of the one-line poems that Chinese and Japanese love. The image evoked is of an impoverished scholar in a hut with no money to fuel a lantern or buy a candle. His passion for study is so intense that each night he heaps snow by his desk and fills his room with netted fireflies. Their tiny glow and the moonlight reflected from the snow enable him to read his texts. Material poverty must never stop you. Another axiom that Takashi learned from his parents goes: A lioness rears the cubs that climb back up the bank. According to the Chinese ancients, a lioness has fierce pride, and after giving birth to cubs, she sends them tumbling down a steep bank. She will rear only the ones with the courage to struggle back up.

As an adult, Takashi said he never remembers his mother making him study. She allowed a love of learning to develop naturally in him. In some matters, however, she refused to wait for natural development. She enjoyed her children's banter and was tolerant of harmless horseplay and nonsense. But should any of them become cheeky to their elders, then beware! Small Takashi talked back to her one winter day. She snatched him up in a flash, whipped off all his clothing and hauled the startled, shivering handful of threshing limbs to the veranda door. She threw the door open and hurled him out into six feet of snow. The lioness had no intention of rearing an inferior cub!

An ancient saying known and loved by every Japanese goes: Send the child you love away on a journey. Immaturity will be the price of parental overattachment. Takashi was sent off to the city of Matsue to do the entrance exams for a very good secondary school. He passed and said good-bye to the simple happiness of the thatched home above the charming valley with its limpid mountain stream. It was 1920, and he was twelve years old.

Takashi went to board with relatives in Matsue. His mind marveled at the whole new world coming to life in one of Japan's emerging modern cities. Close by the Matsue castle moat was a home where a famous Westerner had lived until recently. Takashi had never met a Westerner, and this Lafcadio Hearn was especially remarkable, Matsue relatives told him, because he was a foreigner who understood Japan. Hearn had mastered the Japanese ideographs, read the classics and spent his considerable literary talents explaining Japan to the West. The little country lad was moved by this story of a cross-cultural life and one day he would do something similar. He had bouts of homesickness, of course, but did not allow himself time to brood about it as he set off to catch up with the academically more advanced city boys.

Takashi's father, the once hyperactive Calmness, had given his classmates many a laugh in his brief stay at six schools in Matsue. Takashi caused his classmates mirth during physical education classes. His big country body just wasn't coordinated. He would charge up to the vaulting horse only to crash headlong into it. He would grab the parallel bars, fierce determination written all over his face, and grunt and grimace but never succeed in getting up to the preliminary position. He tried his hand on the baseball diamond but was a disaster at every position. They called him "Daikon", after the thick and ungainly Japanese radish.

Nagai was swept off his feet by the new Western thinking and science that had swept all before them in Matsue High School. The late 1800s and early 1900s were an era when atheism was all the rage among Japanese schoolteachers because it was part of the exciting scientific philosophy coming from the West. The great Darwin had proved that nature explained itself. The hard-nosed atheist Thomas Huxley, the man who gave dictionaries the word "agnostic", had put all religions on the scrap heap of history as far as Nagai's science teachers were concerned. Most Japanese have an inbred courtesy that dissuades them from ridiculing someone else's religion even if they themselves have none. Young Nagai's teachers did not mock Shinto but would make asides about Shinto's sacred stories—about the god who slew the eight-headed monster, for instance. The teachers said that maybe that story originated when an inventive member of the imperial family devised a system of dikes that tamed the eight tributaries of Shimane's Hii River so that it no longer devastated the crops in flood time. They suggested that religious beliefs, appropriate and helpful though they were to past generations, would become totally unnecessary as the sure light of science illuminated every area of man's existence. By the time he had graduated from high school, Nagai was a convinced atheist. Science, the one road that led to rock-hard reality, was the road of the future. He would go to a medical university, absorb all it had to teach him and return to work with his father and mother in their country practice. Together they would make it a medical showpiece!

It was not only science that excited his expanding mind. He was moved by the rich, vague and sometimes heartrending music of German romanticists like Franz Schubert. Then he read *Kokoro, True Heart*, by Japan's most famous novelist of the era, romanticist Soseki Natsume. That book's noble despair set him thinking about the contradictions emerging with the new scientific age. *Kokoro* was a brilliantly evocative book, highlighting human alienation in post-Meiji Japan. The hero contemplates suicide, and author Soseki was soon to do the same. Nagai was disturbed by this first contact with modern angst, but he pushed his uneasiness aside and threw himself into preparation for the highly competitive university entrance exams.

With his examination marks, Nagai could have entered either of the famous Tokyo or Kyoto imperial universities, but he chose the far-less-prestigious Nagasaki University. Had Nagai's parents some intimation of what awaited him in Nagasaki, they would have striven might and main to stop him! But they felt only gratitude as they joined hands before the ancestral gods and sent him off to the warmer south to study medicine.

3

Kublai Khan, Tsune and Pascal

Nagai felt good in the severe black university uniform with brass buttons, looking like a German university student. Meiji Japan, when it planned its great leap forward in the 1870s, selected whatever seemed best in the Western nations. For its navy, it chose the British model; for education, that of Prussia. Japanese have much in common with Germans—painstaking, methodical and orderly ways, for instance. Because the precision and thoroughness of German medical practice appealed to the Japanese, young Nagai would be studying medical books written in German and following German medical techniques.

Nagasaki Medical University was a cluster of white reinforced concrete buildings. Situated at the foot of 1200-foot-high Mount Konpira, it was part of the spreading northern suburbs. To the southwest lay sparkling Nagasaki Bay, and beyond that, rising 1,089 feet like the counterpoise of Mount Konpira, was the green grandeur of Mount Inasa. A third of a mile north of the university stood the big red-brick cathedral, large enough to accommodate five thousand worshippers. Both its massiveness and its penetrating bells that chimed the Angelus three times a day surprised and irritated him. Japan was moving into the age of enlightenment and relinquishing religious superstition. It was bad enough for modern Japanese to believe the inadequate gods of Shinto, but to submit one's intelligence to foreign gods was just too crass, and it angered him. Little did he suspect what part the Urakami Cathedral would one day play in his life. A quarter of a mile south of the university class-rooms was the reinforced concrete university hospital. He went over and walked through to the third floor, where he looked down on the suburbs of Matsuyama and Urakami, marveling at the quiet beauty of a sea of roof tiles all the same subdued gray.

Japanese schools and universities begin classes in April, which is spring, and Nagai was delighted by the color and variety of flowers that greeted springtime in semitropical Nagasaki. A professor showed Nagai's class a corpse in one of the very first lectures and said: "Gentlemen, this is man, the object of our studies. A body with physical properties. Things you can see, weigh, test, measure. And this is all man is." Nagai found noth-ing odd in this denial of the spiritual.

It would be wrong to say he did not believe in anything. He passionately believed in science, sure that science held the key to every door that barred human progress. That faith spurred him on to study with the dedication his father showed thirty years earlier. Nagai believed also in "humanity". Science had dispelled the mists of the long Dark Ages, and the human race was at last coming into its own. *Banzai* for the tremendous future of the human race!

Finally, he believed in Japan. His burgeoning knowledge of the Japanese classics gave him a glimpse of the length and depth of Japanese history and culture. He read with delight and a growing awe the *Manyoshu*—a collection of roughly 4,500 poems, most of them written in the last half of the seventh and the first half of the eighth century A.D. By any nation's standards, the *Manyoshu* is an extraordinary literary masterpiece. The poems are fresh, lyrical and *Nihon-teki*, that is, thoroughly Japanese.[1] Enhancing and even making this book unique is the lowly

---

[1] Japanese call their country Nihon or Nippon.

station of many of the *Manyoshu* contributors. Alongside emperors, empresses, aristocrats and court samurai are a great many lowborn folk, poorly schooled border guards, peasants, wandering minstrels and unpretentious town dwellers. That the nation's first major work of literature was poetry spoke volumes to Nagai about the essence of the Japanese temperament.

The young student Nagai was coming to regard the *Manyoshu* as a kind of holy writ. The *Manyoshu* and several other forms of traditional Japanese poetry exercised so powerful an influence throughout his whole life and appear so often in his writing that a few samples might help a non-Japanese reader.

Most *Manyoshu* poems are highly emotional. Take, for example, the poem of seventh-century Prince Ikusa, forced to undertake a long journey without his wife: "In my grief I have become like a thrush that calls sadly through the night. My poor heart aches. . . . I trudge along all day and have only grass to pillow my head at night. To think that I used to regard myself as bold! Now I stagger about, faint from a heart that burns with longing, burns like those salt fires of the fisher girls on the shores of Ami. . . . Night after night I pine for my beloved, who sits alone by our hearth." A *Manyoshu* warrior expresses soldierly loyalty: "Whether we perish as bloated corpses in the sea, or fall and rot in grass on the mountainside, if we die for you, O Emperor, we die without regret." Many *Manyoshu* poems show a refined love of nature: "On the sea of heaven the cloud-waves stir and the moon, like a boat, sails through the forest of stars." One of the most frequent *Manyoshu* themes is romantic love: "I will hazard a double-edged sword and die content if it be for your sake", writes a samurai to his lady. Sometimes there is wry humor: "As if to say, 'Good, go ahead and die of love!' that cruel girl passes right by the gate of my house." Japanese poetry does not rhyme. The poetic form is a fixed number of syllables, an austere form capable of carrying rich emotions.

This poetry also values simplicity, even severity, in structure. Celebrated Japanologist Edwin Reischauer speaks of the "excessively brief form" of Japanese poetry exemplified, for instance, in the seventeen-syllable haiku of the later poet Basho, 1644–1694, "who can conjure up a whole scene with all its emotional overtones in a simple phrase." A well-known example of a Basho haiku is the following, transcribed into Roman letters with the prescribed 5 plus 7 plus 5 syllable count:

> Shizukesa ya
> I-wa ni Shimiiru
> Semi no koe

Utter stillness ... until, piercing the very rocks, the shrilling of cicadas.

Not long after entering Nagasaki Medical University, Nagai joined a poetry group founded by a well-known poet, Professor Mokichi Saito of the medical faculty. It is not uncommon in Japan for a scientist, politician, admiral or seamstress to be also an accomplished poet.

Nagai entered Nagasaki University in April 1928. That was one year after the big bank crisis in Japan sent shock waves across the land, reaching even the peaceful valley of his parents. By 1929 the whole world was sliding into the Depression. Japanese industry had been expanding vigorously, but within a few fateful years the West levied huge tariffs, even as much as 50 percent, on Japanese exports, threatening to topple her export-dependent economy. The fall in silk prices hit farmers very hard. More and more of his rural patients would bow low and ask Dr. Nagai or his wife to wait a little longer for their payments. The doctor made ends meet by taking on work in a hospital some distance away. Mealtimes and bedtime became irregular, and for the first time in their married lives the Nagais began to find their medical calling a strain.

Dr. Noboru Nagai and his wife refused to allow the worsening Depression to intrude into the life of their son at Nagasaki Medical University. His allowance was not princely, but they sent it each month, telling him to worry only about his studies and encouraging his deepening interest in Japanese poetry. This latter led him more and more into a study of the history and culture of Japan and a deepening of his pride in his race. Intense patriotism is one of the dominant factors in the history of Japan, past and present, and is the cement of that much-discussed Japanese homogeneity and famous Japanese group dynamic. Nagai was no exception, and the following incident highlights his own growing love of Japanese traditions.

He utilized part of one vacation to explore the port of Hakata, which lies beside the city of Fukuoka. He had read much about the thirteenth-century siege of Hakata and wanted to see the seven-hundred-year-old ruins and walk over the ground made sacred by the do-or-die battles against the vaunted warriors of Kublai Khan. This Mongol emperor, grandson of Genghis Khan, set up the Yuan dynasty in Beijing in the year 1264. The Mongols had, since grandfather Genghis' time, swept all before them—central Asia, southern Russia and much of the Near East. The famous Mongolian cavalry had carved up every army set against them in Silesia and Hungary and as far as the Adriatic Sea. Genghis Khan was regarded as one of the greatest generals of all time, and his grandson Kublai was also a mighty conqueror. Thinking the Japanese would be intimidated by his reputation, Kublai Khan sent envoys to them demanding they recognize his suzerainty.

The Japanese gave his delegation short shrift. Enraged by this insult, he assembled a formidable invasion force in Korea, requisitioning Chinese and Korean ships to cross the narrow straits to Hakata Bay, 125 miles east. The Mongols soon captured the offshore Japanese islands and landed at Hakata.

However, the weather turned foul and a cyclone threatened. The Mongol general, fearing the destruction of his fleet in the exposed bay, decided to head back to Korea and return when the weather was good. The Japanese had fought tenaciously, but now the Mongols knew the lay of the harbor and land and were confident of crushing the small samurai force the next time.

Japan prepared for the next onslaught feverishly. The military dictatorship in Kamakura, the imperial court in Kyoto, Shinto shrines and Buddhist temples combined in a national campaign of prayer. One message was preached up and down the land: Japan is a gift to the Emperor and his people from the gods. It must be held as a sacred trust, and to die defending it against heathen Mongol hordes is the highest honor to which anyone could aspire. A ten-foot-high wall was built around Hakata Bay in the hope of stopping the dreaded Mongol cavalry.

In June of 1281 the Mongols embarked 150,000 troops on Chinese and Korean ships in what was then the greatest seaborne invasion in history. As soon as the enemy fleet appeared on June 23, small Japanese craft flew at the lumbering junks and harried them like angry wasps. The Mongols, however, quickly took the offshore islands and slaughtered all the men. They systematically raped the women and, piercing their wrists and passing rope through them, hung them alive from the prows of the ships. That spelled out only too clearly the fate awaiting wives and daughters of the grim samurai waiting on the beaches and sand dunes of Hakata Bay. The Mongols landed, and the samurai flung themselves at the great horde with no thought but of holding them. Hold them they did, from June 23 until August 14. With the aid of the ten-mile-long stone wall the Japanese contained the Mongols and their awesome cavalry. Opposing lines of roaring warriors surged this way and that, but the Japanese did not break. But how much longer could raw valor stop the superior equipment and technique of the Mongols?

On the night of August 14, signs appeared in the southwestern sky that lifted Japanese hearts. The next day, August 15, a typhoon struck Hakata Bay, bringing a hoarse cheer from every samurai throat as ponderous Mongol boats were smashed together or piled up like matchwood on the northern peninsula. The violent winds howled for two days before their fury was spent. The clear and tranquil sunrise of August 17 revealed a sight for sore Japanese eyes. The bay that had been dark with Mongol ships was clear again. The enemy fleet lay below its surface or scattered over the horizon in tatters. Japanese leaders told their jubilant people: That typhoon was no ordinary wind. It was *kamikaze*, divine wind. The event became enshrined in Japanese folklore and gave birth to the belief that Japan would never be subjugated. Young Nagai walked reverently beside remnants of the ten-foot-wall. Though he was a scientific materialist, he believed in *Yamato-damashii*, "the spirit of Japan".

Nagai returned to the peaceful classrooms and laboratories of his university, brimful of confidence in Japan's future and his own. He was doing well in his studies and was a member of the university basketball team. At last he had found a game he could play! He was big for a Japanese, five feet seven inches tall and 157 pounds. He played forward and the cheerleading squad gave him a flattering nickname, "University Wall". His team won the western Japan championship and came in third in the national titles that year. He was popular with the young nurses, and he liked that. He had little interest in politics and was not concerned by the rising star of the militarists. He was not unknown in the bars down by the docks—bars equipped with women of easy virtue—where he sometimes drank large quantities of sake with fellow students, gaining some fame for being able to hold more sake than anyone else in his class.

Walking through the university hospital, he breathed the carbolic-tinged[2] air like a sea captain savoring the tang of the ocean. Yes, he felt like a captain in training. He had finished two years' study, and in just two more years he would be Dr. Nagai, carrying a stethoscope through these corridors, bowed to by nurses and patients. He would have people's lives in his hands: his decisions, his expertise, would actually save their lives! Life expectancy in Japan was still far below that of Western countries. Japanese doctors were now changing that, and soon he would be one of them. He went to the tuberculosis wing to return a book about tuberculosis, a disease widespread in Japan. His classmates used to tease him about the number of books he read, but he tried to read everything he could.

Classes had not been going long when a disturbing telegram came from his father. It stated bluntly, "Come home." He packed hurriedly and uneasily, tossing in the inevitable books. As he sat in the northbound train staring out the window, he thought apprehensively about his mother. During the recent holidays, he had noticed a certain slowing down and had tried to draw more information out of her. She laughed and teased him about searching for a patient to practice on and changed the subject. He grew apprehensive at the thought of anything being the matter with this woman who was so important in his life.

His father met him at the *genkan*, the porch of their home. Takashi was stunned to learn his mother had suffered a stroke and could not speak. She was conscious but very low. She recognized her Number One Son, and her eyes followed him pathetically as he moved to her side. She lay on a futon, or quilt, on tatami, the thick straw matting that completely covers most floors of Japanese homes. He sat shoeless beside her and took her hand. She could say nothing, but he read clear

[2] Carbolic acid, or phenol, is used as a disinfectant.

reflections of her emotions in the dark almond-shaped eyes that gazed into his. To him it seemed that she had held off the final ravages of cerebral hemorrhage until she could say goodbye to him. She died minutes later. The experience was to change his life, and later he wrote: "I rushed to her bedside. She was still breathing. She looked fixedly at me, and that's how the end came. My mother in that last penetrating gaze knocked down the ideological framework I had constructed. This woman who had brought me into the world and reared me, this woman who had never once let up in her love for me . . . in the very last moments of her life spoke clearly to me! Her eyes spoke to mine, and with finality, saying: "Your mother now takes leave in death, but her living spirit will be beside her little one, Takashi." I who was so sure that there was no such thing as a spirit was now told otherwise; and I could not but believe! My mother's eyes told me that the human spirit lives on after death. All this was by way of an intuition, an intuition carrying conviction." *Chokkan*, or "intuition", is an important word in the Japanese vocabulary. It is made up of two ideographs: *choku*, meaning "immediate" or "direct", and *kan*, meaning "feelings"—hence, something that comes directly to the feelings. Far Easterners regard this knowledge very highly.

Since his last year at high school, the physical sciences offered Nagai what seemed the only reliable roads to truth. He was bewildered by this nonscientific "intuition" that his mother's spirit continued to live. Was this an authentic, undeniable experience of what Zen people called *satori*, or enlightenment, that comes like "the flash of a sword cutting through the problems of existence"? Or was his powerful intuition merely a trick of the unconscious, triggered by emotional wishful thinking? He was not sure, but the experience set him rethinking the long tradition of "wisdom" thinkers that were part of the history of Japan and China. Their insistence on the superiority of man's heart over his intellect was ensconced, he noted, in many age-old ideographs that he read daily. The ideograph for "wisdom", for instance, was a composite of two ideographs, one being "intelligence" and the other containing "heart". The ideograph for "knowledge", however, was a composite of "intelligence" and "weaving loom". Did that say that clever people can weave intellectual arguments with mere quick wit, while wise people are in touch with the deeper dimension of the heart? Again, there were two ideographs for "hear". One meant hearing sounds and contained the ideograph for "ear". The other was for hearing meanings beneath sounds and combined the ideographs for "ear" and "heart". Nagai was wondering if his own hearing and understanding lacked "heart".

During a high school class on literature, Nagai had been struck by a sentence in Blaise Pascal's *Pensées*. The seventeenth-century Frenchman wrote: "Man is a thinking reed." The sentence had a Japanese ring to it; it was like something a Buddhist priest might say. The teacher had elaborated on Pascal's literary style as the exemplar of modern French prose, concluding that Pascal was that fascinating type, a poet-scientist. Something stirred in Nagai when he heard that. During his medical studies at Nagasaki University, he came across Pascal again as the inventor of the syringe. Looking him up in an encyclopedia, he discovered that Pascal also invented the barometer and was regarded as one of the leading minds of the seventeenth century and something of a mystic. Because *Pensées* was highlighted in the article, Nagai went out and bought a copy, little realizing the influence the book and its author would come to exercise on him. It was one of the books he slipped into his bag when he set out in response to that blunt telegram from his father.

After his mother was buried, a devastated Nagai left for Nagasaki, choosing to travel part of the way by boat to give himself more time to come to terms with her death. The mood of nature seemed in sympathy with his loss—gray clouds scudded low over a dark and agitated sea. Alone on the deck of the southbound steamer, he took out his copy of the *Pensées* and began to read. This was the first milestone on a new journey.

Pilgrim-poet Basho (1663–1740), the "saint of haiku".

4

The Mouse Who Could Not See the Stars

The *Pensées* contains very little about science. It is a kind of logbook of Pascal's journey in search of metaphysical realities. Much of it left Nagai quite bewildered—words like "grace", "paradise lost", "redemption". Unusual biblical quotations and a host of Western metaphors and historical allusions mystified him. But there were parts that touched something in Nagai's heart and suggested that Pascal might possess a tremendously important vision.

Pascal did not accord human reason the supreme authority given it at Nagasaki University. The Frenchman remorselessly ridiculed anyone who would rely on human reason alone. We dream at night and create a world of fantasies. How does reason know our present waking state is not full of similar illusions? Nagai knew that some of the great Eastern religious thinkers taught that the external "reality" around us is mere "illusion", viewing human philosophy as "a dream about a dream".

There are two false attitudes to reason, according to Pascal. One is overconfidence in reason, which often leads to barren scepticism. The other is resignation to stupidity coming from laziness or disinterest. Truth is reached by avoiding these two pitfalls. It requires hard work, but you are a "deserter" if you refuse to take on the search. Human reason does not reach the highest objective reality, continued the Frenchman, but only the inferior scientific truths. The higher truths, utterly more important than mere scientific facts, are of the order of wisdom and are received rather than grasped. Unlike the rational truths of science, the higher truths are seen "by the eyes of the heart". That expression was familiar to Nagai from Buddhism. Many images of Buddha show a jewel in his forehead, representing the eye of the heart, which sees beyond mere appearances. Pascal's insistence on an order higher than reason was echoed in Buddhism's Hanya, or Wisdom, sutra. "The heart has reasons of which reason knows nothing", added the Frenchman.

Nagai put the book down and listened to the forlorn cry of the gulls following the ship. He realized he was hungry, took out his *o-bento*—his lunch box—and began to eat deftly with chopsticks. Much in the *Pensées* unsettled him. Why? Because it was utterly alien to the Far Eastern way of thinking? Not a few Japanese said that of all Western philosophy and religion. He remembered the first time he sat down in a restaurant to a Western breakfast when traveling with his father. He felt terribly clumsy with a knife and fork and did not enjoy the meal. There was no bean paste soup or flakes of seaweed and above all no rice, absolutely essential to a Japanese breakfast, and it left him feeling unsatisfied. Yet now he was used to Western food and enjoyed a quick Western breakfast. Is it possible that maybe he had to persevere with Pascal a little longer?

He put his lunch box away and strolled along the deck. Pascal said reason was not the highest faculty, but he used reason to prove this. Was not that a vicious circle? Pascal wrote that unaided human reason can penetrate neither the mysteries of life nor those of God. God does, however, reveal the essential truths to the honest believer who prays. Pascal concluded: "Faith is a gift of God. . . . You must pray for it." Nagai leaned on the deck rail, looking vacantly at the horizon, wondering: How can I pray honestly if I am not sure God exists? Surely this is where the Frenchman's line of reasoning falls apart, for to pray is to stop reasoning and to believe in God's existence blindly. That is an abdication of both reason and intellectual responsibility!

Nagai took a new tack: If God existed, he would surely make his existence more obvious to us if he was as interested in us as Pascal claimed he was. Or was it childish to reason like that? Pascal claimed that "there is enough light for those who desire only to see and enough darkness for those of a contrary disposition" and that faith was based on personal experience of God in one's heart. Nagai compared this statement with the conviction he experienced that his mother's spirit survived her physical death. Was that a genuine experience, or did it merely arise from some primitive protective instinct against the despair that might overwhelm one at the death of a loved one?

He took up the *Pensées* again. Pascal drew attention to a contradiction within human history and within the consciousness of every person who thinks deeply. We possess both magnificence and wretchedness. "Our wretchedness is that of dispossessed kings." The sentence stirred Nagai with the possibility of a great universe of eternal meaning and beauty, of which Pascal wrote with a kind of familiarity. Nagai thought sadly of the old proverb: A mouse cannot see the stars, nor an earthworm the flowers. He wanted to believe in Pascal's flowers and stars, but another voice spoke up: The *Pensées* is the beautiful poetry of an extraordinarily compassionate man, distressed by all the pain and loneliness in the world—but as fictional as childhood fairy stories like the bamboo cutter and the moon princess.

His mind went back to comments a teacher had once made about Marx' expression "Religion is the opium of the people": "Lads, the Chinese opium poppy is beautiful, and so is much in the religions of the world. But religion can put you into a dreamworld as fatal as that of the opium poppy, making you believe a god or Buddha will intervene miraculously to save the situation. That is not only simplistic, but it anesthetizes our natural initiative and responsibility which should spur us on to find real solutions. Look at the plain lesson of history, Japanese or foreign. Science flourished only when religion's hold on society was broken. Jesus Christ was a magnificent dreamer, but his flowers of the field that neither labor nor spin turn out to be narcotic poppies. Do not be seduced by them; base your thinking and your lives on hard scientific fact."

Again Nagai returned to Pascal. "The Christian religion has always survived, yet it has always been under attack—Christ has been a sanctuary for some, a stumbling block for others." Yes, the Tokugawa shoguns saw Christianity as an alien thing that must be stamped out of Japan. Tens of thousands of Japanese Christians had been killed in the 1600s. The Tokugawa dictators, and of late the militarists, branded Japanese Christians as traitors to the *kokutai*, the unique national polity. Nagai's strong commitment to the *kokutai* intensified certain feelings of uneasiness he had while reading some uncompromising parts of *Pensées*. They seemed so un-Japanese, so foreign to his beloved Nihon.

Back in Nagasaki, Nagai threw himself into his medical studies, but the problems raised by his mother's death would not go away. Many social scientists, despite numerous signs of male domination in Japan, see the nation as a "mother society". The mother plays the dominant, if sometimes unobtrusive, role in Japanese life. Nagai now realized that it had been his gentle mother rather than his highly respected and authoritarian father who had most influenced him. He regretted that it was now too late to discuss his new spiritual problems with her.

University friends noticed a change in Nagai. Gone was his facile optimism and unquestioning acceptance of salvation through science, of utopia around the corner. He became more critical of his professors. Not long after his mother's death, one of them exuberantly explained human mental processes, including thoughts and emotions, in terms of electric currents passing through the brain. Nagai pressed him for specific details, but the professor was unable to supply them, admitting it was still a hypothesis. Nagai drew up a list of brilliant hypotheses he had read in medical books that were changed or abandoned in later editions. He longed to find what Pascal called "absolute truth". Was there any such thing, or was Pascal just whistling in the dark?

For his previous two years, he had been restricted to lectures, laboratory work, dissecting animals and, finally, dissecting corpses. Now, in his third year, he began accompanying doctor-professors around the hospital wards examining patients. He noticed how the cold manner of some doctors could hurt and even demoralize patients and realized his mother's death had made him more sensitive. He still played basketball, sometimes climbed a mountain and occasionally enjoyed drinking bouts with friends. He felt he now had a better understanding of what poets like the seventeenth-century Basho said—you do not have to travel to a far country to see great beauty; it is all around you. He was beginning to understand what Zen masters call the "suchness" in a bowl of cheap green tea, in a common garden-variety bloom, in the cry of a plover on a deserted beach. His heart was not at peace, however, and in a book he wrote fifteen years later, he summed up this period of his life:

"For five years I was deeply troubled by a little voice I heard, waking and sleeping: 'What is the meaning of our lives?' I read the life stories of all kinds of people in my quest for the meaning of mine, but the more I read, the more complex the question became. Of course it did; I was studying others' lives rather than my own. My life is not theirs. The life of each one of us is different, and its meaning is unique.

"You probably remember the fine lace that women used to make in their homes before factory machines made women's clothing cheap and uniform. They would make the most complicated-looking piece of lace from one unbroken thread. It all looked very mysterious to me, but to a good lace maker the pattern and the weaving were quite simple. Our lives are like lace, appearing unbelievably complicated and mixed up to others. It is essential to remember that your life has to make meaning only to you.

"I did not know that at this time and began feverishly reading philosophers. The more I read them, the more complex the whole question of life's meaning became. Of course, I realize now that some philosophers write for the gallery, for a reading public that is disappointed if things are too plain and simple! The honest seeker is only confused by these less-than-honest weavers of words. I doggedly tried to follow the demoralizing reasoning of a number of moderns who ended up by saying that life is incomprehensible. Yet the more I thought about it by myself, the more I began to see that birth and life and death can be and should be straightforward."

The bamboo cutter and the moon princess.

5

'Tis an Ill Wind

It was 1931, some months after his mother's death, and Takashi was pursuing his studies in the relative calm of Nagasaki Medical University. Some hundred miles to the northeast, his father was anything but calm. The wind from the north, the dark yin direction, howled down like a curse. It was a heartless wind, cruel like the wolves of its birthplace deep in frozen Siberia. Dr. Noboru Nagai had trudged slowly up the hill behind his house through swirling snow but did not notice the cold, so preoccupied was he with emotions of anger, hurt and indignation. He now stood motionless before the pile of snow that covered his wife Tsune's gravestone, his eyes closed in prayer.

The evening before, two unexpected visitors had come from Nagasaki. The bespectacled one turned out to be from Nagasaki Medical University, a professor of ear, nose and throat diseases. The other visitor, dressed in an opulent overcoat and wearing gloves of imported fur, was introduced by the professor as a director of the Nagasaki Chamber of Commerce and one of the city's big businessmen. "He has a charming daughter," the professor said, "and recently I took the liberty of inviting your son Takashi to their villa at the foot of Mount Unzen for two days. The family, and above all the young lady, were very impressed by your son. It seems the warm feelings are mutual, and I believe they would make a wonderful match. My friend is so taken with your son that in the happy event of them marrying, he would send him to Europe to specialize in any medical field he chooses. He would like to invite you, Dr. Nagai, to come and retire in Nagasaki to be near your son. One of the company's finest villas, right beside some magnificent fishing spots, would be presented to you—as a small sign of gratitude for the happiness the proposed union would bring."

Nagai's son Takashi continues the story: "I received a telegram from my father, '*Return immediately*', and set out on the eighteen-hour train journey with apprehension. My father had patients in his consulting room when I arrived, and he sent out an abrupt message telling me to wait. A nurse I didn't know brought me green tea and sweet bean pastries. She bowed and I returned her politeness, while inwardly I was thinking how cold and impersonal my home had become since Mother died."

Eventually the patients left and his father came in, opened his mouth several times without speaking, and blurted out: "How could you sell yourself?" The young man's consternation and bewilderment only increased.

"O-to-san [Dad] . . . I don't understand."

"Don't give me that—quit playing dumb. You think you're a smart, big university student. Did you think your father would agree? Agree? Why anyone who is even half a man would draw the line at exchanging himself for a pot of money!"

His son said in bewilderment: "O-to-sama [honorable Father], please explain what you mean."

"Explain?" the other thundered. "I recognize your right to marry whomever you choose. But to marry for money and as a *yoshi*!" (When a man marries as a *yoshi*, he changes his surname to his wife's. This usually happens when she has no brothers, so her family name would otherwise die out. The *yoshi* belongs to the wife's family rather than to his own.) "What? Me a *yoshi*?" asked the son. Like a vicious card player, his father threw the two visiting cards on the table. "Then explain these!"

"These two came here?" "Yes, with a marvelous story of you and a wealthy girl in love. All you have to do is become a *yoshi*, and your European studies are fixed up. I'm apparently over the hill, so they'll retire me to Nagasaki, where I can putter around fishing!"

Suddenly it all became clear. Takashi remembered the date very clearly when he accepted the professor's invitation to go with him to a friend's house. It was September 18, the day the Manchurian Incident started the warfare in China. Takashi wondered why he was invited to the villa, but he had no idea the visit was to be a *miai*, a meeting to see if a couple suit each other. Takashi categorically denied telling anyone he was the slightest bit interested in the girl.

He asked his father how he had replied to the visitors. "I said", replied the older man: "Begging your pardon for my saying so, but Noboru Nagai, even though he may not be wealthy, hasn't fallen so low that he would sell his son for a fishing villa."

Suddenly the son felt tears coursing down his cheeks. He impulsively seized his father's hand, a hand, he wrote later, that "had taken thousands of pulses but had never taken a bribe". Two hands tightened in a handshake, and the bond between their spirits was stronger than ever.

Takashi returned to Nagasaki, and completing his third year, set his sights on his final examinations at the end of the fourth year. They would be his passport to a life of medicine, and he dropped most of his extracurricular activities to focus his mind totally on them. However, the old bugbear questions of the purpose of life and the existence of God were still with him, and he began the new semester, in spring of 1931, by going off alone into the hills with a picnic lunch and his well-worn copy of the *Pensées*. He sat on a rock by a small stream that came rushing down from the mountains above. He opened the *Pensées* at the Wager.

Nagai shared a common Japanese liking of French culture and was a little flattered by the French appreciation of Japanese art, dress and architecture. He was attracted by Pascal's literary style and depth but was often put out by the Frenchman's smugness. Pascal's absolute claims for Catholicism paled before the realities of the Inquisition, the Galileo affair and the massacre of the South American Indians. Nagai was angered by the last line of the Wager: "Only Christianity makes men both happy and lovable; the code of the gentleman does not allow you to be both happy and lovable." His mother and father, just to name two who came to mind immediately, gave the lie to that. Yet other parts of Pascal promised something that his mother and father had been unable to give him.

Pascal insisted that surer than sense or merely intellectual certainty is certainty experienced in the heart or human spirit. It is not our shallow intellect that can grasp God, continued Pascal; we meet him in our heart, in our spirit—that is where faith is. The Frenchman concluded with some strong advice: If you find anything cogent and attractive in my words, know they come from a man who goes down on his knees. Even though you cannot yet believe, do not neglect prayer or the Mass.

Nagai finished his picnic lunch, put his pack on his back and set off along the unpaved country road that skirted the clear stream. It was a glorious April day, and the little valley echoed with the songs of the bird Nagai had loved most since childhood, the *uguisu*, sometimes called the Japanese nightingale. Something told Nagai that all the beauty around him did not just happen. Was not Pascal's Creator God a reasonable hypothesis? Nagai reflected: I am always ready to test a hypothesis in the laboratory. Why not try this prayer that Pascal is so insistent about, even if only as an experiment?

He was not too sure what Christian prayer was but did not want to call on a priest lest he risk tedious proselytizing by some religious fanatic. Many university students took lodgings in Nagasaki households, so he decided to look for a Catholic family willing to take in a boarder. That would provide opportunities to learn about Catholicism and Christian prayer without committing himself. After some inquiries, he settled on a two-story house half a mile from the university and close to the cathedral. It was surrounded by camphor laurels and huge camelias that must have been over a hundred years old. The name on the front gate was Sadakichi Moriyama. He was a successful cattle dealer who lived alone with his wife. Their only child, Midori, was a schoolteacher living away from home. This Moriyama household was to exercise so profound an influence on Nagai that some background details must be given.

A pilgrim monk, Kobo Daishi.

6

The Hidden Christians

Sadakichi Moriyama's Christian roots went back three hundred years, to the time when Nagasaki was Japan's first and only Christian city. On August 15, 1549, Saint Francis Xavier landed in Kagoshima, and the Japanese people heard the Christian Gospel for the first time. No European had yet penetrated beyond the coast, and there was no Japanese-European dictionary. This led to massive problems for Xavier, and he began by preaching Dai Nichi. Xavier found to his chagrin that Dai Nichi was not Japanese for the Almighty God of the Bible but was one of the manifestations of the Buddha. However, faith is something that is caught more then taught, and many Japanese were so impressed by the energetic Basque aristocrat that they asked for baptism.

There are not a few chapters in the story of Catholic missions in the ages of colonialism that make for disturbing reading. The Jesuit story in Japan is not one of them. The men who followed Xavier attracted many converts, from the ranks of aristocrats and commoners, by the force of their personalities and convictions and by their work for the sick, homeless and orphans. Japanese civil authorities, for instance, have erected statues honoring the Jesuit Luís de Almeida, who pioneered surgery in Japan. Dr. Almeida had become a wealthy investor in the Far East when he joined the Jesuits. Before taking his vows, he arranged for his assets to be put into the lucrative Macao-Japan silk trade, stipulating that the dividends were all to go toward Jesuit hospitals and orphanages in Japan. These dividends were never more than a tiny percentage of the silk trade but led to the wild fiction that the Jesuits were deeply involved in gold and silk transactions. The fiction was repeated in the best-selling novel *Shogun*.

In 1579 the Jesuit Alessandro Valignano arrived as superior of the Jesuit mission and was to prove as effective as Xavier. A physical and intellectual giant, he had received a secular Renaissance education and worked as a lawyer when, aged twenty-seven, he joined the Jesuits. Throwing himself into the *Spiritual Exercises* of Saint Ignatius, he became skilled in prayer, even contemplation, and was made novice master. One of his novices was Matteo Ricci of future China fame. The Jesuit general placed great importance on the missions Xavier had begun in the East and, when Valignano was only thirty-five years old, put him in charge of them all.

Valignano became a missionary centuries ahead of his time. He quickly summed up the dangers in the current situation of colonialism and insisted his men learn and respect the language and culture of the people for whom they worked. He forbade the saddling of Western cultural baggage onto Asian shoulders. Jesuits went to the East to teach the Gospel and not Spanish, Portuguese or Italian culture. By all means, share Western astronomy, medicine and science with the people of the East, but do not identify the Gospel with sixteenth-century European culture. He insisted that his men prepare Japanese to take over leadership and, to the chagrin of some, suggested that Europeans were superior to Japanese only in knowledge of the Gospels. In all other matters, Jesuits were to be learners. Valignano, with rare insight into and feeling for the people, wrote a handbook on Japanese etiquette and customs and insisted on his men following it. Because of the regard leading Japanese men had for the tea ceremony, he ordered every Jesuit house to set up a tea ceremony room. Valignano's (and Ricci's) missionary policies of indigenization and enculturation won over many Japanese (and Chinese) intellectuals.

A sizable number of Japanese daimyo, the feudal barons, became Christians or displayed great respect for the new religion. One of them was Ukon Takayama, sometimes called "the Japanese Thomas More". Like the erstwhile chancellor of England, he was one of the leading political and cultural figures of his day. Takayama was arrested and stripped of castle and lands because he refused to compromise his Christian faith. Dictator Hideyoshi tried hard to woo this outstanding military tactician, calligrapher and master of the tea ceremony to his own cause, as Henry VIII tried to win Chancellor More. Takayama was finally exiled from Japan because he refused to renounce his Christian faith.

Great numbers of samurai and tens of thousands of lowly peasants and townspeople asked for baptism. Dictator Hideyoshi grew apprehensive at this swift increase of Christians, especially when men of the caliber of Takayama began speaking of Christ as their *Shukun*, their leige Lord, who received an absolute loyalty given to no other lord. Did this not jeopardize the samurai code? The dictator, impressed by the Jesuits and their fund of Western learning, had originally favored Christianity. Suddenly, in one of his notorious mood swings, he banned Christianity. All Japanese Christians had to renounce their religion, and all foreign missionaries had to leave. To emphasize the point, he ordered twenty-six Christians to be arrested in Kyoto, the *miyako* or capital city, and force-marched through the depths of winter to Nagasaki, a thirty-day journey by foot. They were to be executed by crucifixion on their arrival.

The choice of Nagasaki was deliberate. Nagasaki had not been an important town until 1571, when it became the chief port for the European ships that carried the new and flourishing trade between China (via Macao) and Japan. The port was part of the fief of Baron Omura, a Christian daimyo. In the past, daimyo had given tracts of land to Buddhist monks for monasteries and schools. Omura decided Nagasaki's harbor dues would help the Jesuits run their schools, churches and houses for the poor. So it became a Christian town, with schools, the bishop's residence and a seminary that saw fifteen Japanese ordained priests before persecutions destroyed visible Catholicism.

The Moriyamas were Christians in Nagasaki when the twenty-six travel-worn, barefoot victims limped into the city. Dictator Hideyoshi, a man of no real belief, thought that a public spilling of blood would quickly convince Nagasaki Christians to abandon their faith. To this end, he ordered the executions to be slow public spectacles. Nagasaki was told of the hour of arrival of the condemned, and a great throng of Christians turned out to cheer them and shout encouragement. The twenty-six were marched to Nishizaka Hill, not far from the present Nagasaki railway station. Twenty-six neatly sawn crosses ran from the brow of the hill down toward the harbor so that everyone could see the show. The victims were fastened to the crosses by iron rings and straw ropes. Two samurai stood beneath each cross with unsheathed bamboo lances, waiting to run their weapons up under the rib cages of the prisoners. This final act was delayed to heighten the terror of condemned and onlooker.

Singing broke out from the line of crosses, "Praise the Lord, ye children of the Lord", and the buzz over the hillside ceased as the crowd stopped to listen. The psalm came to an end, and one of the twenty-six began the Sanctus, that part of the Latin Mass, preceding the consecration, which was sung regularly by all Japanese Christian communities. When the last strains floated across the bay, a Franciscan on another cross began the simplest of litanies, "Jesus, Mary ... Jesus, Mary ..." The Christians in the crowd took up the prayer, four thousand of them. Hazaburo Terazawa was the official in charge of the execution, and he would have to give a personal account to the dictator. He was growing apprehensive, as it was becoming a show of Christian strength rather than the bloodcurdling spectacle Dictator Hideyoshi had ordered.

One of the twenty-six asked leave to speak. He was the thirty-three-year-old Jesuit Paul Miki, son of a general in Baron Takayama's army, an accomplished catechist and preacher. Dying well was tremendously important for samurai, and they often met death with a *jisei no uta*, or farewell song. Miki's strong voice reached the edges of the crowd:

"I am a Japanese and a brother of the Society of Jesus. I have committed no crime. The only reason I am condemned to die is that I have taught the gospel of our Lord Jesus Christ. I am happy to die for that and accept death as a great gift from my Lord." Miki asked the crowd if they saw fear on the faces of the twenty-six. He assured them there was no fear because heaven was real. He had only one dying request: that they believe. He said he forgave Hideyoshi and those responsible for this execution. Then, with deliberation and in a ringing voice, he gave his farewell song. It was the verse of Psalm 31 that Christ quoted from the Cross: "Lord, into your hands I commend my spirit."

Terazawa gave a sign, and samurai moved in with their steel-tipped bamboo lances. The samurai gave deep-throated cries, and their lances ripped into the twenty-six. The deathly silence of the crowd suddenly erupted into an angry roar, and Terazawa hurriedly withdrew to compile his report. The spectacle of humiliation had gone awry. The prestige of Christians rose dramatically, and baptisms increased.

Dictator Hideyoshi died, and a huge power struggle took place among the feudal barons. Ieyasu Tokugawa was victorious, became a more absolute dictator than Hideyoshi and took the old title shogun. The first of the Tokugawa shoguns was deeply suspicious of Christianity, especially Catholicism. He saw missionaries accompanying the conquistadores on colonial enterprises all over the globe and was disturbed that gentry like Baron Takayama and simple peasants disobeyed all-powerful Hideyoshi in favor of this outlawed foreign religion. In 1614 the shogun, having wiped out the last remnant of resistance to his rule, reenforced the prohibition of Christianity. Large rewards were offered for information leading to the capture of priests and catechists. When Christians in great numbers went to death rather than renounce their faith, the shogun introduced refined tortures to break them. Nagasaki and its environs were filled with government agents and soldiers. Priests slipping into Japan to replace the ones who were executed were quickly apprehended, their Western eyes and accents giving them away. Many Nagasaki Christians migrated to offshore islands or remote areas like Urakami and devised ways of keeping and handing on the Christian faith without priests.

Sadakichi Moriyama's ancestors were with the group that went north of Nagasaki to a rough part of the countryside where the small Urakami River ran into Nagasaki Bay. They became farmers and fisherfolk and formed an underground church. They appointed a "water man" to baptize; a "calendar man" to keep the dates of Advent, Christmas, Lent, Easter and so forth; and a *chokata*, or "head man", as overall leader. Sadakichi Moriyama's ancestors were the first *chokata*, and each eldest son assumed the responsibility when his father died. The Tokugawa shoguns remained in power two and a half centuries by setting up a police state, and their total opposition to Christianity never slackened. In 1856 Kichizo Moriyama, the seventh of the line of *chokata*, was snared in a police net. He died under torture but did not betray his trust. His infant son was to become Sadakichi Moriyama's father.

In 1858 Japan, forced to open up to the outside world by Commodore Perry's gunboats, signed a commercial treaty with the United States. Europeans soon entered Japan and took up residence in places like Yokohama and Nagasaki. When they began to build churches, the shogun said only Europeans could enter them. Christianity was taboo for Japanese. In February 1864 Father Petitjean of the Paris Foreign Mission Society completed a church in Oura, a southern suburb of Nagasaki, just below the present Glover Mansion of *Madama Butterfly* fame.

This church was four miles down the bay from the secret Christian community of Urakami. The pro tem Christian leaders, having seen their *chokata* taken off to die violently in prison just six years before, were very reluctant to move quickly. Furthermore, they argued, the new Christian Church might not be that of their ancestors. The latter had handed down some uncomplicated dicta, one of which ran: The Church will return to Japan, and you will know it from others that might come by three signs: the priests will be celibate, there will be a statue of Mary and it will obey Papa-sama in Rome.

Some Urakami Christians went by the new Oura church one market day, one managing to slip into the church undetected and see a statue of Mary holding the Christ child. They questioned locals about the tall Frenchman in black and were told that he lived without a wife. They also saw the ominous government notice board outside the church stating that the church was for foreigners and that any Japanese found inside would incur the full severity of the anti-Christian regulations.

The son of *chokata* Moriyama was too young to make a decision. The elders argued for waiting until they could be more certain about the Oura church. Their wives, accusing them of pusillanimous dilly-dallying, said they had enough proof and were going to meet the Frenchman. On the following day, March 17, 1865, donning straw raincoats against the heavily overcast sky, they set out in several fishing boats, skirted the east side of Nagasaki Bay for three miles and landed just beyond Dejima. They walked up the hill, trying to look like fisherfolk come to the city to buy provisions. When they saw there were no police or officials in sight, they sped up the stone steps into the church.

Inside the church, Father Petitjean was reciting his breviary dejectedly. As a seminarian in Paris, he had been fascinated by books on the Japanese Christians during the sixty years after Francis Xavier's first baptisms. He had read the detailed accounts of the twenty-six crucified in Nagasaki, of Baron Ukon Takayama, Lady Tama Hosokawa and the thousands of Japanese of all classes who chose death rather than renounce their Christian faith. When Japan opened to the West, he had come to Nagasaki with high hopes, expecting to find some surviving Christians. To his sorrow, he found nothing but hostility to Christianity. Today the weather matched his mood as he knelt in his brand-new church alone.

He looked up sharply as the group of roughly dressed Japanese women from Urakami came across the tatami floor to accost him. "Santa Maria no gozo wa doko?" asked a woman named Yuri, which means "lily". "Where is the statue of Holy Mary?" The priest was too startled to reply. Another woman, Teru, meaning "luster", reassured him: "Our hearts and your heart are the same." She repeated the question: "Santa Maria no go zo?" "Ah yes, yes. Doozo, doozo. Please come this way." He led them around to the side altar against the eastern wall. "Ah! It's her! It's her!" There was the relief of centuries of waiting in Teru's voice. "Yes, it is she. She has the Child Zezus in her arms." Some of the pronunciations, the priest was to discover, had changed over the centuries, but when he questioned them on what they believed, he found they had spoken the truth: their hearts and his were the same.

Father Petitjean was told that the spacious Moriyama cattle shed was the meeting place for the Hidden Christians of Urakami. He sent a message to the water man, the calendar man and the elders. They warned him of the danger if the city officials learned of their identity, so he disguised himself as a farmer and went after darkness. He celebrated Mass in the cow shed, with rice straw under his feet to cover the muck.

The Japanese are a people attuned to symbols and marveled at this first Mass being in a cow shed. The story of the dark Advent and Christmas journeys of the little family that was refused shelter by the townspeople and that was hunted by Herod's soldiers had been a favorite during the twenty-five decades of persecution. They even gave the cattle extra hay on December 25!

Nagasaki officials, eventually getting wind of the clandestine Christians and the French priest, asked the central government for instructions. The Tokugawa shogun still ruled the nation, but very uncertainly. Militant daimyo were recruiting samurai for "the glorious cause" of freeing the Emperor from centuries of Tokugawa-enforced imprisonment in his gilded cage at Kyoto and of strengthening Japan against the growing threat from Westerners. In this last year of its life, the Tokugawa dictatorship, which had all but wiped out Japanese Christianity in the 1600s, told the civic officials in Nagasaki to stamp out these smoldering Christian embers. Accordingly, at 3 A.M. on the morning of July 15, 1867, soldiers sloshed through pouring rain and rounded up sixty-eight leading Christians. More were taken later, and finally all of the 3,414 Urakami Christians, ranging from feeble old folk to howling babies, were dispatched to nineteen detention camps specially set up around the nation. The government sent them to scattered prison camps to destroy their unity. If the Christians persisted in their religion, torture and capital punishment were to be used.

Less than a year later, the Tokugawa dictatorship was overthrown and the Emperor was reinstated in the person of Emperor Meiji. In the face of hostile Western colonists spreading through Asia, the new Meiji government saw national unity as a top priority. Christianity was Western and disruptive. Shinto was purely Japanese and, teaching both emperor worship and the nation's sacred destiny, would be the cement of unity. Christians were potential traitors in a Japan bracing itself against the colonists from the Christian West. The efforts to reconvert the Christians in the prison camps were brutal, and many died. Europeans living in Nagasaki alerted the Western press. Articles began to appear and foreign governments made official protests, resulting in the Meiji government abandoning its policy. Just five years after the Urakami Christians were force-marched to distant imprisonment, they limped back home. Six hundred and sixty-four, or just under 20 percent, had died in captivity, and many others were in poor shape physically. As the government had labeled them traitors, there had been open season on their possessions. Their farming equipment, furniture, boats, fishing gear and anything else of value were gone. The wilderness covering the once-neat rice paddies brought tears to their eyes.

Example of Taka-yama's calligraphy.

Christian daimyo Baron Ukon Takayama (baptismal name of Justo).

7

The Bells of Nagasaki

With the coming of the French priests, the traditional roles of head man, water man and calendar man had died out. The last head man died in jail in 1856. His tiny son, who matured during the harsh "exile in Babylon", returned with the exiles to Urakami and resurrected the family cattle business. In due course he married, and in 1907 his eldest son Sadakichi went on a cattle-buying trip to Ukujima. This island, two hundred miles west of Nagasaki, is the most northerly of the Goto Islands. Many Christians had fled to the Gotos when persecution broke out in the early seventeenth century and formed hidden Christian communities that still survived. Ukujima, however, refused entry to Christians, fearing Tokugawa reprisals. Ukujima people still regarded Christians as dangerous. When Sadakichi and an island girl, Tsumo Akagi, fell in love, it caused great problems. Farmer Akagi was adamantly opposed to his daughter Tsumo marrying a Nagasaki Christian.

The girl fled to Nagasaki on a cattle boat. Her father came on the next boat and brought her back. She fled again, and the father disowned her. The only one pleased to see her was Sadakichi. His parents were strongly opposed to Number One Son marrying a *mi-shinja*, an unbeliever. The Urakami women saw her as a rival for the eligible cattle dealer and nicknamed her "the Crow". This was because of her luxuriant, jet-black hair that set off her beautiful face, burnished by the sun and salt air of her island home. Despite the opposition, they married.

In 1908, the year Takashi Nagai was born, they had their only child, a daughter called Midori. When Sadakichi's father died, they inherited the ancestral home and cattle business.

Now, late in 1931, Nagai stood outside that home. Sadakichi and his wife lived there alone. Their daughter lived in another town, where she was a schoolteacher. Nagai had no idea that this two-story house had been the secret headquarters of the Hidden Christians for two and a half centuries. All he knew was that it looked like an ideal place to board. He called out: "O jama itashimasu. Is anyone home?" Tsumo came to the door, her once-lustrous black hair now flecked here and there with gray. Nagai introduced himself as a student from the nearby medical university, looking for lodgings. He wondered if the Moriyamas had a spare room. He made a good presentation in his severe student's uniform with brass buttons, well-polished shoes and easy smile. Tsumo responded pleasantly, telling him to wait while she consulted her husband. He was out in the cow shed, and they quickly decided they did not need a boarder. She went back and gave a polite refusal.

Nagai was never one to take an initial refusal to heart. Two days later, he was back at the front door and asked, with a deeper bow and a broader smile, if they would not reconsider his request. Tsumo smiled at his friendly persistence and went to the living room to consult her husband. They were not long back from Sunday Mass, and Sadakichi said: "Maybe it's like today's sermon, and the Lord sent him. It wouldn't do to refuse. Tsumo, how would you feel about taking him?" She already liked the student and readily agreed. Some hours later that day, Takashi hummed one of the colorful Kyushu folk songs as he unpacked in a spacious second-floor room, feeling very pleased with himself.

Nagai's stay in Christian Urakami was to prove decisive, and he wrote of it at length in a later book. He would be awakened daily at 5:30 A.M. by the two big bells booming from the nearby cathedral. Soon he would hear the voices of the Moriyamas below praying aloud in Nagasaki singsong that is almost chanting. At noon and 6 P.M. the bells would ring out again, and he would see people stop and recite the Angelus. Sometimes he would be invited to join the Moriyamas for a meal and quickly discovered that Sadakichi was eager to talk about the Christian religion. Nagai found his intensity, sometimes fueled by hot sake, rather off-putting. He wanted to investigate the beliefs and practices of Christians at his own pace and on his own terms.

About three months after he began lodging with the Moriyamas, a professor made a passing reference in class to the Nagasaki martyrs. That in itself was not extraordinary because the twenty-six who were crucified on Nishizaka and the thousands who were killed in and around the city were featured in all books about Nagasaki and in the official guidebooks and tourist pamphlets. The professor had dismissed the martyrs as "fanatics". The Christians in Urakami did not strike Nagai as fanatics. He thought they were even ahead of others in several areas of "enlightenment". For instance, every Sunday was a free day, when workers put down their tools and families relaxed together. The rest of Japan was decades away from a weekly day of rest for workers. The kindergarten the nuns ran not far from the cathedral was sixty years old, making it one of the first in Japan. The orphanage and several schools the nuns ran seemed certainly as good as ones run by the state. The Japanese sisters, brothers and priests he saw around Urakami touched a chord within him. Their lives of poverty, chastity and dedication were like those of Buddhist monks in Japan's past when Buddhism had been the soul of Japanese life and every village had its o-tera, or Buddhist temple, a building of architectural beauty and a center of classical learning. But, time and again in Japanese history, when Buddhism became powerful, it interfered in secular government affairs and had to be repressed. European

Christianity seemed to have a similar fatal flaw, thought Nagai, which appeared in the Crusades, the Inquisition, the Galileo affair and the blessing the institution gave to the slave trade and the rape of South America, Africa and much of Asia. Maybe the professor was right: religion was dangerous because it always ended up in fanaticism. Religion was too costly if the price was fanaticism and the loss of common sense.

Nagai heard that the cathedral bell ringer had a collection of Christian relics three hundred years old. He went to see him, and the asthmatic old man took him to a large room where he kept seventeenth-century crucifixes, Rosaries, paintings and images of "Maria Kannon". The latter excited Nagai's interest. Kannon is the Buddhist Merciful One, found all through Asia—Kuan Lin in China, Avolokita Ishvara in India and Chen-resigs in Tibet. No woman can enter Nirvana and become a Buddha but must first be reborn as a man in an intermediate stage of salvation. Kannon, therefore, is a man, but the face is always feminine to emphasize Kannon's gentleness and all-embracing compassion. When the government officials intensified house-to-house searches to hunt down Nagasaki Christians, the latter began making ceramic images of Mary that looked like Kannon. A small cross was placed inside or behind the image, and often Maria Kannon carried a child. When officials saw Christians kneeling before these images, they presumed they were Buddhist devotees of Kannon and left them alone.

Nagai accepted the bell ringer's offer to give him a guided tour of the cathedral. The cathedral was 230 feet long, making it the biggest in the Far East. It accommodated five thousand worshippers, and its two bell towers were over one hundred feet high. The bell ringer told Nagai how much pain it cost to build the cathedral, and he himself had been part of the story. He was just a boy in 1872 when they came home to Urakami from years of privation in the camps scattered over

Japan. The first years back were primitive, for all their implements had been stolen, and they had to dig their overgrown fields with broken roof tiles and pottery shards. They had their eyes on the spacious house overlooking Urakami that had belonged to the government official responsible for interrogating their leaders and for sending them all off to the prison camps. After slaving to make enough money, they bought the residence, demolished the house and built a wooden church there.

By 1895 they had scrimped and saved enough to tear down the wooden church and to begin building a cathedral of stone and brick under the direction of their amateur architect priest. Almost every family was involved. Men manned barges to ferry huge foundation stones from Kumamoto and hauled them up the hill. Others went up the mountains to fell and dress timber; women and children worked in shifts to make hundreds of thousands of red bricks. The Christians' French pastor taught them how to make cement and plaster statues, and natural artists among them sculpted images and architectural ornaments from granite. It was all done by people just above the poverty level, and any number of times they ran out of money and materials and had to stop. Finally, twenty-two years after dragging the huge foundation stones up the hill, their cathedral was completed. The year was 1917, when the economy was improving and Japan was one of the Allies in the war against Germany, at very little cost to herself.

Nagai had read how famous Gothic cathedrals like Chartres and Cologne had also been built by the volunteer labor of untrained common folk. Sometimes it took a century to build a cathedral full of all kinds of constructional discrepancies! Opposing walls, matching windows and roof sections are often out of alignment. Yet they have stood for six centuries and more, uplifting achievements of the human spirit. When Nagai came to Nagasaki, this Urakami Cathedral had been the first jarring note.

Everything from its noisy bells to its oppressive shape and color was offensive to his sense of the *Nihon-teki*, the purely Japanese. But now his judgment softened as he learned it was not built by foreign money but by poor Japanese farmers and fisherfolk. He felt pride that Japanese whose only training had been on rice paddies and fishing boats had created something noble.

Nagai walked a roundabout way home from the cathedral, skirting Mount Inasa, letting his eyes drink in the rice fields and thatched farmhouses. They carried the fingerprints of the Japanese workmanship he loved: even in common everyday things, sensible practicality was combined with artistic beauty. Nagai loved this *Nihon-teki* tradition that he saw even in these Urakami farmhouses. He loved the severe beauty of their tatami mat floors set off by the inexpressible loveliness of sunlight captured in the snow-white paper of *shoji*. *Shoji*, the sliding windows and partitions inside all Japanese homes, are made by stretching snowy paper across small square frames of unvarnished softwood. The *shoji* partitions can be lifted out, opening up the whole house into one large room to accommodate the many guests at those important events in traditional Japanese life, wakes and anniversary liturgies for the dead.

Nagai thought that Japanese owed their strong feeling for beauty to their mothers. As girls, whether they came from wealthy homes or poor ones, they had all been trained in Japan's thousand-year-old tradition of feminine refinement and grace. Learning that tradition was regarded as one of the essential preparations for marriage and was the reason why every town and village had flourishing classes in *ikebana*, or flower arrangement, and *cha no yu*, or tea ceremony. His thoughts winged back to his own mother. Everything she did, from the way she served common green tea at a meal to her bows of welcome and farewell to patients and callers, was done with grace. To Nagai it was obvious that the mother was the central figure in Japanese life. The strong appeal of the motherly and the feminine was highlighted in the universal popularity of the images of the Buddhist Merciful One, Kannon. Even the Hidden Christians had Maria Kannon, and he had noticed the prominent statues of Mary in the cathedral—a stone one of Mary by the Cross outside the entrance and one of a softer mood inside. The Moriyamas had a statue of Mary in their *tokonoma*, the tastefully simple alcove in the main room of every Japanese house of any size where the family's best objects of art are displayed.

An hour later, Nagai was in his own tatami mat room in the Moriyamas'. He pulled open the *shoji* and slid back the glass window, leaning on the sill and gazing at the huge red-brick cathedral. On the street just below him, a girl in a faded kimono was walking slowly up and down. She looked about ten and had a baby strapped snugly on her back. Nagai was taken by the peculiar melody she sang as she rocked back and forth to keep the baby from crying. Was it one of those haunting Kyushu folk songs? Ah, now he could make it out: Kyrie eleison, Christe eleison! He recognized the words from his passing acquaintance with Beethoven and Bach Masses.

Boom ... boom ... boom. The cathedral bells suddenly sounded the 6 P.M. Angelus. Several workers in fields between Nagai and the cathedral went down on their knees to say the ancient prayer to Mary. The ten-year-old girl stopped still too. A quaint fantasy came to Nagai that the bells had changed Urakami into a hamlet in Brittany and that he was looking at a painting by a favorite artist, Millet. Just as suddenly, he felt sad because Urakami Christians and Millet's peasants had faith, but he was a complicated student who had only questions.

A young plow beast started bellowing down in the shed. When it had been brought in from the Goto Islands last night, it had tried to bolt, and Moriyama-san had to tie it up in a stall, where it continued bellowing all night. It was just as cross-grained and bent on escape today. Was he like that stupid cow, wanting to break away and escape home but not know-ing where home was? He went back to his desk and took out a medical book to prepare tomorrow's lectures. He began read-ing the German text and thought: Here is my home, here is my terra firma—science and the verifiable facts of medical sci-ence! His mind was convinced, but his heart felt something was missing.

8

Dew on a Morning Glory

Like the dew on the morning glory is man and his house. Who knows which will survive the other.

—*The Ten Foot Square Hut*, Kyoto, thirteenth century

Nagasaki citizens celebrated the beginning of the new year, 1932, with *o-mochi*, the traditional pounded-rice cakes. Families doffed their workaday clothes for magnificent kimonos and visited Shinto shrines to thank the gods for the old year and ask protection on the new. Parents smiled proudly at kimono-clad children playing traditional battledore[1] on the streets. Little did they suspect that the violence brewing over in Manchuria would soon become a raging conflagration that would leap across the Yellow Sea and ignite Japanese cities. Dull military uniforms and women's shapeless *monpe* trousers would replace bright kimonos. Many of the boys playing pleasant games of battledore on Nagasaki streets would die in vicious hand-to-hand fighting in Chinese mountains or Malayan jungles.

China was again growing restive over the undue influence foreigners exercised in her affairs. In retaliation against the latest occupying force, the Japanese in Manchuria, she began a

[1] An oriental precursor to badminton.

boycott of Japanese goods in the pivotal port of Shanghai. Japan's exports, already suffering from Western tariffs, were massively affected by this Shanghai blockade. On January 28, Japan's military forces in Manchuria, the Kwantung Army, moved south and attacked Shanghai. The Chinese put up heroic resistance, and a stalemate developed. On March 3 peace was signed. But the treaty signed with ideograph brush strokes would only paper over the top of the rumbling volcano. Soon red-hot lava would burst out and burn a path all the way to Nagasaki.

Young Nagai, however, hardly gave world politics a thought. His exams loomed before him, the crucial steep hill after a marathon of eighteen years of study. Japanese students of that period began six years of primary schooling at the age of six. If they went on to secondary schooling, they did five years of middle school. High school was another three years, after which, aged about twenty, they could go on to university. Nagai, a month away from his twenty-fourth birthday, prepared to take the national exams to qualify as a doctor.

He and his classmates took little time off during the 1932 New Year's holidays. From early January until mid-March, they would sit for stringent exams in nine subjects—internal medicine; surgery; ear, nose, and throat disorders and treatment; psychiatry; ophthamology; gynecology; dermatology; urology; and pediatrics. After the written exams, each student would be allotted patients to treat, and a gimlet-eyed attendant professor would give marks according to the standard of treatment. Nagai, having been near the top in all subjects for four years, passed brilliantly, was awarded a university medal and was chosen to deliver the address on graduation day. He wrote and told his father, adding that he planned to return home after graduation and work under him. The latter, although now feeling the strain and sorely missing his wife's moderating care, refused the offer. "Your mother worked and sacrificed so that you could become a top doctor. I happen to know you have been invited to work on at the university, so seize the opportunity. But I appreciate your offer."

For the moment young Nagai forgot about everything else, including Pascal's disturbing questions, and set to work gathering ideas for the graduation speech. It must have intellectual depth and be scientific but not coldly so. It must reflect the new *Yamato-damashii*, or spirit of Japan, modern but warm with the emotions of the ancient *Manyoshu* poetry. He was ashamed that, medically speaking, Japan was still among the undeveloped nations. Diseases like tuberculosis were rampant. He would end his address with a stirring call to his fellow graduates to work with all their might until they could hold their heads as high as doctors in the West. Having decided the content, he sat down to write it with a brush and Chinese ink. Freed from the heavy German of his medical textbooks, he wrote with speed, glad that his native language had been created by poets.

He never gave the speech. Several days before the graduation ceremony, tragedy struck. It looked like anything but tragedy when it began at the sayonara party held in Nagasaki's fashionable Chinese restaurant, Tsutenkaku, "the heavenly palace". They had been under great strain during the previous two months of study and examinations, and the moment they walked through the glittering entrance, the students were out for a night of fun. Young geishas appeared like brilliantly painted snow geese. At first impassive and wooden behind their heavily whitened faces, they came to life when alcohol began flowing. There was a lot Nagai did not remember about that party, but he did remember the alcohol they consumed in great quantities—beer, Chinese spirits, Japanese sake and expensive European wines. The geisha began singing and dancing and dragged the students from their tables with shrieks of laughter and not a few spills.

Nagai had never been more confident in all his life. The world was a ball in his hands, to be twirled as easily as that pretty geisha from Sasebo who had lavished attention on him most of the night. The little kitten thought she could get him drunk, but she gasped and spread dainty fingers when he tossed back every drink she served him. He realized he was tipsy, however, when he rose to do his forte, the Dance of the Mud-fish Catcher. The toasts followed, and he consumed much more alcohol.

The restaurant closed when it was well into the small hours. The students loudly congratulated each other out onto the street, chatted with a group of apprentice geisha passing by and sent one another home with rousing student songs. Home? Where was home? Ha ha ha! All of Nagasaki was spinning. Was he a mudfish in a fishbowl? Was he still, but the fishbowl revolving? Ah, that's it—get his fishbowl onto a tram seat. Trams go straight even if fishbowls don't. Here's the tram stop. What, no trams? Oops! What a stupid mayor, letting trams go to bed so early. Well, even though the mayor is stupid, the taxi driv-ers aren't. They never go to bed. Oh no! It can't be. Yes, broke! That dumb treasurer! He didn't bring enough to pay the bill, and we had to help him out. Well, who cares. I'm giving the graduation speech and getting the medal, and that girl from Sasebo liked me the best, and a samurai poet loves walking in the rain. Yippee!

It was only a misty spring drizzle, but by the time Nagai reached the Moriyamas'—and went around to shush the cows and tell them not to wake up Sadakichi and Tsumo—he was soaked through to the bone. But it was all right to be wet. How could you be a mudfish in a fishbowl if you weren't wet? He half-crawled, half-swam up the staircase, dragged out his futon, the fluffy mattress that is spread on the tatami mat floor, and muttered: Mudfish all, let's lie on the bottom of the lake for a while.

A roaring headache dragged him out of his drugged sleep. The sun was high in the spring sky, and the light was harsh on his eyes. His ears were paining and his limbs leaden. A voice called from the foot of the stairs. No, he replied hoarsely, he didn't need any meals and would appreciate not being disturbed. He would stay in his room today. Left again to himself, he decided it was just a bad hangover, took some headache powders, changed out of his damp clothes and lay down again. Darkness mercifully came, but it ushered in the most fitful night of his life.

The next day, long before the sun appeared over Mount Kompira, he struggled into some clothes and went groggily downstairs. His head pounded so badly that it seemed to block out all other sound. Wait—all other sound? He realized he could hardly hear a thing! He was glad the Moriyamas were out in the cattle shed and did not see him. He struggled the half mile or so to the hospital and collapsed shakily onto a chair, where his old friend the matron[2] took one look at him, got him onto a bed and brought an on-duty doctor.

It didn't take long to diagnose acute middle-ear inflammation and possibly meningitis. The doctor told the matron that if Nagai's illness turned into meningitis, he could die. Nagai was very special to her and was that year's star graduate. She immediately had him transferred to a private room, telephoned a professor who was a top ear specialist and asked if he could come immediately. Young Nagai looked up as the specialist touched his shoulder and saw it was the very man who had tried to marry him off to a millionaire's daughter! Nagai felt too drained to see any humor in the situation.

The professor drew fluid from Nagai's spine and gave a low whistle at the telltale signs of meningitis. Young Nagai, of all people—sturdy, always on the go, the top of his class. Now it could be all over for him! Hemolysis had already begun destroying Nagai's red blood cells, leaving no choice but a dangerous

---

[2] Senior nurse who supervises the nursing staff and patient care.

operation. Even if the patient pulled through, it could be with a brain so damaged he would be mentally retarded for the rest of his life. That was a risk that had to be taken.

The operation averted the immediate crisis, but for some time Nagai was dangerously ill and in and out of delirium. There is a custom in Japan of a woman relative remaining in hospital with the patient. She is called a *tsukisoi*, or attendant. The *tsukisoi*, though disappearing from modern Japanese hospitals, was always much appreciated by patients. She was beside the patient all day, ready to assist by moving a pillow, bringing a glass of water or massaging a hurting back. At night she slept on a mattress on the floor beside the bed, a very comforting presence. Nagai had no relatives in Nagasaki, so the Moriyamas found a somewhat elderly woman to be his *tsukisoi*.

She was from Urakami and was like one of those Breton peasant women Nagai admired in Millet paintings. She did not know Nagai but was deeply moved to see the fine young man at death's door. She spent much of the time saying the Rosary, half-aloud in Nagasaki singsong. It did not distress him; this sound he often heard in the Moriyama home. He knew he was hanging between life and death and gained comfort from the old lady's prayers.

Gradually the crisis lessened and his mind cleared, but he was deaf in his right ear. Someone else had given the graduation speech, and Nagai felt, for the first time in his life, physically and psychologically spent. The classical Japanese literature that he loved was full of allusions to the evanescence of glory and the impermanence of life. Nagai found himself thinking of the first lines of Chohei Kamono's *The Ten Foot Square Hut*. Written about A.D. 1212 and only twenty-one pages, it is so profoundly in tune with Japanese feeling that it has endured as one of Japan's most-read books. Its opening paragraph is its theme: "Ceaselessly the river flows. . . . The eddying foam gathers and then is gone, never staying for a moment. Even so is man and his habitat." These words, once beautiful poetry, were now crushing reality. The cherry blossoms, bewitching when they suddenly appear on dark leafless limbs, draw immense crowds for *hanami*, flower viewing. But within three days the delicate petals lie on roads and footpaths, and busy people walk roughshod over them. His graduation speech too lay trampled under the feet of the fickle audience who enjoyed themselves just as much without him. A feeling of nausea swept over him. Was it because life could be so heartless and unjust? Or was it nausea at his own shallowness and conceit? The last lines of *The Ten Foot Square Hut* came back to him:

> Sad am I at heart
> When the moon's bright silver disk
> Disappears below the mountain ...
> How peaceful it will be
> Amida's perpetual light!

Did Amida Buddha live in perpetual light? Did Jesus Christ? Did his Mother? Or was there no such thing? Was all reality as impermanent and meaningless as flecks of foam on the Uji River? Was Kamono's poetry merely another noble attempt to console the poor human heart in the *ukiyo*, the floating world, where our lives rise, fall and disappear like waves on the open sea?

Seiza, *the formal sitting posture.*

9

Silent Night and a Precious Life

About the same time that year, 1932, Professor Itsuma Suet-sugu sat down heavily in a shabby office at Nagasaki Medical University, feeling depressed. He had come to this university last year to pioneer, he had believed, a radiology department. There had been great difficulties to overcome in the course of mastering this new branch of medicine that, even in Europe, was still in its infancy. It had been all the harder for Suetsugu because his study and research were done in German, though Saint George's Hospital in Hamburg had been a first-rate place to study and work.

The professor thought he had prepared himself for everything, but he had not taken into account the unpredictable human element. Lurking in the hearts of not a few influential Nagasaki University professors, who seemed so dedicated to medicine and truth as they lectured eloquently in their classrooms, was an old demon, professional jealousy! Maybe there was fear too, fear that Professor Suetsugu's new x-ray machine might make obsolete their hard-won stethoscope art. He was stunned by the coldness of the reception he and his machine received. The understanding had been that he would be given everything he needed for a separate department when he returned from Germany. He found himself and his equipment, however, shunted into a few obsolete rooms. There was not even a bathroom. He was told offhandedly to use a bathroom in the neighboring department. Nor would the

University Council authorize him to put up the sign "Radiology Department". The medical students soon picked up the vibrations coming from the other professors. The students already had more than they wanted for the final exams and spent little time on the assignments Dr. Suetsugu gave them. Radiology was not accorded much space in the examinations, another slight to Suetsugu, but he had his revenge in marking the papers. He gave many of his students what he thought they and the administration deserved—zero! Nagai had been one of those who had gotten a zero.

It was now late spring. Nagai was recovering but still in the hospital when a messenger came from University Administration with a proposal requiring a prompt answer. The visitor sat on the left because Nagai was quite deaf in his right ear. Bending closer, he told Nagai that because his hearing was permanently impaired, stethoscope work would be impossible. The administration suggested he become the assistant to Dr. Suetsugu in radiology. The latter's complaints about the completely unsatisfactory treatment of radiology had at last been heard. His zero marks, which he refused to reconsider, had finally goaded the administration into doing something. Nagai was flabbergasted but also cornered. If he did not accept, they would withdraw the invitation to work at the university. Though he thought Suetsugu was not a little odd, he said yes, he would accept the offer.

Some weeks later, Nagai listened as the professor outlined his plans: "X-ray technology is the wave of the future. Japan has to face the fact that in radiology, we are nearly forty years behind Europe. Nagai, I will be frank with you. X-ray technology is already revolutionizing medicine and will do so all the more. But ..." The professor suddenly became somber and looked steadily into the young assistant's eyes—"we can't fully control the rays yet. See this photograph. It's of Dr. Holzknecht of Vienna. He taught me while I was overseas. He was one of the great pioneers and literally gave his life for radiology. He lost one finger from radiation exposure and then another. Finally, they had to amputate his right arm. Look, here is a copy of notes he made on better ways of protecting doctors and technicians from radiation."

Nagai took the notes. He read German but found the writing almost illegible. "Oh yes", added the professor. "It's hard to read. After the amputation, he had to write left-handed. I've seen a stone monument in a garden at Hamburg University with at least a hundred names on it, names of people who have died from radiation contracted during radiological research. There are professors, doctors, nurses, technicians, even a nun scientist. They are martyrs, every one of them, martyrs for scientific truth, dying for all the patients around the world who will be saved by x-ray technology. On that stone there are names from many nations—Poland, Germany, Belgium, Denmark, France, England—but none from Japan. We have an obligation to join this dangerous scientific quest until there is a safe x-ray unit in every major hospital, Nagai-kun." (*Kun* is a suffix men often use in place of *san* when not addressing a superior. It is a familiar form of "Mister".)

"Look at the miserable rooms they've given me here. They've absolutely no notion of how important radiology is going to be, and we will have to grit our teeth and work at it until the fools understand. I'm sure you've heard of Pierre and Marie Curie. They were so poor before they received the Nobel Prize for isolating radium that Marie had to get a side job in a girls' school to make ends meet. Imagine that—the world's best woman scientist forced to teach equations to schoolgirls! Nagai-kun, I can promise you little more than hard work and an abysmal lack of appreciation from university staff and students." He gave the younger man a sharp look that found its mark. "Add to that, Nagai-kun, serious risks to your health. But you'll be a Japanese pioneer in a vital medical field."

Suetsugu became animated. "We will uncover new truths that will last forever. Forever! If something is true, it is eternal. If you became a politician, you'd be working for very temporary things that are often false." With obvious reference to the militarists, who were on the way to dominating Japanese politics in that summer of 1932, he added somberly: "Look at Genghis Khan's Mongols. They conquered Asia and part of Europe, but today they have no land to call their own. Natsu kusa ya tsuwamono domo no yume no ato!" The latter was a haiku poem by one of Nagai's favorite poets, seventeenth-century Basho, and was composed on a field where two huge armies once clashed. Proud banners, gilded helmets of commanders, even the bones of slain warriors and horses had long since been reclaimed by nature, and only a peaceful field of grass remained. Pithiness and rhythm are lost in translating a haiku, but the English meaning is: "Ah, summer grasses. All that remains of those military dreams!" Nagai soon became Suetsugu's enthusiastic disciple.

He now stood beside the professor as the first patient came into the darkened room. She was an attractive young woman, her hair done with a permanent wave, still a novelty in Nagasaki. Suetsugu spoke to Nagai in German and traced the barium fluid to show him that intestinal worms were the cause of her pain. Nagai wondered if there was a young man in love with her and whether his admiration would be dimmed if he could see what they could see! The next patient was a teacher who looked tubercular. He begged them to give him a clean bill of health, as he had a wife and family to support and would be fired if he had a serious illness. Japan was now deep in the Depression, and woe to anyone who lost his job!

Suetsugu took up the subject of finances at lunchtime. "In America, both big business and the government help scientific research. We still have to battle for recognition, let alone help. One x-ray costs seven yen. That's about four days' salary for you. Nagai-kun; we have to get money for research and find a way of x-raying more cheaply. Do you know what the American scientists are now doing? Atomic research. That's a natural development of our field, of course, and there is colossal atomic energy just waiting to be liberated. Ernest Lawrence of the University of California has a cyclotron for the purpose of atomic transmutation. It's a huge machine about four times the size of all our buildings here." This was the beginning of what would soon develop into an absorbing interest for Nagai, the study of atoms, radiation and the possibilities of atomic energy. He would become something of a specialist in the theories of atomic structure and nuclear fission.

Mid-December 1932 was exceptionally cold. Nagai used to stay at the hospital after the day's work, absorbed in radiological research despite the poorly heated rooms. He was amazed that he could once have been so disinterested in the new science Dr. Suetsugu had introduced. Tonight he was going home early because it was December 24, and he had accepted the Moriyamas' invitation to join them in a special Christmas Eve meal. Christmas was not a public holiday in Japan, and the militarists discouraged people from celebrating Christmas because it was "un-Japanese and alien". Nagai had never celebrated it but would do so tonight out of friendship and respect for his good hosts.

The Japanese-style dining table was only a foot above the tatami mat floor. Everyone sat in formal *seiza* style, with the back straight and with insteps and feet flattened underneath the buttocks. When host Moriyama said, "Dozo, O raku ni. Please sit comfortably", the men sat more easily, with their legs crossed in front of them. Polite women never relaxed the severe but aesthetic *seiza* style. On this particular night the Moriyamas' only child Midori was home for the winter holidays. Midori means "verdant", but what immediately took Nagai's eye was the raven-black hair of extraordinary sheen and luxuriance, a legacy of Midori's mother, Tsumo, "the Crow". Midori's dark complexion and strong supple limbs too came from her mother's people, who had lived outdoors as Ukujima farmers and fisherfolk since the early 1600s. Midori waited on them that night, and although she did not speak much, Nagai noticed how attractive she was when she smiled. A proud Tsumo had once shown him school-album photos of Midori as sprint champion and middle blocker in the championship volleyball team. He could see an athletic girl still in the graceful flow of her movements.

The father, soon aglow with hot sake, did most of the talking and spoke enthusiastically about his Christian ancestors during the persecutions. They would meet in the Moriyama cow shed on Christmas night, which they called *natara*. *Natara* was an example of the strange words that had evolved among these Hidden Christians, words found in no Japanese dictionary. The words were Latin or Portuguese in origin, but their pronunciations had changed over three centuries of oral tradition. *Orassho* was their word for prayer, derived from the Latin *oratio*. Before Christmas Eve, continued Moriyama, the stalls and the shed would be cleaned and food laid out with hot water standing by on a charcoal stove. Police or government agents might be on the prowl, so there would always be lookouts to give the signal. If police did come to check on what was going on, as they often did during the harsh Tokugawa dictatorship, the Christians became a group honoring, in traditional Buddhist style, a departed Moriyama. The highlight of the night would be one of the elders retelling the story of Mary and Joseph, who were refused lodging and roamed in the winter darkness until they found a shelter for farm animals. The telling of the story made Christmas happen again, giving the Christians courage to go on through another year of danger. "We are having our own troubles with the police right now," said Moriyama, "but considering that we can celebrate public midnight Mass in the cathedral tonight, we have it very easy compared with our ancestors."

Cowherd Moriyama exchanged more hot sake with Nagai and then leaned forward until his ruddy face was close to that of the doctor. "Sensei [Doctor], why don't you come with us tonight to midnight Mass?" Ever since that Sunday when the persistent student had requested lodging a second time, Moriyama had encouraged his wife and Midori to pray that Nagai become a Christian, adding: "Maybe God sent Nagai to us just for that." Midori had taken this to heart. Now she turned toward Nagai sharply to see his reaction to the invitation to midnight Mass. "But I am not a Christian", answered Nagai. "That doesn't matter", replied the father. "The shepherds and Magi who came to the stable were not either. But when they saw him, they were able to believe. You can never believe if you don't come to the church and pray." Two phrases from Pascal flitted across Nagai's consciousness: Get down on your knees; go to Mass. He surprised himself by replying: "Yes, I'd like to accompany you tonight."

Though it was snowing that night, nearly five thousand people crammed into the cathedral for midnight Mass. Even rough-looking farmers and laborers had dressed well, and women's and girls' kimonos splashed gorgeous colors across the throng. Nagai was struck by the power of the congregational singing and by the stillness each time they stopped. In his book *Horobinu Mono Wo*, he writes at length about this first Mass and his unexpected "intuition that there was a living Someone present in the Urakami Cathedral". Nagai was familiar with the famous Buddhist word and concept *Mu*. The ideograph for *Mu* is written: "a man burning a bundle over a fire" and is variously translated into English as "Emptiness", "the Void", or "No Thing". Buddhism insists that each of us is, in a real sense, a void, a nothing, because everything we possess has been received from another. My body, my face, my words, my very accent came as gifts from my ancestors, parents, family and teachers. Every ounce of food I eat, everything I use, is from others. Nagai found himself thinking, during the long moments of silence, of this ancient Asian concept.

His mind went to another Buddhist concept that always amused and delighted him: nature deliberately put our navel right where we see it daily as we bathe. It was placed there as a sign, as a symbol that our bodies and every part of us came as gifts. We literally lived from our mother for nine whole months. We did absolutely nothing to deserve this, being passive recipients of her nourishment and care. Therefore, of ourselves we are truly *mu*, we are nothing, we are the void. But there is another *Mu*. It is not *nothing* but No Thing, absolutely above and beyond the "things" accessible to our limited minds. Nagai wondered if Pascal's "Absolute, Infinite God" was the same as Buddhism's "No Thing" and "the Void". He had read in the *Pensées* that "God is inexpressible, and so the Bible is full of metaphors" and that "our minds, like our senses, are very limited—too much light or too little light and we are blind; too much noise or too little noise and we are deaf." Pascal had concluded with a statement in tune with the magnificent thirteenth-century Japanese Zen monk Dogen: Even though we cannot grasp the Truth with our tiny reason, we can have a heart-experience of it. Nagai groaned inwardly: the only sure path for any man was that of reason. Yet Pascal and Dogen were saying reason can never arrive at the full Truth. Was this the fatal blind spot in religious believers? Was this disastrous apparent rejection of reason behind the fanaticism and wars that seemed to invalidate the claims of every religion Nagai had read about? Yet Pascal and Dogen possessed something magnanimous that mere "reasonable" people seemed to lack.

The old priest ascended the pulpit and interrupted Nagai's reverie. Five thousand people became utterly still as the priest's reedy voice extolled the wonder of God choosing a poor carpenter and his virgin wife. "Here is the humility that our minds know is the truth to make us free. Here is the salvation for which our hearts yearn. How can we complain about hardships when the Holy Family accepted the darkness and pain of this night because it was the Father's loving plan?" The words struck Nagai like the blow a Zen master gives a sleepy disciple, making him conscious of all the selfishness, materialism and sham in his heart!

The priest left the pulpit, and everyone rose to sing the Latin Credo. The words, occurring in Masses by the great composers, were not wholly unfamiliar to Nagai. Tonight's Credo, however, unsettled him because its stark dogmatism was unsoftened by the glorious polyphony of Beethoven or Mozart. This Credo from five thousand Urakami throats was more like a defiant roar and battle cry. Why did he feel disturbed? Was it a sane reaction to "fanaticism", all the more unsettling because expressed in a very un-Japanese way? Or, he reflected ruefully, was he disturbed because ordinary people could take an uncomplicated stand for goodness and truth, while he was a footloose academic and ethical dilettante who could not?

The singing stopped, and incense swirled about the candle-lit altar. It reminded him of *haru-gasumi*, the faint blue haze that hangs over Japanese mountains in spring, always suggestive of something infinitely tender. Silvery bells pierced the *haru-gasumi*, and again everyone knelt. Looking across the hush to the pinpoints of candlelight on the altar roused a memory deep within him. It was the memory of a university vacation when he and a few friends went tramping through great silent mountains. Each night, they would sit by the embers of the campfire, often in silence. Nagai would gaze up into the clear night sky, picking out his favorite constellations, listening to them like sections of an orchestra you could hear only in your *kokoro*, your heart. Those constellations, and now these candle glints, suggested a mystical Beyond.

The cathedral Mass came to an end, and Nagai was back home in his room in the Moriyamas'. He lay snug under a heavily padded Japanese quilt but despite a long day of almost twenty-four hours was wide awake. His mind was as restless as Nagasaki's skies during the April Hata-age, the kite-flying festival, when hundreds of multicolored kites soared, dived and swerved as their operators strove to sever each other's strings. Conflicting thoughts and emotions struggled against each other, banishing sleep. Flashbacks of that night's rich medieval ceremonial clashed with a scientist's inbred fear of emotionalism. He admired a faith that inspired five thousand people, mostly of the laboring class, to alternate the deepest silence with the exuberant singing of Schubert's *Ave Maria*. His doctor's common sense warned him, on the other hand, that religions of strong discipline and of black-and-white answers are precisely the ones that have become the most militant and destructive. The Crusades, Nichiren Buddhism and Islam came to mind. The memory of his intuition of a loving Presence at the Mass faltered as voices echoed from the past, voices of professors cautioning their students about the pathologic effects of autosuggestion, hysteria and psychological manipulation. And yet . . . Pascal was aware of those dangers, and he was sure of the loving Presence in the Urakami Cathedral. Pascal in Urakami? No, that wasn't right—it was Saint George's Cathedral in Hamburg. He frowned mentally, but before he could get it straight, drowsiness overwhelmed his mind and emotions and turned out the light of consciousness.

The next day, he worked in the radiology department as usual but returned home ready for an early bedtime. He had hardly changed into his *nemaki* and slithered under the fluffy futon than he was sound asleep. He did not hear the movement down below when Midori woke her parents around midnight, gripped by terrible stomach pains. Her mother immediately suspected intestinal worms. The Japan of the early 1930s had not achieved fully hygienic standards. The farmers were poor and in no position to buy chemical fertilizer, nor did any but the richest homes have sewage laid on. The solution to these two problems was to empty the contents of toilet pits onto vegetable gardens and farmlands. A regular sight on the Japanese landscape was a farmer hurrying along vegetable rows carrying over his shoulder a pole with a malodorous "honey bucket" on either end. One unfortunate result of this process was a high incidence of intestinal worms from eating vegetables. Tsumo always had worm-medicine handy and immediately gave Midori a dose, but it was no help. Midori was now moaning and writhing in pain.

It was snowing heavily and would take ages to get a doctor at that hour, so Sadakichi went upstairs and woke the young Dr. Nagai. With a profusion of bows and apologies, he explained the crisis. Takashi went straight down and quickly diagnosed acute appendicitis. Midori must be operated on immediately. When he turned from Midori's bed, he saw Sadakichi kneel in front of a statue of the Virgin Mary and light a candle. Poor Sadakichi mumbled to no one in particular, "It's all God's will, and who knows what good will come from this", a remark that struck Takashi as odd.

Telling them to get Midori ready for moving to the university hospital immediately, Nagai hurried to nearby Yamazato Primary School, careful not to slip in the snow. The night watchman answered his knocking and said yes, Dr. Nagai could use the telephone. "Moshi moshi. Hello, hello. Three two double-o, please. It's urgent; hurry, please ... Ah, moshi moshi. Nagai here. Who's on hospital emergency tonight? Good, good. Would you call him, please. Nagai from x-ray speaking." A friend came to the phone, and Nagai asked him if he could do an appendectomy immediately. With warm assurances lingering in his ear, Nagai was out in the snow again and back at the Moriyama's door. Midori was rolled up in a blanket, moaning softly.

"It would take too long to get a taxi in this snowstorm. We can't risk the delay." Sadakichi had been in poor health for some months. Tsumo was still out in a back room bundling up the things Midori would need in the hospital and that she herself would need as *tsukisoi* to her daughter. "O-to-san", said Nagai, using the term that family and close friends used for Sadakichi. It means "Dad" and sounds very intimate but is quite respectful. "If you carry the lantern in front, I can manage Midori-san easily." Midori received such a shock that she forgot her pain. Be carried through the streets by a man? But then she reflected, Who would see us at this hour? Her Japanese propriety reassured, she allowed herself to be lifted onto Nagai's back. They stepped out into the swirl of large snowflakes, Sadakichi leading the way through fleeting pools of soft yellow light spilling from his wax-paper lantern. Their footsteps were almost noiseless on the snow-muffled streets, and the city seemed wrapped in peace until a dog rushed out barking at them. The startled party stopped in its tracks, and Nagai roared back at it. As it slunk away, he became conscious of Midori's rapid heartbeats and her hot breath on his neck. As her life was now in danger, Nagai immediately set off again in a hurry, trying not to jolt her, while puffing Sadakichi did his best to keep ahead with the light. They entered the hospital, and their footsteps echoed eerily down the unlit wooden corridor. Nagai turned the corner and saw the lights on in the operating room. Steam was escaping from the room's exhaust pipe and rose as delicate gray spirals through the shaft of yellow light coming from a window. "How beautiful it all is," he thought, "lights burning, steam heating on, operating table ready, instruments laid out—everything in readiness to save a precious life".

Seven minutes after they laid her on the operating table, the operation was all over. The appendix had been on the point of bursting. A nurse put it in a bottle of formaldehyde solution and handed it to a bemused Sadakichi, whose emotions had been through the four seasons in the space of half a night.

Tsumo had also arrived by now with sheets, a futon and toiletries slung on her back. She also carried a bulging *furoshiki*, that ubiquitous square of colored cloth that Japanese use for carrying things. She gave it to Nagai, saying it was a little something for the good doctor who had operated. Nagai took it to the surgeon's room, and the surgeon opened it, revealing several bottles of wine, a ham and homemade sausage. The surgeon poured out glasses of wine for Nagai and for himself. Raising his glass, he said: "To the speedy recovery of your sweetheart." Nagai flushed and protested that Midori was not his sweetheart. "Come on, friend", laughed the young surgeon. "Do you mean to tell me she would consent to being carried through the streets of Urakami if she were not? And the oh-so-gentle way you carried her! It's not a matter to be embarrassed about. You are to be congratulated on your choice. Let's drink to her."

Silent night—Nihon-teki *style.*

10

The Virgin and the Prostitute

In January 1933, Nagai was staggered to receive a plain official postcard calling him up for military service with the Eleventh Hiroshima Regiment. The Japanese generals, who initiated the Manchurian campaign without consulting the elected politicians in Tokyo, assured them that victory would be swift and cheap. They were wrong; the Chinese had been humiliated enough! Their resistance sent shock waves across the Sea of Japan, reaching even the radiology rooms at Nagasaki University. In his medical work, Nagai had come to learn the horrific casualty figures in China. He realized his call-up could well be his death sentence, and a great melancholy swept over him. His first real research project, the effects of x-rays on rabbits, had absorbed his whole attention for months. It would have to be left behind, inconclusive. He had a chilling premonition that this was how his life would soon end—inconclusive.

On January 21, his last night in Nagasaki, old friends from the university basketball team gave him a farewell party. It began in high spirits, but the daughter of the restaurant proprietor ruined the mood by bursting into loud sobs as she was filling his sake cup. She had hosted too many farewell parties for fine young men like Nagai. Everyone had *banzai*ed them off with sake and assurances of quick victory only to hear of their deaths in action a few months later. Nagai's party went flat and broke up early.

Light snow was falling as he walked home to the Moriyamas'. Just weeks before, he had traveled this same road carrying Midori. He vividly recalled her heartbeat on his shoulder. Was his doctor friend right, was Midori his sweetheart? Well, even if she was, he must leave her, and everything else that had given promise to his life! They were just beautiful dreams, perhaps to be buried forever in an unmarked grave under Manchurian snow. He opened the Moriyamas' front door and trudged up to his room, disconsolate. He thought he might just sit there all night, relishing the last hours of his youth and his hopes. Or maybe he would get drunk to dull the pain. Suddenly, light footsteps were coming up the stairs, and then he heard a low "Gomen kudasai. Excuse me." He got up, opened the sliding door and found Midori, dressed in one of her tasteful kimonos, sitting upright on the wooden corridor floor in formal *seiza* fashion. Placing her two hands flat on the floor in front of her, she bowed so low that her lustrous hair fell over them. "I have come to say good-bye and to thank you again for saving my life." He sat in formal style too and returned her deep bow but found himself at a loss for words. She held out a thick woolen cardigan. She knitted it while she was convalescing, she said, as a practical way of saying thank you as he embarked for freezing Manchuria. In her heart, there was the echo of a prayer she had been saying all day: Please, Lord, don't let this young man be cut down by bullets. Please, Lord, bring him back.

He just stared at her. She was like a beautiful flower by the wayside, but he was on a forced march and must pass her by. Everything within him rebelled against it as he gazed at her, a well-nigh perfect example of womanhood, the cardigan resting on her outstretched hands. He put out his own hands to take it and felt her warm hands under his. A great yearning surged through him, and, in one movement, he grasped her hands and drew her close. This time her heart beat close to his as he kissed her passionately. Then, just as suddenly, he released her. He searched her eyes for her reaction but learned nothing, seeing only tears. She bowed low, her beautiful hair falling in disarray on the wooden floor. "Please come back safely", she whispered. "I shall pray for you every day." He listened to her kimono swish down the stairs, and it left him feeling alone, weak and guilty. If Midori had responded to his advances, how far would he have gone? Would he have betrayed the trust the Moriyamas had given him?

There were many university friends at the Nagasaki station the next day to see Nagai off, and he responded to their call for a performance of the Dance of the Mudfish Catcher. The "all aboard" announcement was lost in their cheers, and the stationmaster uttered uncomplimentary words about "those idiots from the ivory tower". Others besides Nagai were going off as rookies, and the Neighborhood Associations were there to see that each recruit left with a good showing of well-wishers waving Rising Sun flags and singing patriotic songs.

The train headed east with Nagai feeling painfully alone. He had seen rousing send-offs before, but the Rising Sun flags were no magic wands warding off Chinese bullets. He had treated wards full of wounded and dying soldiers, but the Neighborhood Associations had not come to show them how to die in peace. Common soldiers were expendable, and when one died, the hospital staff removed the soiled sheets and replaced them speedily for the next soldier. They put a new name above the bed and just as promptly forgot the one that preceded it.

That morning, Midori, who was still recuperating, was sitting on the glassed-in veranda in the weak sunshine, knitting heavy woolen gloves. She was a woman of deep faith to whom praying was as natural as breathing. While her needles moved deftly, she was talking to the Lord: "Please don't let him die in Manchuria; please bring him back safely. He doesn't know you yet, dear Lord, but everyone at the hospital spoke of his great generosity and dedication to his patients. Mary, he looked so sad last night when he was alone. You know that he has lost his mother. Please take her place. I promise I'll say the Rosary for him every day and try to write him the kind of encouraging letters his mother would have written. Please help me do it well."

Hiroshima was not an old city like the ancient places in Nagai's native Shimane Prefecture. In what is for Japan the recent date of 1594, a local daimyo, Baron Mori, selected this strategic site, overlooking a protected bay, for his castle. Hiroshima means "broad island". The Ota River, flowing down from a maze of mountains in the north, forks out into six streams on the plain near the sea to create the Hiroshima delta. Over the centuries, six slender islands were formed in this delta, and the present city straddles them. Toward the end of the nineteenth century, modern port facilities were constructed to handle large ships, and Hiroshima was selected for a main station on the brand new railway between Osaka and Shimonoseki. When the Sino-Japanese War broke out in 1894, Hiroshima Castle became Imperial Military Headquarters, and Hiroshima remained a key military base until 1945.

As Nagai's eastbound train sped through the mountains west of this city, an announcement came in good time, as it usually does on Japanese trains: "Soon we will stop briefly in Hiroshima. Thank you for traveling with us. Please check the luggage rack to make sure you haven't forgotten any personal effects. Once again, thank you, and we hope we can be of service to you in the future." Nagai looked out the window and saw the tributaries of the Ota River coming into view.

In just thirteen years' time, U.S. Colonel Paul Tibbets would strain to see the same tributaries. He would be thirty-two thousand feet up in the B-29 bomber he named Enola Gay after his mother, hoping to honor her with a perfect drop of "Little Boy" in the world's first atom-bomb attack. Weighing four tons, the bomb would explode with more force than twenty thousand tons of TNT. The blinding moment of nuclear fission, August 6, 8:15 A.M., would be seared on the memory of the city like a brand. Though decades would pass, its citizens would painfully relive that moment every anniversary, still finding it hard to believe. They would leave at the epicenter the skeleton of a gutted concrete building, a dark and dead silhouette forever set against the city's evolving skyline, an empty tombstone for one hundred and twenty thousand carbonized citizens. Little children would look on the dread monument like the skeleton of a weird monster that had once come and devoured one-third of Hiroshima's people and pulled down nine-tenths of its buildings. Citizens who lived through "that day" would have nightmares for years, seeing again and again the Ota River choked with blistered, skinned and bloated corpses.

However, on that first day of February, 1932, Nagai's express train slowed to a stop in a Hiroshima supremely confident of its sprawling army base and proud of its folk crafts, wax-paper umbrella factories and sake breweries. The peaceful waters of the Ota River flowed gently into a bay teeming with a famous delicacy, Hiroshima oysters.

Nagai went straight to Company no. 1 of the Light Machine Gun Corps, Eleventh Hiroshima Infantry Regiment, and entered the office. Soldiers sat around a stove talking loudly over sake. No one took the slightest notice of him. He announced himself: "Takashi Nagai, reporting for duty." A voice roared back: "And just what do you think your hat's doing?" "Ah! Beg your pardon, sir", said Nagai, grabbing it with his free left hand.

"Don't you know what hand you take a hat off with?" came another voice, this time very soft-spoken. "Oh yes, sir. It should have been my right hand", said a somewhat rattled Nagai, in a voice low like his new questioner's. "Speak up, man! Do you think you're in a girls' school?" "Begging your pardon, sir", shouted Nagai. "I should have taken the hat in my right hand, sirrr!" A lance corporal who sat reading at a table roared back: "Nagai, who in the hell do you think you are, a general, shouting like that?" The tormenting continued, and by the time the soldiers tired of it, Nagai had no illusions about pulling rank as a doctor and assistant to a pioneer radiology professor! He was no Doctor anything, just Private Nagai.

The army and navy created by the Meiji Restoration drew most of its officers from the old samurai families. The rank and file, especially in the army, came from the huge and impoverished peasant population. The rights and indeed the personal value of the peasants had been effectively denied during the 267 years of the Tokugawa shogunate, making them a completely subservient class. From 1868 the new oligarchs under Emperor Meiji began telling downtrodden peasants that they could join a glorious and invincible race of warriors. If they enlisted in the armed forces, they could actually become samurai, truly members of that lofty and once-forbidden elite.

Right up to the present, Japanese have found in *bushido*, which literally means "the way of the *bushi*"—that is, of the samurai—the great energy-giving ideals that Carl Jung calls archetypes. Here is the stuff of heroic legend and the Japanese equivalent of the tradition of chivalry that grew up around Arthur and the Knights of the Round Table—or a more modern Western equivalent, the Virginian, that lone, upright, self-reliant, deadly-on-the-draw hero of the American frontier.

Army candidates, the majority leaving impoverished farms to enter army schools—some at the age of fourteen—were thoroughly indoctrinated in neo-*bushido*. The most glorious thing a soldier, a modern samurai, could do was give his life for the semidivine Emperor, who sat on the Chrysanthemum Throne. The military forces punished commoners who did not lower their gaze on the rare occasions the Emperor was in public. The trouble was that the army knew the Emperor's will better than he did himself! They manufactured the Manchurian Incident, which precipitated the Sino-Japanese War in 1931, without consulting the Emperor. Although he became livid with rage when he heard the news, they publicly congratulated themselves on being his "purest" subjects, prepared to risk life and limb for him. The same bloody-mindedness would eventually lead to war with the United States, even though the Emperor told Prime Minister General Hideki Tojo that it must be avoided at all costs. In effect, the Chrysanthemum Throne was as helpless as chrysanthemum petals in midwinter winds.

A samurai had to be tough. The farmhands who joined the army found a certain compensation for their poverty-ridden backgrounds and mediocre education by excelling in this school of toughness. Rookies were often punched by corporals and sergeants. Sometimes the first instruction to a newly arrived group was brutally simple: they were lined up in their army uniforms, and one by one they were knocked to the ground by a burly sergeant. Right from the start they recited daily the Meiji Military Rescript,[1] which included the old dictum: A true samurai never surrenders. In the war in the Pacific, Japanese soldiers would find it very hard to respect the many Allied soldiers who surrendered. Educated in blinkered army schools, they had no idea of the West's long tradition of honorable surrender. Every Japanese who went as far as middle school had studied a book of essays called *Tsurezure-gusa*, written by Kenko, a court official turned Buddhist monk. His book, written around A.D. 1330, has had a profound effect on subsequent Japanese culture to this day. One of the work's seminal

---

[1] A rescript is a written message from the Japanese emperor that defines the position of the state. The letter carries temporal and religious authority.

sentences runs: "Only if a man accepts death calmly when his sword is broken and his arrows spent, to the end refusing surrender, does he prove he is a hero."

The new recruits of Light Machine-Gun Corps Company no. 1 were soon made painfully aware of just how raw and stupid the drill sergeants thought them to be. Stern discipline dogged them day and night, even when not on parade. Punishments were meted out for the slightest and inadvertent offenses. On the first day of leave, Nagai and a group of fellow rookies left the camp gates with relief and headed for those little eating places you see in every Japanese town and city. At the first one, they had cooked eel washed down with plenty of beer. Then, down a block, tempura and more beer. On a few hundred yards, and into a seedier place for o-den, a thick Japanese stew, and more beer. They lurched to their feet, faces aglow, but their geographical progression had not been haphazard. A hundred yards along, they reached their objective—the brothels. "Hora! Here it is, lads. Up and at them!"

Nagai was alone in a small room talking with a nineteen-year-old prostitute. He found out she came from an island in the Inland Sea between Hiroshima and Shikoku. Her makeup had wilted in the noonday heat, and she carried an unmistakably jaded air. Was that herpes around her lips? As he watched her stuffing food into her mouth, all desire for a prostitute left him. He leaned forward and, taking her free hand, put the fee into it. Then he opened the *shoji*, the sliding paper door, to go out. She was startled and snorted: "Don't you fancy me, you bastard?" and hurled food at him. "At that precise moment," he was to write in his book *Horobinu Mono Wo*, "a young woman was praying for me before a statue of the Blessed Virgin in the Nagasaki cathedral." He discovered this when a letter arrived from Midori Moriyama several days later.

Shinto shrine near Hiroshima.

The kaya thatch home in Mitoya where Nagai was born.

Stone on the site of the Moriyama ancestral home, which was destroyed by the A-bomb. The inscription says "Chokata [head persons of the Hidden Christians] lived here."

Takashi and Midori Nagai, with their son Makato.

The Nagais with Makoto and their relatives.

Bedridden Nagai with his two children.

Part of Nagasaki University Hospital after the A-bomb.

Saint Paul Miki, Twenty-six Martyrs Museum, Nagasaki.

A Maria Kannon.

Nagai's daughter Kayano (right) with her daughter Kazuko (meaning "child of peace"). Kyoto, 1990.

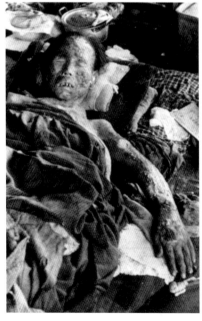

Two photos showing the effects of the A-bomb's infrared rays. The boy carried by his elder brother died the next day.

His medals, after the A-bomb.

Nagai wearing his medals, after his second return from the China war front.

The melted Rosary Nagai found with the charred skeleton of his wife.

Nagai's younger brother Hajime with Midori's melted Rosary, now displayed in Nagai Museum, Nagasaki.

Peace Park statue, Nagasaki. The right hand points to heaven, the left hand to the Urakami Cathedral.

The Urakami Cathedral and southern cupola after the A-bomb. Four months later the bell was unearthed intact.

Nagai's hut, Nyokodo.

Statue of Mary by the Cross, damaged but left standing in the ruins of the Urakami Cathedral.

Bronze of a Yamazato schoolgirl praying in the A-bomb flames. A present-day pupil is seated alongside.

Father Ichiro Okura, who was the agnostic doctor involved in the flag incident in the aftermath of the A-bomb.

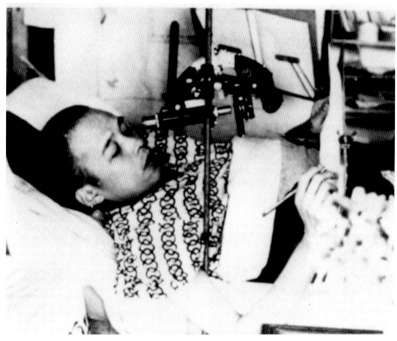

Bedridden Nagai continues research into the effects of A-bomb radiation.

The hidden Christians of Urakami, Nagasaki, declare themselves to Father Petitjean in the Oura church on March 17, 1865.

Nagai with silver sake cups and a document sent by His Imperial Highness, Emperor Hirohito.

Ichitaro Yamada, who dug up the cathedral bell on December 24, 1945.

Inside a Japanese home. A sliding paper-frame wall (shoji) is on the right. A scroll (kakejiku) hangs in the built-in alcove (tokonoma). The women are sitting in the formal seiza posture on a tatami mat floor.

The Oura church in Nagasaki, saved from the A-bomb by the hills. The hidden Christians declared themselves to Father Petitjean in this church on March, 17, 1865.

The Urakami Cathedral today, rebuilt like the cathedral destroyed by the A-bomb. Note the original statues, scorched by A-bomb heat rays.

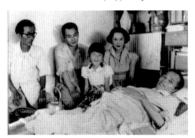

Bedridden Nagai in Nyokodo, with movie director Hideo Oba and stars Masao Wakahara and Yumeji Tsuioka, discussing The Bells of Nagasaki.

A scene from The Bells of Nagasaki, a top box-office movie.

A scene from the second Shochiku movie about Nagai, Children of Nagasaki.

11

The Great Pan Is Dead[1]

Several days after his visit to the brothel, Nagai was summoned to the commandant's office and directed to a subordinate's desk. Nagai saluted and was immediately startled by the question: "Who is this Midori, and what's your connection with her?" "No special connection, sir, just an acquaintance." "Just an acquaintance, is she? Then why have you gone red? You can keep the gloves she sent but not this book, *A Catholic Catechism*. Special Affairs will check it, and you're in trouble if they find something subversive."

The enclosed letter from Midori was short, and Nagai read it quickly. However, when he opened the package containing the gloves, he immediately noticed the faint perfume. He held them to his face and inhaled. The perfume that had remained in his memory since the night he kissed her!

Three days later, he was called to the commandant's office and handed the catechism. "It's full of complicated ideas about Christianity. Special Affairs notes there is nothing leftist, but if you have time to read useless stuff about Western gods, you had better know your Soldier's Manual thoroughly!"

A little later he sat down to the catechism, a straightforward book in question-and-answer format. The book put into precise if sometimes quaint words the very questions that had

[1] Plutarch, priest of Delphi, A.D. 100.

been puzzling him for years. "What are the most important things in life?" "Why were we born?" "What is the meaning of suffering?" "What lies beyond death?" Since moving from atheism to agnosticism, Nagai had done some thinking about several of Japan's outstanding religious figures, like ninth-century Kobo and thirteenth-century Dogen, who made perilous sea journeys to find spiritual masters in China. Returning to Japan, they refused prestigious positions and led ascetic lives, ceaselessly teaching, writing and counseling never-ending streams of wisdom seekers. Their lives had been uncompromising quests for answers to the questions posed rather naïvely in Midori's catechism. Quests and questions, yes, but who had the answers? Were there any?

He came to the Ten Commandments and read them with embarrassment. "I suddenly felt dirty. If there was a God and if there was a devil, I had spent my life observing the devil's ten commandments—pride, lust, covetousness, gluttony, anger. . . . I had done everything the book said was wrong." On his last day of leave, he won the plaudits of his mates by putting away half a dozen bottles of sake and then sitting down in the crowded main street at Senda Machi. Suddenly this and so much of his past seemed utterly cheap. And his future? An untimely death in Manchuria? One narrow ray of light penetrated the gloom—a faithful woman in Nagasaki who had promised to pray for him daily. Her promise gave him comfort, though he himself could believe in neither God nor Buddha.

Nagai's diary continues the story from a Manchuria acrid with cordite.[2] It was now two years since the overconfident Japanese army had attacked Chinese troops, assuring a stunned Prime Minister Wakatsuki that this "Chinese incident" would

[2] Smokeless explosive powder that has been gelatinized and pressed into cords resembling twine.

be concluded in next to no time. However, it had become the terrible "Chinese swamp", and Nagai was working on field operating tables that were bloody around the clock.

He writes of how painful it was to explain to an increasing number of amputees why he amputated. He describes one soldier caught by a bursting shell who was rendered totally blind and deaf. Much later, when the soldier regained consciousness, he thought he was a captive of the Chinese and begged them repeatedly to finish him off. When Nagai's unit advanced behind artillery barrages, his stomach turned as they passed mangled Chinese dead, many of them elderly and infants. Most disturbing of all were the small orphans holding desperately onto the corpses of their parents, sobbing and looking dumbly into space. Was the firmament that he once thought so beautiful just a never-ending void of meaninglessness?

Formerly, his vision of science and human progress had been a source of energy and optimism. Now that vision was receding like a mirage as he operated around the clock, trying to focus his bloodshot eyes on the victims of scientific warfare. His faith and confidence in the two-millennia sweep of Japanese history and culture faltered too. He had accepted army propaganda in the Hiroshima staging camp: "Japan has a sacred responsibility to occupy the vacuum in Manchuria and stop the advance of inhuman Bolshevism. Japan must also liberate Asia from Western colonists and usher in the Asia Co-prosperity era." The brutality of the Japanese army left him deeply troubled.

Nagai lit his hurricane lamp and wearily opened the *Pensées* to the place where Pascal quoted the sad words of the Greek writer Plutarch: "The great Pan is dead"; the pantheon has degenerated into "crass superstition or complete atheism." He thought of the Japanese pantheon, the eight million Shinto gods. They had once been powerful rallying symbols in the Meiji Restoration and standard-bearers for the militarists.

Japanese soldiers all bowed before them in the Shinto shrines that dotted the Japanese landscape, before marching off to war. But when those same soldiers lay in his wards awaiting death, which Pascal called the moment of ultimate honesty, few were able to turn to the gods for comfort.

Pascal went on to insist that you could discover the living God only "if you went down on your knees." Midori and her parents, and the salty old bell ringer who helped build the Urakami Cathedral, went down on their knees. Midori's catechism insisted that prayer was as essential to the human spirit as air is to the lungs. Nagai wanted to believe this because he wanted to believe there was some meaning to the universe and to the deaths of young soldiers dying in a foreign land— and to the deaths of his mother and the Chinese mothers and children and soldiers. If there was no ultimate meaning to life, he might end up like that deaf and blind soldier, begging his "captors" to finish him off! He had a doctor friend who coped with the war by using morphine. He sympathized with the man's anguish but regretted his behavior. The serenity of Pascal, the Moriyamas and spiritual giants like Dogen and Kobo was very attractive, but if he plunged blindly into faith and prayer, would it not be the cowardice of surrender? Faith might be a more subtle form of surrender than morphine, but was it not just as much a surrender?

Chinese dragon, a symbol of transformation.

12

At the Feet of a Janitor-Sensei

Richard Wagner in his opera *Tannhäuser* draws on medieval symbolism to tell a powerful story. The knight Tannhäuser, wearying of the griefs and uncertainties of life, offers himself body and soul to Venus, the goddess of carnal love. Alas, he grows weary of Venus too and falls into despair because he lacks the power to break free of her jealous hold. The faithful maiden Elizabeth, who has never ceased loving the feckless knight, pours out her heart to the Blessed Virgin, begging her to intercede for Tannhäuser. The knight escapes the smothering love of Venus and wins eternal salvation. Nagai describes his return from the Manchurian front with a similar metaphor. He returned to Nagasaki disillusioned and near despair as he descended the gangplank. He stood on the wharf looking up at "the two Nagasakis.... One is the Nagasaki of carnal love, and you can find it down in suburbs like Maruyama, Hama no Machi, Ohato and Minato Machi, places of the night dedicated to loose women, sake and fun. Close by this carnal Nagasaki is the other city, the Nagasaki of Mary, also a place of love, but a love sustained by prayer, sacrifice and service. You can discover this second Nagasaki in the Urakami Cathedral, on the Hill of the Twenty-six Martyrs, in the Oura pilgrim shrine and in the monastery built by Maximilian Kolbe."

Nagai stood on the wharf trying to make up his mind. Climb the steep hill to the cathedral or go to downtown Nagasaki for solace in the familiar places of Venus? The maid Elizabeth swung the balance for Tannhäuser, and the thought of Midori did it for Nagai. He would go immediately to her and apologize for his behavior on that last night. He had hoped to marry her one day, but she was a faithful believer who had never lost purity of heart. He was hopelessly confused, a man who had lost his integrity doing everything his passions urged him to. Marriage prospects or not, he would go and apologize for grabbing her as if she were a plaything of Venus. Then he would go up to the cathedral and seek a ray of light for the darkness in his heart.

Midori answered the door, gasped involuntarily and just stood there. Nagai, uncharacteristically, found himself at a loss for words. He was not used to apologizing. As men will sometimes do when they do not know what to say, Nagai tried to hide his confusion by doing something. Removing his army overcoat, he peeled off the woolen pullover she had knitted him and put it on the tatami floor, where Midori remained motionless in her kneeling-sitting posture. Standing on the ground, two steps below the tatami, he gave a jerky bow and said abruptly: "Thanks to you, I didn't once come down with the flu. Thanks." Midori carefully bent down and took the frayed pullover, feeling the warmth that clung to it. She held it in both hands, saying nothing. It was a bleak winter's day, and he began to shiver. Worse than that, he was still unable to find adequate words to begin his apology. The silence had become oppressive for Midori too, equally at a loss. Suddenly, grasping the pullover to herself, she bowed and stood up. "Where are you going?" he blurted out. She said, "I don't suppose it's of much use to you now", and he listened to the patter of her bare feet as she disappeared to the back room.

He put on his overcoat, mortified at clumsily ruining a simple apology. Midori's reaction indicated there was no hope of marriage. She had merely pitied him for the directionless person that he was. Now that he was back from the front, her duty was finished! Heavy in spirit, he walked through the Moriyamas' front gate and down the hill and climbed the steep stone steps to the Urakami Cathedral.

"Gomen kudasi. May I come in?" he called out nervously on the rectory porch. The frail priest who came to the door was the one who had celebrated the midnight Mass at Christmas. Father Moriyama took the soldier's hand in his own as if he were a long-lost brother and ushered him into his study. Nagai noticed the book-lined walls and felt more at home. The priest handed him his card, and Nagai saw that the ideographs for "Moriyama" were different from Midori's surname, though *yama*, or "mountain", was the same in both names.

Nagai politely asked Father Moriyama if he was related to Jinzaburo Moriyama, who lived near Sadakichi Moriyama. "Yes, he's my father. Has he ever cornered you and told you some of those interminable stories?" They both laughed, but Nagai's laugh was nervous. The war had left him drained of optimism and exuberance. Now he must tell this stranger how morally depraved he was. Maybe Father Moriyama would recoil angrily.

"Shinpu-sama [Father], I am not sure what I am doing here and really have no right to be taking up your time. I have lost peace of heart. Maybe I have forfeited all right to it—I have done almost everything your catechism says is wrong. Maybe I have even committed what it calls the sin against the Holy Spirit." It was all Nagai could do to complete the sentence, for his voice and breathing had become strained. The priest said nothing, but his heart went out to this tired soldier just back from the front. He took the kettle off the wood stove and made a pot of that Japanese panacea, *o-cha*, or thin green tea. Nagai drank a cup gratefully, regained his composure and, encouraged by the warmth in the priest's eyes, told the story of his life. He spoke of his old cocksure atheism, of the doubts that followed his mother's death, of his struggle to understand Pascal, of his bouts of drunkenness and visits to brothels. "At times I think there must be a God and an afterlife," continued Nagai, "but I never feel sure for long. Shinpu-sama, what made you so sure of these things that you became a priest?"

Father Moriyama, being an Eastern wise man, responded with a story. His grandparents and their family, he began, had been rounded up in 1864 when the anti-Christian edict was reinforced. His grandmother died in the Sakura Machi prison in Nagasaki; his grandfather died soon afterward in the prison in Tsuwano. Their eldest son, Jinzaburo, unmarried and only twenty-two, succeeded his father as Christian leader. Tsuwano prided itself on its pure Shinto tradition, and the prison officials assured the central government in Tokyo that they would soon bring the ignorant Christian farmers back to Shinto. When lengthy philosophical persuasion failed, refined torture was adopted. In a bitterly cold winter, Jinzaburo and other Christians were plunged through the ice of a frozen pond, held under with hooked poles and fished out just in time to stay alive. They were then shoved close to a fire. The process was repeated, and the victims often passed out. Some of the Christians broke down, agreed to join Shinto and were put into comfortable quarters with plenty of food. However, rock-solid and eloquent Jinzaburo was the one the police had to break if they were to demoralize the Christian group. The commandant was an ex-samurai, Morioka, who had made the original boast that every one of the Christians would quickly return to Shinto. Increasingly frustrated by Jinzaburo's intransigence, he tried a more subtle method. He had noticed how solicitous Jinzaburo was for his fourteen-year-old brother, Yujiro, the youngest in the family and obviously spoiled.

The boy was taken a short distance from Jinzaburo's cell, stripped and whipped mercilessly. He groaned in pain but held out. He was tied up naked on a cross, jabbed with bamboo poles and taunted for belonging to a foreign superstition. He was fastened onto bamboo slats that cut into his knees, and ice-cold water was poured over him until he turned blue. For fourteen days the boy endured such brutalities on a near-starvation diet. Finally, his body could take no more, and he fell into unconciousness. Morioka had intended to break Yujiro, not kill him, but now the boy was dying, and Morioka found himself asking: "Am I a samurai, am I a man, torturing a mere youth to death?" He had the unconscious boy carried to his older sister Matsu in the women's prison. She cradled him, trying to revive him with the warmth of her own body. Yujiro opened his eyes and saw she was crying and asked her to forgive him for crying out like a coward when he was whipped.

Before he died later that day, he told her things the family would never forget, believing they were not delirious ramblings but words of encouragement from the God "who reveals things to children". He told his sister she would return to Urakami and asked her to care for children. Upon her return, she began caring for Christian children orphaned in the persecution, became one of the first Catholic nuns in modern Japan and spent her life looking after children. The boy said that Jinzaburo would return safely too and that his son would become a priest. Jinzaburo did survive the persecution, married back in Urakami and, on the day his Number One Son was born, rushed with him to the French pastor's residence. "Shinpu-sama, a boy. Please pray he will become a priest." The red-faced bawling mite that the Paris missionary blessed was none other than Father Moriyama.

The priest continued: "My faith was something I received from my parents. However, since I became a priest, I have known many who traveled from atheism to belief. You admire Pascal, and I think he has made a priceless contribution in his insistence on prayer if you want to meet God. You mentioned the Zen monk Dogen. Thirteenth-century intellectuals would come from Kyoto out to his monastery deep in the Eiheiji Mountains hoping for a philosophical discussion. He used to refuse lengthy discussions, however, and say: 'Tada suware. Just meditate!' A French priest who helped me a lot in the seminary loved to quote a kind of Christian Dogen, Origen, who died about A.D. 250 and who had a profound influence on early Christianity. Origen used to say that the Gospel according to John is the quintessence of the Bible and is understood only 'if you lean on Jesus' breast', in other words, if you pray. Christianity is all about God's revelation of mystery. This is not something that is grasped intellectually like radiology but is something that is experienced prayerfully. I shall give you some hints on prayer later.

"You said you feared you have sinned against the Holy Spirit. Surely not! That sin is the deliberate and total rejection of the Holy Spirit, and I think it is very rare. The God of the Bible is the one my French seminary professor called the good God. He is the father who runs out to embrace the returning prodigal. Jesus, whom we believe is his Son, said he came to save sinners, not to judge us."

Midori was a woman of considerable strength of character and composure who rarely became flustered in her schoolroom or anywhere else. The man Nagai, however, had thrown her completely off balance. When he had appeared without notice below her porch step, emotions surged through her that she could not control. Back alone in her room, she now laid the cardigan at the foot of the Moriyamas' most prized possession, the crucifix that her family had guarded through seven generations of persecution. Tears coursing down her cheeks, she prayed: "Jesus, here is his cardigan. I begged you to bring him back, and you did. Thank you. You know that I love him, Lord, but that someone far more academic than I must be his wife. I suppose you smile at me, Lord, for even dreaming of marrying him! Now that he is safely back from the war, I shall meet some of the men my parents and the go-between suggest.

I offer you the pain he has brought me, Lord, as a prayer that he will receive the gift of faith."

She felt drained. She tried to busy herself but finally slipped out of the house and walked the quarter mile to the cathedral. At its entrance was a stone crucifixion scene. She glanced up at the Sorrowful Mother and murmured interiorly as she passed: "You always said yes to God. Help me, Mother, to say yes. But why does God make life so painful? I feel lost. Show me the way." She entered the dim cathedral, knelt and took out her Rosary. It was Friday, the day for the five sorrowful mysteries. That matched the pain in her heart. Twenty minutes later, she lifted her head as she rose from her knees—and froze on the spot. Nagai was kneeling up at the front of the cathedral absorbed, it seemed, in prayer. It seemed that Christ was saying: "Midori, your task is finished. Now that he is home with me, you must forget him." Her genuflection was the heaviest she had ever made.

It was not easy to forget him. He began attending Mass on Sundays, and she would notice him immediately. She was now twenty-five, an age at which most Japanese girls are married. She had refused a number of proposals without telling her worried parents that she would not marry while Nagai was still risking his life on the Manchurian front. She did, however, agree to their request to resign from full-time teaching, come home and take a few subjects at a local Catholic girls' school, Junshin ("pure heart"). Spring came, and the liquid notes of the *uguisu*, the bush warbler, again filled the air, and the cherry trees burst into blossom. All of this was lost on Midori.

Nagai went back to his old job in the x-ray department but spent all his spare time reading the Bible and the catechism and speaking with Father Moriyama. He was getting extra lessons in Catholic practice, liturgy and prayer. His *sensei*, a word that is used for both "teacher" and "doctor", was an old resident of Urakami who knew little about philosophy but, Nagai soon discovered, was an unassuming fountain of wisdom and goodness. This *sensei* also worked at the university hospital—as a janitor!

Yujiro Moriyama (lower right) with fellow prisoners.

Jinzaburo Moriyama.

13

White Australia and the Yellow Peril

Swallows darted gaily over the shimmering green countryside of Japan in June 1934, but liberal sociologists looked glumly at the mood of the populace. The "progressives" (the ones who were in favor of Roosevelt's New Deal in the U.S. elections of 1932) were now swinging to the far right. The Japanese had been rocked by the world Depression in the late 1920s. When Western nations slapped huge tariffs on Japanese manufactured goods, they felt vulnerable, isolated and discriminated against. Very conscious of being the only strong nation in all Asia and Africa that was not a colony, they also believed the West looked on them as an inferior "colored breed". When Japan sat among the victor nations at the Versailles Peace Conference after World War I, she tried desperately to have included in the final communiqué a clause decrying racial discrimination. Australia's Billy Hughes led the bitter opposition that quashed the Japanese motion. He said it was the thin edge of the wedge to change "White Australia", a phrase the Japanese resented. There was another phrase they found hurtful and racial: "the Yellow Peril". Germany's kaiser Wilhelm II had coined the expression in 1895 after he had a dream in which he saw Oriental hordes devastating European cities. He spread this "prophetic" warning with religious fervor. The Japanese resented the ready acceptance of this prophecy from a man who had devastated so many European cities himself! "The Yellow Peril", however, stuck, and the Japanese press duly reported its frequent use in the West. More and more of the Japanese became convinced that the West had no intention of allowing Japan to remain the one powerful "colored" nation.

The Japanese who formed public opinion—writers, journalists, professors, schoolteachers, public servants—had warmed to the concept of Western democracy after World War I through the 1920s. The events of the early 1930s, however, cooled their ardor. Not only were the democracies proving racist, but they were bogging down economically, and moral anarchy was taking over: divorce and delinquency were rising alarmingly, and Chicago-style gangsters could thumb their noses at the police. The West's brassy new music, dancing and risqué fashions were further signs of decadence to the conservative, Confucian Japanese.

Japanese ultrarightists and militarists were quick to utilize all of this in aggressively promoting their simple thesis: only when Japan becomes as powerful as the West, economically and militarily, is the nation safe. The Western democracies, they argued, were preparing to reduce Japan to a third-rate power like China and India. The West was now the enemy! Japanese who embraced Western ideologies like Communism and Christianity were traitors to semidivine Nippon in her hour of peril.

The strong resurgence of nationalism and Shinto was soon felt in Christian Urakami. Father Moriyama and the cathedral began receiving attention from increasingly rightist police, and Dr. Nagai realized that interest in Christianity could jeopardize promotion in the state-run medical university. When his father got wind of his son's new interest, he ordered him home immediately. For several days, Nagai Senior used his authority as head of the family as well as his considerable personal powers to dissuade his son, insisting that as *chonan*, or Number One Son, he had very special obligations to the other family members, living and dead. "The ancestors", thundered the older

Nagai, "could not be more offended than by a *chonan* who abandoned filial piety and the old religion." The son replied that the ancestors joined Taisha Shinto because they sought truth and would not be distressed at him becoming a Christian if he found the truth in the Gospels. Had not the ancestors left another religion when they became Shinto believers? The father grew livid and thundered: "Shinto goes right back to the very beginning."

Takashi respected and loved this father who had pointed out the right path to him from childhood to adulthood. And yet, like father, like son! Maybe the ancestors were smiling because years before, this same father had made up his own mind and gone off on a strange journey to become a doctor of the new Western medicine. The aging Dr. Calmness, however, remained implacably opposed to his son's baptism.

Nagai returned to Nagasaki very disturbed and immediately called on the janitor-catechist. The latter carried cruel childhood memories of the exile in Babylon. The recent resurgence of anti-Christian feeling in Japanese society reopened the old scars, and resentment toward *mi-shinja*, or non-Christians, was rearing its ugly head. Having heard Nagai's predicament, he replied bluntly: "The Master said: He who does not hate mother and father for my sake is not worthy of me." That shocked Nagai and left him more disturbed. The next day, Nagai called on a man well known for sound counsel, old Jinzaburo Moriyama. Moriyama listened to Nagai without interruption, sympathetically nodding his head, and responded with the following tale.

Quite some years after he and the Urakami Christians were released from the prison in Tsuwano, a letter came to him from a Brother Morioka. The writer said his father was the official in charge of interrogating the Christians at Tsuwano and thus was responsible for the death of thirty-six Christians, including Jinzaburo's young brother Yujiro. He, Morioka's son, had become a Christian and joined a religious order. He enclosed money to cover travel expenses in the hope that Jinzaburo would do him the great favor of meeting him in Tsuwano. Jinzaburo went and met him at the Tsuwano railway station, and the two walked twenty minutes in silence to the site of the prison camp, just beyond the town. Jinzaburo's nimble mind quickly reconstructed the old scene. The main prison building was gone, but there was the pond! And that low stone wall behind it—that was where a dear friend, twenty-six-year-old Yasutaro, had died in a box too small for him to sit, stand or lie down. He was nailed up in it and left there in the depths of winter until merciful death took him home to God, twenty days later.

Jinzaburo sank to his knees. In a flash, Brother Morioka was kneeling beside him, his forehead almost to the ground, sobbing out his sorrow for what his father had done to them. Jinzaburo turned and embraced him. "Your father thought he was doing his duty as a government official. He really believed the Christian faith was subversive and a danger to Japan. He confessed his mistake in his own way when he carried my brother to my sister Matsu. You know, I have prayed for your father ever since, and I am sure Yujiro prays for him from heaven. Knowing that you have been given the Faith makes my brother's death all the more meaningful. It is another example of the great truth that you understand better than I, Brother—God is always in charge; difficulties, darkness and suffering become opportunities for new graces if we keep trusting." Jinzaburo had finished his story. He called out to the kitchen for a fresh pot of green tea and changed the subject.

Nagai walked home slowly on a road skirting Mount Konpira. To receive baptism would wound his father and go against filial piety, the Confucian ethic he had imbibed with his mother's milk. There were other negative aspects. For instance, some German Bible critics suggested more research was needed before we knew with certainty what Jesus taught. Or again, would it not be prudent to delay baptism until his father accepted the idea? There was also his duty in the pioneer field of Japanese radiology. Why not delay baptism until his position in the state university was better than mere assistant to the professor? After promotion, he could be baptized and do more for Christianity.

He was now home and sat down by the low table on the tatami floor. He took up Pascal's *Pensées* and had hardly read a paragraph when he came across a sentence that riveted his attention: "There is enough light for those who desire only to see, and enough darkness for those of a contrary disposition." Suddenly it became obvious—for him to delay baptism was to keep company with darkness!

He made his decision, but it did not take away the pain. With feelings like those he had had setting out for the battlefront in Manchuria, he called on Father Moriyama: "I am very conscious of my inadequacy, but I come to ask for the great favor of baptism, Shinpu-sama." The priest wondered if he had given himself enough time; baptism was not something to hurry. But Nagai replied, "Shinpu-sama, I am convinced—and my father is just as convinced I am wrong. We had a painful confrontation, and the longer I delay, the worse it is for both of us. Please examine me and decide if I am ready for baptism." The priest did just that, then and there, and was left in no doubt as to Nagai's comprehension and commitment. Father Moriyama agreed to baptize him in a few weeks' time, before the early Mass.

That was June 1934, just after the beginning of the *tsuyu*, the month-long rainy season that is vital for the young rice planted in May. Nagai arose in predawn darkness and trudged to the cathedral through the relentless downpour. The foreign-style building came dimly into sight, only emphasizing his father's accusation that he was deserting his family and his culture. The priest, the catechist-janitor and a third man were waiting in the sacristy. The latter was the ruddy-faced, ham-fisted farmer whose medieval choir garb struck Nagai as some-what ludicrous at that first Christmas Eve Mass. This man, whom Father Moriyama had chosen as Nagai's godfather, was Midori's cousin, a factor of considerable future bearing.

The four of them went to the poorly lit baptistery, and Nagai later wrote of the panic that seized him as the priest prepared the font. He knew he had to "renounce Satan and all his works and pomps". Suddenly the consequences of that promise seemed inhuman. How could he renounce things he had done most of his adult life, things his contemporaries regarded as part of normal living? How could he promise to be a half man, a half Japanese? The priest placed salt on Nagai's tongue. Nagai prayed to be free of the old concupiscences, and peace gradually came. The Latin ceased to sound alien. Rather, it was the harmonious mother tongue of a worldwide family made up of every culture and race. It was the sublime language that carried the incomparable Masses of Beethoven, Bach and Haydn. The self that he renounced for Christ was the "little self" that ancient Eastern sages spoke of in contrast to the "Big Self", which gave a heartbeat to the universe and meaning to our individual little selves.

For his baptismal name, Nagai had chosen that of the Jesuit martyr Paul Miki, one of the twenty-six crucified in Nagasaki in 1597. Nagai admired both Paul Miki's dynamic spirituality and his feeling for the *Nihon-teki*, things thoroughly Japanese—something Paul Miki learned from his father, a general in Ukon Takayama's castle.

Father Moriyama, who had often been asked by Midori to pray for Nagai during his time at the Manchurian front, suspected their feelings for each other and mentioned it to Nagai's godfather. The heavily built and slow-moving farmer proved to be a fleet-footed *nakodo*, or marriage go-between. Having confirmed the mutual interest, he arranged a formal meeting.

Following upon that, he asked them separately if they wished to pursue the matter further. The only problem came from Nagai, who told him: "I am specializing in x-ray diagnosis. It is very important for the future of medicine but is still an uncertain science. Many radiologists have contracted cancer and died. I must live with the risk of dying young too. Midori must understand that clearly before she agrees to marry me."

There is a passage in the Book of Ruth that Midori loved and had sometimes read to the girls at Junshin School. For her, it summed up marriage. "Where you go I will go, and where you lodge I will lodge; your people shall be my people, and your God my God; where you die I will die, and there I will be buried. May the LORD do so to me and more also if even death parts me from you." Nagai had become one of her people and had chosen her God. It was a small thing on her part to share the risks entailed in his pioneer work aimed at saving lives. He had already saved her life. She bowed low and replied to the go-between: "Donna koto de mo, doko made mo, go issho sasete itadakito gozaimasu. It will be my privilege to share in his journey, wherever it leads and whatever happens on the way."

Having received Midori's consent, Takashi went to see two old acquaintances, Dr. Furuse and his wife, close friends of his father. Nagai told them he had become a Christian and was going to marry a Christian, Midori Moriyama, things hard for his father to accept. He venerated his father, and it pained him to do something against his will. But these two choices were matters of conscience, and he must follow the true path as he saw it. He asked the Furuses if they would be gracious enough to explain this to his father. He was sure his father would find Midori an honorable daughter-in-law, and he and Midori would be ever conscious of their debt to the Nagai family, living and dead. The Furuses, left in no doubt as to Takashi's determination, invited Midori to their home and were very favorably impressed. They went northeast to distant Mitoya, and their mediation won the elder Dr. Nagai's grudging approval of the marriage. However, Nagai's father and family attended a wedding ceremony that did little to win sympathy for Nagai's new religion. The Latin language summed up the foreignness of everything they saw and heard at that ungodly hour. A wedding solemnized before breakfast!

Midori gradually changed them. From the outset, she set about establishing a relationship of *wa* with the Nagai family. *Wa*, a vital word in Japanese, is rather like the biblical "shalom". The Kenkyusha Dictionary defines *wa* as "peace, harmony, reconciliation, unity of comfort". Nagai and his wife traveled as often as they could to the ancestral home in Shimane Prefecture. By the time their first child lay peacefully in the arms of grandfather Nagai, his animosity was gone and *wa* had returned.

Wa, "peace", is composed of ideographs for "grain" (rice) and "mouth"; that is, if you are not hungry, you do not fight.

14

Typhoons and Graceful Bamboo

In 1934 Takashi was assistant to the chief of the subdepartment Radiology on a salary of forty yen a month. The cattle business had died with Midori's father, and forty yen was not enough for her husband, her mother and herself in the worsening Japanese economy. Between 1930 and 1936, exports dropped dramatically while imports rose 29 percent. The yen was twice devalued in those six years and was only half its 1930 value by 1936. To help make ends meet, Midori began putting the pastureland to use by growing vegetables. Tsumo, her mother, laughed. Midori means "verdure", and she certainly had a green thumb! She loved nothing more than a day working in the garden. Well, maybe there was something she loved more—sewing—and her skill delighted Takashi. From the time they married, he never bought store clothes. She found out he did not like anything made from artificial cloth, like rayon. When his bachelor clothes gave out, he found himself wearing everything—from gloves and socks to underwear—in pure cotton, wool or silk, all Midori-made. She made him a tweed overcoat that became a standard item in Urakami dressmaker displays. He was discovering that Midori had much in common with the ideal wife described in the Book of Proverbs 31.

Foreigners visiting Japan are usually impressed by the gentleness and gracefulness of the women. This feminine refinement has a long and recorded history. Whereas European women first began to read and write in the sixteenth century, their Japanese counterparts were writing highly polished *Manyoshu* poetry in the eighth century. In the first decade of the eleventh century, the court lady Shikibu Murasaki wrote the nineteen-hundred-page *Tale of Genji*, a classic in world literature and called the first great novel since Homer's *Iliad* and *Odyssey*. This early and widespread phenomenon of feminine literature created clear-cut ideals of womanly grace for the upper classes. Given the unique homogeneity of Japanese society, it quickly flowed to the lower classes.

The ideal Japanese woman was to be like the bamboo, graceful, gentle, sensitive and strong. The slightest wind will stir the bamboo's filigree leaves, but autumn typhoons will not uproot it. Though giant cedar and cypress lie uprooted after a storm has passed, the slender bamboo stands serene.

Besides having an extensive literature inculcating feminine ideals, every Japanese city and town runs well-attended classes in *cha no yu*, or tea ceremony; *ikebana*, or flower arrangement; and fine needlework. The classes are very serious affairs, essential stages on the *michi*, or the way preparing for marriage and motherhood. Nagai was delighted to discover his wife had a teacher's diploma in *ikebana* and in fine needlework and that she loved the tea ceremony. After their marriage, she opened a night school in their spacious home, teaching *ikebana* and needlework.

Midori's larder never lacked fresh vegetables. She grew potatoes, Chinese and Western cabbage, onions, sweet potatoes, mustard greens, radish and whole fields of barley, much of which she gave away. Nagai kidded her about his fears that one day monstrous green tendrils would seize the whole house and gobble them up. One common sight never ceased giving him delight. Midori would be out working in the garden dressed in *monpe*, the baggy work trousers that became standard women's work wear with the wartime government austerity measures. Well-to-do girls from Junshin, where she taught, would pass by in splendid kimonos. They would stop and solemnly bow, calling out: "Sensei, konnichi wa. Good afternoon, Teacher." Never showing the slightest embarrassment, she would stop her hoeing, stand erect and solemnly return their bow with a pleasantry or two. Then there were grave sayonara bows from both sides. He loved this woman whose strong fine hands were as much at home with the classical tea ceremony as with rough hoeing.

At the university, they won their battle to become an independent Department of Radiology. Work multiplied, and Nagai's research on kidney stones was published in a medical journal. Midori noticed with amusement that he was becoming an absentminded professor. When he was on the trail of a medical breakthrough, he would hardly talk for days. He would take off articles of clothing and leave them where they fell. His study desk would disappear under patients' cards, magazines and books. Sometimes he would call a little sheepishly: "Midori, are you free for a moment? I just can't find that report from Kyoto University." She never showed annoyance during his periods of scientific abstraction, telling her mother that his radiology work must get top priority. He let her reign supreme in household affairs, budgeting, buying, banking and deciding everything concerning Junshin, her night school and the ever-expanding vegetable garden.

At Mass on Sundays and feast days, the Nagais often heard Father Moriyama speak on the beauty of the simple family life at Nazareth. It showed, he said, the great worth of ordinary family life and the grace of God present in humdrum daily work. This reminded Nagai of his boyhood, when his mother taught him how to find the universe in a bowl of rice: "Look at the rice carefully, and discover behind it the countless generations of farmers who pioneered wild land and nurtured rice paddies through droughts and floods, poverty, war and pestilence. See generations of artisans too in the simple, practical beauty of the bowl and chopsticks and in all the merchants who handled them. See your parents too, who worked hard to be able to buy and cook the rice." Nagai's mother would conclude her lesson by joining her hands and bowing in a gesture of profound gratitude, reciting a prayer that explained all this, and the universe as well: "Namu Amida Butsu. We depend on you utterly, Amida Buddha."

Young Nagai's family was Shinto, but it is not the least surprising in Japan to hear a Buddhist prayer on Shinto lips. Like most old samurai families, Takashi's mother's family was Zen Buddhist. She told him how the bonze[1] at their Zen temple used to teach the deeper meaning of ideographs. For instance, the two ideographs that form *arigato*, "thank you", literally mean "this came into existence with difficulty". Behind everything we receive, use or possess, the bonze went on, lie difficulties overcome by great effort. *Shigoto*, "work", is made of two ideographs meaning "something that is a service". All are the beneficiaries of countless other "workers", and we owe it to the community to do our own job well, not primarily for material recompense but out of gratitude. This was the boy's introduction to Japan's famous work ethic. Nagai the Christian recalled his mother's gentle homespun spirituality with gratitude.

Professor Suetsugu, dean of the new Department of Radiology, had many irons in the fire. More and more doctors were clamoring for lectures on x-ray diagnosis. Nagai was asked to help and began a series of talks for general practitioners. His audience quickly grew and with it the dean's confidence in his assistant. Nagai was asked to contribute sections of a university textbook. The administration, impressed by Nagai's energy and ability, appointed him chief of medical staff in the university hospital.

A leading Urakami Christian named Tagawa invited Nagai to join the Society of Saint Vincent de Paul. Nagai never liked

[1] Buddhist monk.

taking on anything new without studying it thoroughly. He borrowed several library books on the society, which was founded by Frenchman Frederick Ozanam in 1833 to help the poor. Ozanam, an academic like Nagai, was a professor in the Sorbonne. Before becoming a convinced Christian, he went through a harrowing time of doubt, leaving him with a life-long sympathy for atheists and agnostics. Nagai read on with aroused interest.

Ozanam, while still a student at the Sorbonne, spent an after-noon walking through Paris slums. In a despondent mood, he went into the dingy parish church of Saint Stephen and was startled to see André Ampère on his knees praying! Ampère was one of the foremost scientists in the world. When Ampère was leaving, Ozanam said: "Professor, I see you believe in prayer." Ampère replied: "Everyone has to pray." The reply struck Nagai with force. It reminded him that he had found God through prayer but was doing precious little to help others do the same.

Nagai joined the Society of Saint Vincent de Paul and was shocked on his first field trip to discover that every person in the hamlet of Kaminoshima had trachoma. He began orga-nizing regular trips on Sundays, coaxing university doctors and nurses to join him in giving free medical service to the poor. One Sunday he visited a woman who had contracted gonor-rhea and had fled in shame to the mountains with her five-year-old son. She was almost blind, and the two survived in a lean-to, shared with their only friends and means of support, laying hens. When Nagai first walked in on them, she was hostile and refused to talk. He came the next week with cloth-ing, food and kind words. Before he left, the woman said: "Doctor, I can smell plum blossoms nearby. Aren't they beau-tiful?" He clambered up the mountainside, picked a branch and left her inhaling the delicate fragrance. Assistance is authen-tic, he jotted down in his journal, when it helps restore a person's dignity.

One cold February night in 1935, he worked late in an unheated laboratory and woke up the next morning with a sore throat and an elevated temperature. Midori suggested he stay in bed, but he had promised to assist with a complicated operation that day. Feeling ill when he arrived at work, he had a throat specialist give him an injection. Ten minutes later, he was in the operating theater feeling unwell when suddenly his vision blurred, his stomach began hurting and his heart began palpitating. He realized he was going to be sick, and with a slight bow of apology, he staggered outside, vomited several liters of blackish blood and began gulping air asthmatically. Professor Suetsugu got him onto a bed and administered a powerful injection to his now-unconscious assistant. He diagnosed anaphylaxis, a condition of hypersensitivity to certain injections that can cause internal hemorrhaging, swelling and death.

Nagai was covered in blood, his eyes almost closed and his whole face swollen like a soccer ball. A cathedral priest was soon bending over him. Nagai strained to stop his asthmatic rasping to catch the words, feeling the end was near. "Child of God, acknowledging all the sins of your life, ask forgiveness because they were in opposition to a God who is all love ... Turn to Christ, who suffered and died for our sins ... Accept your sickness with gratitude because you can offer it with Christ's sacrifice on the Cross ... Let us pray to the Father that you may be restored to health...." Nagai whispered his sins to the priest, who recited the prayer of absolution and anointed him. The comforting aroma of spiced oil seemed to come from another world. His mind was clouding now. He felt death was near but was at peace.

Someone had his hand. A woman? She was holding his hand in hers and crying. Ah, Midori. Suddenly he did not want to die. A tense voice said: "Pulse 130, breathing 36." Another injection. He reflected: If I am to die, this is a good place, with Midori and my colleagues beside me. A saying of

Confucius floated into his consciousness, one he had learned and loved as a schoolboy: "If you have found the way of truth in the morning, you can meet death peacefully that evening."

He recovered, but that experience changed him profoundly. Until then, he had never believed death was imminent, not even during the toughest fighting in Manchuria. Now, however, he had looked into its cold eyes. One injection, he says, convinced him of the central theme in ancient Japanese literature—life is as transient "as the dew of Adashino, and the smoke above Toribeyama", places for cremating the dead of Old Kyoto, littered with crumbling tombstones centuries old. Nagai for the first time "tasted" his own mortality and began spending more time reading the Bible or alone in the cathedral.

The episode also left him with asthma. Cool air, laboratory rabbits, his own hearty laughter, sake and a heavy meal, a tobacco-filled room, or sudden exercise could start him wheezing. One snowy night when he was congested, Midori talked him into going to bed early. He was hardly in bed when a caller came with the message that the old farmer at Ippongi whom the doctor had visited on Saint Vincent de Paul calls was so bad with asthma that he could hardly breathe. Nagai said he would go immediately, despite Midori's strongly voiced misgivings. He was not listening, so she helped him into his clothes and put his padded kimono and a cloak over them. She added two pairs of socks despite his protests, gloves, and a cotton mask over his nose and mouth. She gave reluctant approval and helped him into his Wellington boots. With his doctor's bag in one hand and a stout stick in the other, he set out, looking, he writes, like an Eskimo.

The farmer lived a mile and a quarter up in the hills, and Nagai regulated his pace and breathing carefully. He found the old fellow sitting up, his shoulders heaving each time he struggled for a rasping mouthful of air. He was beyond talking, but his eyes pleaded for help. "It will soon be all right, old friend", Nagai said as he took the leathery arm and injected adrenalin and bitter camphor. Within thirty seconds, the tight face began to relax and the breathing began to ease. The doctor gave him packets of medicine for the next five days and said good-bye to him: "O genki de. Get well". The old man bowed gratefully and gave the doctor "two bright diamonds, one in the corner of each eye".

Nagai went out into the night again. The snow was heavier now and the moon completely hidden. I'll be all right—it's downhill, he thought, and foolishly hurried. He had not gone far when his lungs were seized with asthma. He saw a big hole in the hillside right beside the road, dug for storing potatoes. The snow was getting into his eyes as he staggered into the hole and collapsed onto the ground, gasping for air with his body shaking. He wanted to inject himself with adrenalin but knew he could not do it with trembling hands in the pitch blackness. Panic came, which was more fuel for the asthmatic fire in his lungs. It must be seven hours to daylight, he thought, and no one will travel this road in a snowstorm like this. He was no longer a doctor but a frightened patient.

Not long afterward, he saw light outside—then a lantern and someone's heavy stick. Then, above the sound of his short, rasping breaths, came a pinched voice: "It is you, it is you, isn't it?" "Yes", he gasped. "Quick, Midori, the light." She opened his bag, filled the syringe and jabbed the needle home. The terrible boulder started to slide off his chest. As he waited there, his head leaning on Midori's breast, he thought: This is how a soul must feel when led out of Purgatory.

Midori told him she would carry him on her back. Though she called him Shujin, "Lord", as most Japanese wives called their husbands, there were many areas in family life where she and most wives reigned supreme. The pay envelope, for instance, was handed over unopened, and the monthly budget, including the husband's pocket money, was decided by

her. Right now Midori adopted a tone that told him he was
going to be carried on her back. She went down on one
knee of her heavy *monpe* trousers, and he leaned wearily on
her back. A forward and upward movement, and they were
off. She even managed the lantern, its warm and mellow light
capturing the wonder of the silent snowfall. His weary mind
went back to that emergency journey to the hospital. She
was light, while he weighed over 150 pounds! The graceful
bamboo, however, did not break.

15

A Christian Nenbutsu and the Dark Night

Gigantic upheavals were taking place in Japanese public life during the first few years of married life, but Dr. Nagai was too busy with lecturing, with writing medical articles and with x-ray research to worry about politics. His Number One Son was born on April 4, 1935. They called him Makoto, which means "honesty".

There were three power bases in Tokyo in the mid-1930s. First, there was Emperor Hirohito's, which was an ambiguous one. Hirohito's grandfather, Emperor Meiji, had exercised real power, but his heir was the feeble-minded Emperor Taisho, who became a national embarrassment. As a result, Taisho's son Hirohito was rigidly groomed from youth to be an emperor who would "reign but not rule". The second power base was held by the politicians, financiers and industrialists, relatively new groups in a still-emerging democracy where fewer than half the citizens had the right to vote. The third and most powerful base was held by the militarists, convinced they held a semidivine trust to lead Japan to military and economic greatness.

When some politicians and business figures objected strenuously to the militarists' annexation of Manchuria and their huge expenditure on armaments, retribution was deadly. Seven of those who objected were assassinated. Twice Emperor Hirohito raised his voice in protest at this bloodshed, only to receive stinging rebukes from his mentor, Prince Saionji. The latter, though opposed to the militarists, reminded the Emperor of his stern duty to reign, not rule. The murders intimidated the opposition, and Japan became a military dictatorship. The media came under total censorship, and the police force became an arm of the military. The dreaded *kenpeitai*, the thought police, began turning up everywhere. Father Moriyama's name went in their dossier because "Christianity was an alien ideology breeding potential spies."

Daughter Ikuko Nagai was born in 1937. On the night of July 7, Nagai was hurrying home to see this bundle of delight. His eyes drank in the colorful scenes of Tanabata, a folk festival loved by young and old. This was the night of the tragic lovers, Shokujo the beautiful princess star and Kengyu the lowly cowherd star. They fell so hopelessly in love that Shokujo stopped weaving imperial brocade. The infuriated empress cast the Milky Way between them, but each July 7, magpies formed a bridge of wings so the two could cross and meet. Japanese honored the night by setting up bamboo branches festooned with tinsel and bands of colored paper carrying poems—marriageable youth asking for faithful spouses and children requesting help in the arts of music, poetry, calligraphy and needlework. Nagai stood and watched clear-eyed children dressed in bright cotton kimonos singing the plaintive Tanabata song that he had loved in his own childhood. The soul of the folk song was *akogare*, or the longing for something beyond man, he reflected, and he felt sad that so many of his people did not go beyond the *akogare* of the Star Festival—nor had they seen the pure light of the Star of Bethlehem. Indeed, right now they seemed more interested in the harsh red light of Mars, the god of war!

The radio carried grim news the next morning. Full-scale hostilities had broken out between Chinese and Japanese troops near the Marco Polo Bridge, less than sixteen miles from Beijing. Nagai walked despondently to the university, struck by the irony of Japan attacking her cultural mother on July 7. Tanabata, like so much in Japan, was a gift from ancient China!

In contrast to Nagai, Japanese army officers were jubilant, confident of quick victory now that it was full-scale war.

The Japanese army lost no time in mobilizing everyone with war experience. Midori's heart sank when she saw the official postcard in the mail not many days later. Before the month was out, Nagai was sailing for China as a first lieutenant and chief surgeon in the Fifth Division Medical Corps. The following thirty months in China, almost continually at the front, would open his eyes completely to the neobarbarism of the militarists and leave him feeling guilty that he had done nothing to stop their seizing power. Nagai would write much during this second period of war service by way of letters home and jottings in his journal, making it possible to trace the fortunes of the Fifth Division up and down China.

They had just arrived in China when on August 19, 1937, marching through a valley in the north close to the Great Wall, they came under withering fire. By the time they regrouped, four hundred Japanese soldiers were dead or wounded and all radio equipment was destroyed, together with much of their weaponry and medical and food supplies. They were hopelessly cut off from their base camp. Nagai's hastily put-together field hospital was full of groaning men in need of medical help he could not give. He went to the commanding officer and told him the medical situation was desperate. The officer said that without reinforcements, they would all be dead within forty-eight hours. "We have lost contact with headquarters. Our only chance is for someone to slip through the Chinese lines tonight and get help", he added. The doctor replied: "Sir, I request permission to try it." Nagai was competent and resourceful, so the commander agreed.

That night, he moved out under cover of darkness. Japanese headquarters was twelve miles away, but the real problem was the first few miles, now held by Chinese soldiers. He crawled, he slunk along mountainsides, he lay still for long stretches of time, he used a river current and floated down like a corpse. Finally he reached headquarters and reported on the desperate situation. The commanding officer promised relieving troops would set out that night and told Nagai to accompany them. Nagai replied he wished to return immediately because he was the chief medical officer.

He felt exhilarated as he set out, overconfident from the earlier success, and found himself marveling at China's natural beauty. To his right, the Great Wall ran up a mountainside and became lost in mist. To his left was a great fertile plain, laden with fields of millet and sorghum. He noticed something red on a tree in a millet field ahead. Apples! He was hungry and ran through the grain and shook the tree. Apples cascaded down. He was hot from running but suddenly went cold all over as a bullet moaned just over his head, probably from the gun of a farmer. Nagai forgot the apples and fled for cover like a frightened rabbit.

Japanese relief troops came and the Chinese withdrew. The wounded were evacuated, and Nagai had time to jot down his reflections. He had been trying to forget home, he wrote, and to keep his mind on his job, but it was impossible. The Chinese children looked like his own children; everywhere he saw Chinese mothers who reminded him of Midori, and older men who looked like his father. "You look at their faces and see they are good people who think and feel just as we do. We have been told that killing members of an enemy group is not murder, that this is a just war waged to preserve justice and peace. Yes? Well, where are justice and peace? I am finding it harder to see them."

Some weeks later, operating in the large field tent, he became aware of a furious argument going on beside him. He listened: "But I must amputate. Look, which is more important to you, your life or your left arm?" The soldier sobbed as he replied: "My left arm; I am a violinist." A man was carried in with a bullet through both sides of his jaw. "Try to get him some liquid food", Nagai told a medical corpsman. The fighting was raging, and food supplies had run out. The young corpsman decided he would search for birds' eggs, but he found none because it was autumn. He saw a bee and followed it. Hours later, he returned with his pack full of honey—but terribly stung all over his face and hands. War, wrote Nagai in his notebook, brings the best out of men as well as the worst.

In that age of racial and theological intolerance, it is refreshing to find Nagai's attitude to men of other nations and beliefs. Having made a diary entry about finding strength and peace in his pocket New Testament, he added a poem he composed for a non-Christian friend who died that daybreak: "As fair dawn lightened the eastern sky, my comrade-in-arms ascended peacefully to heaven." He added: One finds real love among common soldiers, often men from poor farms or city slums and with little education; was not this the kind of love Jesus spoke of in Matthew 25, love that gains entrance into the Kingdom of his Father?

Nagai remembered his inner turmoil during the 1933–1934 fighting in Manchuria. Yet now, though the fighting was far worse, he enjoyed peace and freedom in his heart. He had certainly changed! One night, he jotted an entry in his notebook about the exhilaration that flooded him that day when he was washing the gangrenous foot of a Chinese soldier-prisoner before an operation. He suddenly realized that he felt the same compassion for a wounded Chinese as for a wounded Japanese, and he wrote: "I now know I have come to China not to defeat anybody, not to win a war. I have come to help the wounded, Chinese as much as Japanese, civilians as much as combatants."

Chinese civilians were often caught in the murderous shelling and cross fire. The Japanese would take a town or village and find adults and children left behind with limbs missing.

Nagai set up a medical group that undertook to do all they could for wounded civilians and children. Nagai sent photos of this volunteer group back to Nagasaki. His Saint Vincent de Paul friends at the Urakami Cathedral spread the word, and soon food, clothing and children's toys started arriving. Nagai had discovered a surprising number of Saint Vincent de Paul conferences in China and distributed the parcels through these Chinese Vincentians. When he set up his first-aid post for Chinese civilians, there was suspicion on both sides. Was that old Chinese approaching them with his hands in his sleeves carrying a grenade? But the old man was just as nervous about the Japanese physicians in military uniforms! Gradually mistrust disappeared, and many came for treatment.

The war dragged on, and Japanese casualties increased. The Chinese generals were no match for the superbly equipped Japanese and refused to fight big battles. Their strategy was to spread ever more widely and westward, ambush Japanese forward troops and flee before reinforcements came. Japanese lines became thinly stretched, and supplies of all kinds became a problem. The severe Chinese winter worsened the situation, and soldiers began dying of exposure. Sake became the main solace for many soldiers, but not for Nagai. After marrying Midori, he never drank wildly again. He did find solace in writing, though he had a new problem with Japanese poetry: "I found my poems were blunt and explicit, whereas a good haiku or tanka[1] leaves much to the heart of the reader." An example: "Corpses of Communist soldiers, mere boys, lying on that mountain grass and beside them bell flowers bursting into bloom!"

Sometimes his journal entries are angry and bitter. After sadly closing the eyes of a soldier he had come to admire, he commented

---

[1] An unrhymed Japanese poem of five lines. The first and third lines are of five syllables each, while the second, fourth and fifth lines are of seven syllables each.

on the self-centered nationalism and empty propaganda of generals and politicians that killed this youth who had so much to offer the world. Usually, however, Nagai wrote of positive things, such as the nobility he kept discovering in ordinary foot soldiers and low-ranking officers. His entries also captured China's great natural beauty and the magnificence of her culture.

Nagai's Christianity was deepening, but its style was becoming more Japanese. His childhood had been Shinto, and he had often attended the austerely beautiful Taisha Shinto liturgies. However, like most Japanese, he had also attended innumerable Buddhist funerals and memorial services for the dead, where he joined in the prayer most common in Japanese Buddhism, the Nenbutsu. The Nenbutsu is simplicity itself, consisting in the continual repetition of the prayer "Namu Amida Butsu", "I depend on you utterly, Amida Buddha." Nagai began praying a kind of Christian Nenbutsu. He would choose a short phrase from the Psalms or from the pocket New Testament he always carried and repeat it over and over. He writes of occasions when badly wounded soldiers were brought into his operating tent by the dozen and waited in lines on the ground. His body and mind became almost numb as he worked around the clock, but he kept his spirit at peace by continuously murmuring: "The Lord graciously restores the dead to life." Another of his biblical Nenbutsu was a line from Isaiah, prophet in exile: "For your sake we are massacred daily and reckoned as sheep for the slaughter."

The ideograph for "Nenbutsu" contains the ideographs for "heart" and "now". To pray the Nenbutsu is to escape preoccupation with the past or future. It is to escape the noisy, busy head and to find the eternal, peaceful Now, the Absolute One, in one's heart. For Nagai, this meant resting in the One who called himself "I am who am." Practicing this ancient way of Eastern prayer brought Nagai deep peace in the most unpromising places and helped him understand Pascal's words: "Don't just study the Scriptures, pray them." "I discovered that the words of Scripture are real," Nagai commented, "even more real than what was happening in the war around me.... I discovered great peace in entrusting myself and my men to God's Providence. It is the uncomplicated way of the One who said: Look at the birds of the air and the lilies of the field!"

Buddhists often recite the Nenbutsu on a string of beads, not unlike a Catholic Rosary, which they may pray as they walk, or sit in a bus. Nagai discovered the Rosary was a great help in prayer, calling it his "pocket church" and praying it on forced marches and during lulls between battles. It helped him pray when he was too distracted or agitated to "think". The following Rosary incident is one of a number he jotted down.

On Christmas Eve 1939, the Chinese mounted a surprise attack and knocked 300 Japanese out of action and had the remaining 240 hopelessly surrounded. The commander told Nagai: "It will be the end if they attack tonight. I have a job for you—gather the wounded around the flag and pour gasoline over their bedding. If the Chinese attack in force, set fire to the gasoline so they won't take any prisoners or our flag. I loathe giving this order, but I have to." Days without a decent meal or sleep had left the commander emaciated and tense.

Nagai was in a dilemma. Every Japanese soldier was duty bound to die honorably by suicide rather than be captured. Nagai told his orderly: "Tell the wounded to be ready to be moved and leave me alone to pray. Call me only for emergencies." He went off a short distance, knelt and began the Rosary, forgetting about the consequences of disobeying orders, forgetting about death and about his wife and two children, just handing everything over to God. Making that simple journey around and around fifty-four beads, he became so absorbed that he did not notice the runner come up some hours later. The messenger coughed, bowed deeply and said: "Sir, begging your pardon. A message from the commander. A large relief force has just engaged the enemy. The crisis is over."

Not long after that action, mail came, bringing letters from Midori. A letter from her was usually a ray of light, but it was different this time—their daughter Ikuko and his own father were dead! Suddenly the years of struggling through bloodied swamps and frozen mountains hit him. He was so physically and mentally drained that he wanted to crawl into a hole like an animal and sleep until death claimed him. He was tasting a Dark Night of the Soul.

Bamboo festooned with poems and prayers for the festival of Tanabata, the night of July 7.

16

Arrogant Heike Tumble[1]

When Nagai went to China, he was delighted to see in Chinese scrolls, paintings and ceramics many of the symbols and motifs Japanese artists use. There were, for instance, the old favorites, bamboo and pine, denoting endurance and fidelity. No matter how cold the winter or how torrid the summer, they remain green and vigorous. Nagai liked best the symbol of the plum blossom, the first harbinger of spring. Every year about the end of January, when snowdrifts still lie about, delicate white blossoms appear on the dark, bare and angular plum branches like miracles. Just when the mountain plum blossoms of January 1940 were cheering the hearts of Chinese and Japanese soldiers, a postcard came that melted the snowdrift that had formed around his heart. He was to proceed immediately to Canton for repatriation. A week later, he was standing alone on the deck of a transport ship, nearing Japan. Recognizing the faint Dannoura shoreline, he knew they must be in the waters where ancient Japan's greatest sea battle was fought. The twelfth-century saga had always fascinated him. The Heike clan was ruling Japan with such arrogance and ruthlessness that the clan of Genji rose up, drove them from Kyoto and annihilated the remnants in the sea battle off Dannoura in 1185. A new proverb was born: Arrogant Heike tumble. Nagai

[1] Japanese proverb.

compared the Heike with the present militarists and felt a shadow pass over his heart. He had witnessed total, merciless war in China, yet the Japanese army was badly overextended and without victory. It had not helped him when a senior officer addressed them before embarkation, forbidding any talk of the real war situation upon arrival in Japan: "We have to help keep up the national morale!"

The pier at Shimonoseki appeared as a blur. The boat drew closer. He saw hundreds of people, but he picked her out almost immediately! Midori was drawn, and close to tears. She had suffered two heartbreaking deaths while he was in China, his father's and their child Ikuko's. The war had brought severe civilian rationing; food, fuel, medicines and even doctors grew scarce, and many infants died. Ikuko, the tiny daughter that gave him such joy before he left, was dead, and Midori blamed herself. He left her in charge of the children while he was at war, and she failed him!

As he came down the gangplank, he had a great urge to sweep Midori up in his arms and rush back with her to their home in Nagasaki. The army, however, permitted no such indulgence. There were a thousand things he wanted to say to her, but he was not given time for a dozen. Almost immediately she was saying good-bye as he boarded a train for Hiroshima.

He sat smoldering in a Hiroshima barracks while an officer gave them another lecture about helping national morale when speaking about China. Faces came before Nagai, the smashed faces of young Japanese and Chinese soldiers, of Chinese mothers like Midori, of children like Ikuko and of old folk, terror-stricken as they fled they knew not where. He thought with bitterness of overdressed generals and of fat civilians who ran the *zaibatsu* business cartels in Manchuria and China. They were modern Heike, and he shuddered for the future of Japan. Amid much military fanfare, medals were awarded to the specially brave, Nagai receiving the prestigious Order of the Rising Sun.

After demobilization, Nagai made the short journey to Mitoya to pray at the graves of his parents. Tears came to his eyes as he stood there recalling their lives in the light of a favorite Gospel passage, Matthew 25, where Jesus says that those who have loved and served others will enter paradise. He felt at peace as he gazed down on the thatched home that had been a place of hope for poor farmers. "The communion of saints" was something very dear to Nagai. He bowed low and thanked his parents for praying for him while he trudged through Chinese mud and asked for their support in his new work at Nagasaki.

Nagai took the first train for Nagasaki and found he was too distracted to concentrate on planning or even reading. Faces from the China front kept coming before his eyes. Some were Japanese, like Kawahara his orderly; others were Chinese, like the sixteen-year-old girl who stumbled toward him, still in shock from the shell burst that had blinded her. Nagai took his Rosary from his pocket and began to pray for each one of them. Suddenly Mount Unzen appeared to his left. Ah, the green mountains of home! Soon he was alighting at the Isa-haya station. He swept his son Makoto into his arms and hugged him ravenously, but the boy stiffened in his father's embrace. Nagai's eyes moistened at the sad thought of what war does to families.

Later that night, when he had a moment alone, he was con-scious of conflicting emotions—of wonder at being back home and of the wretchedness of the ongoing war. He opened his dog-eared Pascal and read: "Only in Christ can the paradox of man's wretchedness and his greatness be solved." The resolu-tion of the paradox, continued the Frenchman, was "living for the glory of God". Nagai took his brush and wrote: "The Son of God has graciously brought me back safe to Nagasaki so that I can work for the Father's glory."

Nagai resumed lecturing in radiology and quickly became a professor. He felt certain that Japan was rushing headlong toward a colossal crisis when good doctors would be in huge demand. Though he was unrelenting in demanding hard work in class and gave plenty of assignments, his lectures were very popular with students. The Japan of the 1940s had the highest rate of tuberculosis among the developed nations. Nagai initiated mass x-raying in Nagasaki to discover tuberculosis in its early stages. It proved the most effective countermeasure to date.

He threw himself into radiation research with several interested colleagues. "Microscopes brought a breakthrough into the vast microscopic world, once thought the ultimate frontier, but the atomic world is utterly smaller. The size of planet earth is to an apple what an apple is to an atom! Will x-rays make it possible for us to see this ultramicroscopic world?" He experienced "a sense of exhilaration because we are in pursuit of truth, which is eternal! Our laboratory is actually the threshold of the house of God, who created the universe and its every truth." On one occasion, while studying a kidney case and looking at the brilliant formation of urine crystals, he "felt a great urge to kneel". He clearly saw "that a laboratory could be the same as the cell of a monk". His voracious appetite for science was one result of the long exile from the university. The depravity of war and lying jingoistic propaganda gave him a fierce desire to discover more and more truth. Articles for journals began flowing from his pen again.

Midori still insisted on reading his published articles. He was both amused and touched at the way she would read the article full of nearly incomprehensible medical jargon almost as if it were a script from the Emperor! He used to steal a look at her sitting up straight on the tatami floor in the formal *seiza* posture, dressed simply and wearing no makeup. Though she made beautiful clothes for friends on occasions like weddings, she took seriously the government's call to live simply so more could be sent to soldiers at the front. Her hands were rough from long hours in the vegetable gardens, but she retained the femininity that attracted him the first time he saw her. He would pretend he was busy with papers but would peep at her as she struggled with his article. Tears would come to her eyes, so proud was she of the man who had written this! He was proud of her too. This gentle, sensitive woman could be amazingly forceful and decisive. When Tokyo ordered every city, town and hamlet to set up a Women's Neighborhood Association to help the national crisis, Midori was elected both president of the local branch and overall president of the eighteen branches covering their entire suburb.

Nagai became interested in politics, Japanese and international, after his second interlude in China. He jotted down serious forebodings about Mussolini and especially about Hitler. It gave him little comfort when Japan's volatile foreign minister Matsuoka signed an alliance with Germany and Italy. He was disturbed when Japanese cabinets fell one after another and General Hideki Tojo became premier on October 18, 1941. They had not nicknamed him "the Razor" for nothing!

On Saturday, December 8, 1941, Nagai and his wife rose early to attend the 6 A.M. Mass of Mary's Immaculate Conception. He voiced his worries to her as they climbed the cathedral hill in the winter darkness, worries about the stalemate in the Washington talks between Japan's Nomura and Secretary of State Hull. During Mass he prayed there would be no war with America, "with the same intensity of feelings I had that night in China when I was ordered to pour gasoline over the wounded". Nagai had not been impressed when America forced Japan into a corner by cutting off her petroleum supply. He agreed with Admiral Yamamoto of the dove faction that this was most regrettable and a belligerent act that threatened Japan's existence as a nation. However, should Tojo seek a solution through war, America would pour gasoline over Japan and set the nation on fire! Nagai had no illusions about American resources and military potential.

Hurrying home from that Mass, the Nagais passed many workers on their way to the Mitsubishi war plants half a mile north of their home. Altogether, there were seven Mitsubishi complexes in Nagasaki, including a big shipyard. Remembering the Chinese air raids, he thought: If war comes, Nagasaki will certainly be a target.

He quickly ate the breakfast Midori put before him, bean-paste soup, rice with flakes of dried seaweed, and fresh grilled bream. The bream was a treat for our Lady's feast day, a Christian custom Midori always honored. He finished with light green tea, and five minutes later he was on the streets heading for the university when a street loudspeaker crackled out, "At dawn this morning our Imperial Forces engaged the combined forces of Britain and America ..." A nearby youth cheered: "Banzai! At last, at last!" A chill numbed Nagai, and with it came a terrible presentiment that these buildings around him would be destroyed. He was shaking as he stood there, little suspecting he was 200 yards from what would be immortalized as "ground zero", the epicenter of the A-bomb.

17

The Machine That Turned on Its Master

His first lecture that morning was x-ray diagnosis for third-year students. He looked at them somberly and warned of difficult times ahead. They would all be involved in the war, many at the front, others as medical officers in places that would certainly be bombed. "Look, it's a war with the American colossus and a very powerful Britain. Most of us will have close relatives among the casualties. You've no idea what war in China was like. War against America and Britain will be ten times worse.... Japan will be cut off from the international flow of medical research. We will just have to study and research all the harder." He concluded darkly, "I feel sure that some of us in this room will be killed or maimed." As he said that, a vivid scene flashed uninvited onto the screen of his memory. It was the children's ward in Kanansho Hospital near the Yellow River, where he had taken toys and sweets from the Nagasaki Vincentians. There were children without arms or hands, and others without feet or legs. He offered them sweets, but they just stared at him dumbly. The bombing had robbed them of something more precious than limbs. When he snapped out of the reverie some moments later, his students were staring at him, shocked. As much for his own encouragement as for theirs, he quoted a favorite saying of Confucius: "If you have found the way of truth in the morning, you can meet death peacefully that evening." Brightening, he said: "Now let's get down to x-ray diagnosis."

The military government files noted that Nagai had been twice at the front, distinguishing himself under fire. Almost immediately he received orders to organize air-raid measures for the suburb of Urakami. One of the first groups he called together was the women of the eighteen Neighborhood Associations. Government propaganda had lulled most Japanese into a false sense of security, and they were stunned by his opening words: "We may be bombed any time now. You must learn how to stop bleeding, how to carry the injured to a first-aid station. You will need courage, but above all you will need love ... love great enough to lay down your lives for your fellow citizens!"

Nagai now turned his energies to building an underground operating theater that included an x-ray room. He had operated for days under artillery fire in China inside a makeshift underground theater, with a light strapped onto his head like a miner. When he assured the university faculty that the same could happen in Nagasaki, some smiled patronizingly.

All this unhappiness was somewhat alleviated by the birth of a daughter. Nagai and Midori called her Kayano, meaning "of the miscanthus reed". Miscanthus is the tall, graceful reed used to thatch houses, especially in the country. The choice of this name reveals something about Nagai that was well known to Midori. He had a passionate love of the harmonious blend of genuine folk craft with nature. He discovered it every summer, for instance, in the verdant rice paddies descending terraced hillsides. In autumn, when mists rolled down from the mountains like something otherworldly, he stood and gazed at vermilion Shinto shrines rising like ships from their green and gold sea of cedar and gingko trees. Thatched roofs filled his earliest memories of the tranquil valley of his boyhood. He found roofs of miscanthus thatch very beautiful whether standing against the iridescent mountain skyline of spring, or set off against the red, yellow and auburn flames of autumn, or frozen in dark silhouette against bare rice fields covered in snow.

Chinese and Japanese names appear bare like deciduous trees in winter, if you write them in English. They appear as prosaic as "Jones" or "Betty". The ideographs, however, transform them into poetry. The ideographs for "Kayano" conjure up images of waving miscanthus reed and thatched country homes. The ideographs for "Nagai" mean "the well that lasts".

In the first flush of Japanese military success, Nagai's grim warnings seemed cowardly and laughable. But the confident smiles would have frozen had his students known the American Navy had cracked the Japanese code. Tokyo's plans for Midway were studied in advance by the United States and in June 1942 a huge Japanese task force steamed into the gray jaws of a steel trap set by Admiral Nimitz. Losing four big carriers and the best of their aircraft division, the Japanese were not able to regain naval initiative for the rest of the war. Censorship, however, kept the debacle of Midway from the Japanese media. The U.S. Marines landed on Guadalcanal in August 1942 and halted the Japanese advance southward.

By early 1943 Allied air superiority was severing Japanese supply routes to far-flung bastions like Lae and Rabaul. Japanese shipping losses became greater than tonnage launched. It was a bad year for Nihon, but far worse was soon to come. Air raids on the Japanese mainland had been carrier-based or launched from distant Chinese airfields. In November 1943, the British and American chiefs of staff who were meeting at Cairo decided to seize the small Micronesian island groups of the central Pacific, the Gilberts, Marshalls, Carolines and Marianas. The Japanese defended their territory every inch of the way with desperate heroism, but Tarawa, the Biak airfield, Saipan, Tinian and Guam fell before the typhoons of American steel. Saipan was taken in July 1944, with thirty thousand Japanese soldiers and twenty-two thousand civilians killed. The

U.S. Marines, backed by a huge air force and navy, lost over fourteen thousand men. With Japan's carrier-based striking power already ineffective, the taking of these islands meant that giant American B-29 bombers could raid Japan around the clock. Hiroshima and Nagasaki would soon come to learn of a tiny island called Tinian!

When Nagai had been preparing for baptism, he asked about the Catholic teaching on war. Father Moriyama explained the tradition outlined in the fourth century by Augustine: one could fight in a "just war". Nagai had long since doubted that Japan was in a just war, though he did not think the Western Allies were paragons of justice either. He came to the practical conclusion that caring for the wounded, whether soldiers or civilians, was in no fashion immoral and with peace of conscience poured all his energies into air-raid drills. He built up an emergency supply of medical essentials in his underground theater in case the hospital was bombed.

Sparkling Nagasaki Bay is well protected on three sides by wooded mountains and faces southwest into the East China Sea. That was good protection if enemies marched over land or came in ships. But when their planes roared in from the sea, it was entirely different. Without warning, U.S. fighters would appear low over the city, and huge B-29s glinted like foil high up in the sky. From August 1944 the air raids became almost daily affairs.

His journal notes of April 26, 1945, describe a particularly fierce raid. When it was over, a truck filled with badly wounded people roared up to the university hospital. He helped carry them inside, washed human brains from his fingers and sent those with suspected fractures to be x-rayed. Then he went down to the morgue to clean up the corpses and to sew up their wounds, to make them decent-looking when family or friends arrived. His radiology staff loathed this job, saying it was not their responsibility. However, as he always went down to do it even if no one else came, they had begun going regularly too.

With sickening frequency news bulletins carried the names of graduates who had been killed on active duty. Nagai had come to hate names like Luzon, Leyte and Iwo Jima as he had hated the bad places in China. Wartime food shortages worsened, and tuberculosis increased. Suspected cases were sent in droves to be x-rayed, a great many being x-rayed by Nagai. He was also absorbing radiation when x-raying hospital patients and teaching his students. After many radiologists, like Professor Holzknecht, had died of cancer caused by gamma rays escaping from x-ray machines, radiologists agreed it was dangerous to be exposed to more than 0.2 roentgen units a day. Nagai was now well over that limit, but when a worried colleague questioned him, he replied: "Yes, I am aware of that, but I am responsible for training our students and I am ultimately responsible for discovering tuberculosis cases. People all over Japan are in situations of risk, and I can't avoid risks if I am to do my job." He did not shirk danger areas in China and had never been wounded, which had given him a false sense of security. With more hope than prudence, he continued his dangerous flirtation with gamma rays.

But he began to notice ominous signs on his hands and to suffer extreme exhaustion, sometimes shaking as he climbed stairs. Night raids meant little sleep when he was air-raid warden. He wrote in his journal that sometimes when he felt utterly spent he would close his door and sit alone before the statue of the Blessed Virgin on his office desk. He would say the Rosary, and tranquillity would slowly return. The nurses noticed he was beginning to fall asleep everywhere. He would wake with a start and begin working furiously to make up for lost time. A colleague eventually persuaded him to be x-rayed, and in his book *Horobinu Mono Wo*, Nagai describes the outcome.

He stood holding the x-ray frame, conscious of how cold it felt and how alone and frightened he was. If only Midori were beside him! He had examined ten thousand patients in this room, and how eager he used to be to see the results of a medically interesting case. How could he have been so cold and clinical? Now he was terrified because he might be incurably ill. Many of his patients had been too, but he had called out orders and thrown switches with ice-cold objectivity. Now the ice was around his own heart. His mouth was dry and his heart like a desert.

He and the radiologist looked at the picture together, and a gasp escaped Nagai involuntarily. There was an ominous shadow over the right side of his stomach, and his spleen was significantly enlarged. The top right section of his liver was swollen, and his intestines and stomach had been forced downward. Upward pressure had moved his heart slightly sideways. The radiologist could not speak. Nagai tried to ease the heavy silence. "Call your assistant, and let's give him a chance at diagnosis. There is a lot of good study matter here." The assistant came but was struck dumb when he looked at the chief's x-ray. Suddenly the door was flung open, and a young nurse breezed in, all smiles and efficiency. "Professor Nagai, the fourth-year students are ready for their lecture." She wondered why the other two doctors turned away from her. But the professor's smile and prompt answer reassured her. "Good, Nurse Oyanagi; I'll be right there."

After the lecture, a detailed examination showed that his white blood cell count was 1,000 percent above normal, and his red blood cell count was 40 percent below normal. He took the data sheet and read aloud the medical prognosis: "Patient Nagai has incurable leukemia. Life expectancy, two to three years. Death, lingering and painful." He smiled at his glum friends. "Doctors, we have to be realists, and one day every one of us must become a patient, a terminal patient."

He saw their embarrassment and ushered them out of the room. Now alone, he took off the mask of senior doctor and began to tremble. He turned to prayer: "Lord, you know how weak I am. I don't know if I can take it! O Lord, why must it be so early? My wife and my children! And all the unfinished work here!" His thoughts turned to the Christ of Gethsemane. "Lord, I know you said we all have to carry a cross, but . . . I am very tired, and this cross seems so heavy."

Before leaving, he turned and gazed at the x-ray machine that had sown seeds of death in his blood, and he became calmer. This machine had helped him through his doctoral thesis. This machine and he himself had lit a way in the darkness for thousands of his fellow human beings. If it had a soul, he thought, it would feel great compassion for its companion, Nagai, and share his burden. The machine was no longer the shiny new thing Professor Suetsugu had brought. It had paint chipped off here and was worn there, just like Nagai! Was not that the best way to end up, worn out in the service of your fellow men? Nagai realized he was no longer trembling. Peace had returned and even a sense of gratitude for a full life.

A very gentle knock disturbed his reverie. It was the university president, come to sympathize. Nagai bowed and apologized for his carelessness. "No, Nagai-kun, you were not careless. You are sick because you cared for those long lines of patients needing help, with no one to x-ray them but you."

18

But Midori Will Be beside Me

He now faced his hardest task, breaking the news to Midori. He walked slowly home, again in a somber mood, not noticing the bright colors the June sun had poured out all over Nagasaki. Marrying him had meant a hard life for Midori. He had not set up a small surgery at home to supplement his mediocre salary like other professors. No, he used all his free time to do what he liked, research. He mostly came home late from the university, sometimes in the small hours, and yet she always waited up for him and never complained. He rarely took her out, and only recently she laughed about it, saying: "When things are better, we can go to all the restaurants and theaters we like." Now, thanks to his presumption and carelessness, the only future for Midori was the hard road of a young widow.

Midori heard the front door slide open and came with the cheerful patter of bare feet on tatami. Her face lit up. "Well, aren't you home early! This is a pleasant surprise!" She took his shoes and helped him out of his Western suit into a kimono, all the while humming a tune, chatting about having fresh raw tuna and clams for supper. Did Midori sense bad tidings, he wondered, and talk on like this in a subconscious effort to drive them away? Why had he thrown himself into radiology like a man possessed? He remembered the times when he would be working on an article for a periodical, carrying on like a bear with a sore head—demanding she make no noise, calling for green tea and then forgetting to drink it. He even passed her on the street once without recognizing her! She only laughed when she told him about it later. Yes, he had let himself get absorbed in what he liked so that he could play the big scholar. He looked across the table at the crow's-feet beginning around her eyes and at the work-coarsened hands. She looked up sharply, disturbed by his silence. His eyes met hers, beautiful, sensitive pools of honesty.

He told her, and she seemed to listen without emotion. Then, quietly rising from the table, she lit the candles on their family altar. She knelt there in the austere *seiza* fashion, her head bowed before the crucifix her family had guarded through 250 years of persecution. He followed her and knelt likewise behind her, now noticing that her shoulders were shaking. She remained there in prayer until the emotional turbulence had subsided. Remorse flooded him that he had flung himself recklessly into his own pursuits, taking Midori for granted. She turned her head and spoke quietly with composure. "We said before we married, and before you went to China the second time, that if our lives are spent for the glory of God, then life and death are beautiful. You have given everything you had for work that was very, very important. It was for his glory." Nagai was stunned. This woman had never failed him. He was fighting to hold back tears, not for himself, but tears of gratitude. He sensed he was in the presence of holiness. She seemed at that moment to personify the persecuted Urakami Christians, still believing and hoping despite 250 years of persecution.

He had walked into his home depressed that night. He returned to his x-ray department on the next day, he writes, "a new man. Her complete acceptance of the tragedy, and her refusal to hear any talk of blame, had *freed* me!" The fatigue of body and spirit of the last months seemed to vanish. Once again, she had lifted a heavy stone from his chest. His thirteen years of radiology, his time at the front and the last few years of austerities and air raids seemed worthwhile and, yes, beautiful! Midori had said the previous night that one of their children might continue his x-ray work and research, and he wanted to bow at her feet for that! It told him she bore no resentment. He could almost embrace the x-ray machine, he writes, experiencing great peace and a surge of energy for whatever there was left to be done. Was this the joy that comes from "abandonment to the will of God" that Pascal wrote of? he wondered.

Okinawa had fallen, and rumors flew that the next American move would be a landing on the island of Kyushu. Nagasaki was a vital port in Kyushu, and more *kenpeitai* descended on the city. The parish priest of Urakami was taken to police headquarters and interrogated about the "prayers for peace" being said in the cathedral. "Are you praying for Japan's defeat?" asked the police chief. "No. Christians all through the world are praying for peace. Everyone agrees that war is not good. I'm sure you do." "Yes," replied the policeman sharply, "the war will stop because Japan will win! You can continue that prayer in your church only if you put in Tenno Heika, the Emperor, in place of your Almighty God." The pastor had to answer carefully if he was not to be imprisoned like some priest friends, leaving their churches without Mass. The aging priest replied: "But sir, we have it on the authority of our glorious Emperor Meiji that the Emperor is not Almighty God who made the universe. In his Imperial Rescript for Soldiers, he wrote: 'I, in obedience to the grace of heaven'. That heaven, which even he obeys, sir, is what we call Almighty God." The angry official told the priest to go home.

The army surmised the Americans would soon hit Kyushu and Tokyo Bay and with their dreaded air power get a foothold. But that would be only the beginning! The Americans had surrounded the small island of Okinawa with ships, bombarding it at will, but it took them three months and 12,500 dead to capture it. Japan could not be surrounded by battle-ships and was over 90 percent mountains. The Americans might land on coastal plains, but the Imperial Army and the total adult population would fall back as the Chinese did, to the next mountains and then to the next. The Americans would have to fight for years and lose millions of men—or drop those "unconditional surrender" terms with the blasphemous possibility of executing the Emperor. Every Japanese would die a thousand deaths rather than allow that. Even were the race wiped out, it would be preferable to such a dishonor.

In the middle of July 1945, a group of Nagasaki Catholic lay leaders were ordered to report to army headquarters. They were savagely berated as potential fifth columnists, direly threatened and told to report immediately to Nagasaki police headquarters if the Americans landed. Dr. Nagai was among them and writes of how the Christians concluded that they must now ready themselves and their families for the worst, even death. Nagai walked the long way home, passing along the road traveled by the twenty-six Christians who were crucified in 1597. He prayed especially to Saint Paul Miki, whose name he took at baptism, for help to die like a true Christian.

Back at the hospital the next day, he jotted down his fears about the slow, painful death of patients with his type of cancer, adding: "But Midori will be beside me. She will be there praying and will press the crucifix to my forehead. I'll breathe my last in her arms. She will close my eyelids and take me to the grave. Selfless Midori! You will transform my dying moments. Thank you, Midori."

The Americans had dropped many leaflets on Japan. At first the Japanese was crude and sometimes laughable; but now, in 1945, it was sophisticated. The police forbade people to read the leaflets, but many did. A recent leaflet dropped on Nagasaki contained a grim poem: "In April Nagasaki was all flowers. In August it will be flame showers." It was now

August. On the evening of August 6, Nagai heard a report about a new bomb that had devastated Hiroshima. He and Midori had previously tried to persuade their three-year-old Kayano and ten-year-old Makoto to go off with Grandma to the country. The children made such a fuss about it that the parents desisted. However, the events of August 6 decided it. The next day, Grandma and Midori loaded up knapsacks of gear and set off with the children on a four-mile walk northeast to a rustic house in Koba overlooking a peaceful mountain valley. A shrill orchestra of cicadas and a singing mountain stream welcomed them.

Midori returned home early the next morning, the eighth. An air-raid alarm sounded, so she and Nagai headed for their shelter. He was in bad shape physically, with his spleen swollen and his legs unsteady, so she put his arm over her shoulder and her arm around his waist. He started to laugh, and she joined in. They sat in their shelter, he writes, like lovers on a picnic. They forgot the war and spoke of the coming feast of the Assumption, August 15, a big day for Nagasaki Christians and the day Francis Xavier arrived in Japan. Midori said she would make the traditional bean-jam cakes, and he laughed about how many their boy Makoto ate last Assumption Day. Nagai asked the times for confession in preparation for the feast day. Midori told him she was going tomorrow morning. He said tomorrow afternoon would be a better time for him.

The all-clear came, and they walked back to the house. He was amazed and grateful that Midori's mood was one of "positive gaiety". She ate breakfast with him, laughing about their young imps up in the mountains and poor Grandma trying to cope with them. Midori wanted to walk him to the university, but he said no, that he felt fine now. At the *genkan*, the front porch, she helped him into his white shoes. She was wreathed in smiles, he continues, as she knelt on the tatami and bowed low to him with the traditional and mellifluous farewell, "Itte irasshai mase." He bowed and warmly gave the response, "Itte mairimasu", and walked off using his stick, trying not to appear unsteady, thinking: This is wonderful; she's in such fine spirits despite everything.

Not a hundred feet down the street he remembered his *o-bento*, his lunch, which he had left in the kitchen. He retraced his steps to the *genkan* and received a terrific shock. Midori was lying on the tatami, shaking with sobs like a child!

He was on air-raid duty that night, August 8, refusing an offer to be excluded from the roster. "Look how magnificent the student wardens have been during the air raids, and some of them have died for it. No, they have asked for no concessions; neither will I." The dean of radiology wanted to lead his students and young staff by personal example.

August 9 opened with an air-raid alarm, but it was a lone plane, and the all-clear sounded at 10 A.M. "Time wasted on a plane not interested in Nagasaki", someone remarked. He was wrong—it was very interested and radioed precise information back to a B-29 named Bock's Car that was rushing northward to Japan from Tinian.

Midori came out of the shelter after that 10 A.M. alert with two relations, Tatsue and Grandma Urata, and they sat chatting on Midori's veranda. "Your children must be lonely", said Gran. Midori was spreading out a bag of beans to dry in the sun in preparation for making bean-jam cakes. "Yes, Gran", she replied. "Kayano, anyhow. That urchin Makoto will be swimming in the river, as happy as a frog. He'll grow webbed fingers yet!" Gran laughed, and then her face clouded: "And the good doctor, how is he, Midori?" "I'm afraid he's bad. Anyone as sick as he is just couldn't work as he does and not get worse. He was on air-raid duty last night, so I haven't seen him since breakfast yesterday. I'm really worried about him. Please keep up your prayers for him." Gran nodded gravely. If she were younger, she would accompany the younger woman on the four-mile pilgrimage Midori sometimes made to the Lourdes Grotto behind the monastery on the eastern outskirts of the city. Father Maximilian Kolbe had built that grotto when he came to Nagasaki in May 1931.

Just then, another young cousin breezed into the yard. "O-hayo gozaimasu. Good morning", she fairly sang. "Who is up to a walk to Topposui Mill for grinding wheat? Won't someone join me under a blue sky on a beautiful country road that is just waiting for travelers?" Tatsue smiled at the exuberance of her younger relation and said yes, she'd go. Kikue clapped her hands and turned to Midori: "Now, illustrious head of all the Women's Associations of Urakami. Just last meeting you said—and I can quote it—'It is important that children develop freedom and grace of bodily movement, and a sense of beauty.' Therefore, you must join us as we swing our arms and legs freely and gracefully to Topposui and drink in acres and acres of beauty." Midori enjoyed the banter and said she had wheat to be ground but would go to the mill on her way to see her children later in the day. She had to make her husband's lunch and take it to him at the hospital, as he was not home the night before. In the book *We of Nagasaki*, Tatsue Urata writes poignantly of their parting. "This was how we separated into two groups, the ones that were going to be safe and the ones that were going to be killed."

19

When the Sun Turned Black

Major "Chuck" Sweeney had an extremely risky takeoff before dawn, loaded as he was with the 4.5-ton A-bomb, "Fat Man". Now they were over their primary target, Kokura. He had made three runs over the hopelessly clouded city when he made a shocking discovery: the auxiliary gasoline pipe was blocked. Unless they dropped the bomb soon, they would never get home. He turned his plane southwest for the secondary target, "Nagasaki, urban area".

His B-29 was over Shimabara just before 11 A.M. A radio announcer saw this and excitedly broadcast a warning, and Nagasaki people who heard him ran for their shelters. Moments later, Sweeney and his crew saw Nagasaki right below them through a cloud break, immediately recognizing the Urakami River and the Matsuyama Sports Ground. That put them almost two miles northwest of the planned drop, but time had run out. Bombardier Kermit released the bomb. It was just 11 A.M. when Fat Man went plummeting down onto the city of two hundred thousand souls, of whom more than seventy thousand would die, many without a trace.

Inside the Urakami Cathedral, Fathers Nishida and Tamaya were hearing confessions again after the all-clear. The cathedral was only a third of a mile from where Fat Man detonated and was reduced to rubble in an instant. No one would be sure how many perished inside.

Less than two miles away from the cathedral, Chimoto-san was working on his rice paddy on Mount Kawabira. He heard a noise, looked up and saw a B-29 emerging from the clouds. It disgorged a huge black bomb, and he threw himself to the ground. He waited a minute. Then came an awful penetrating brightness, followed by eerie stillness. He looked up and gasped at the huge pillar of smoke, swelling grotesquely as it rose. Suddenly he realized that a hurricane was rushing toward him. Houses, buildings, trees were being cut down before his startled eyes as if by some enormous, invisible bulldozer. Then came a deafening roar, and he was hurled like a matchbox into the stone wall sixteen feet behind. Shaken to his very soul, he gaped at the pines, chestnuts and camphor laurels torn from the ground or broken off at the trunks. Even the grass was gone!

Midori's nineteen-year-old cousin Sadako Moriyama had just found her two small brothers chasing dragonflies in the Yamazato school yard. She told them their mother wanted them. At that moment, she heard the plane and ran with them to the school shelter. As they entered, they were picked up and hurled to the far wall, and she blacked out. Coming to, she heard the two children whimpering at her feet and wondered why it was so dark. As a little light began to penetrate the gloom, she was paralyzed with terror. Two hideous monsters had appeared at the shelter's entrance, making croaking noises and trying to crawl in. As the darkness lifted a little, she saw they were human beings who had been outside when the bomb exploded. In less than seconds, they had been skinned alive, half a mile from the epicenter, and their raw bodies had been picked up and smashed into the side of the shelter.

She went outside. The light was weak, as if it were barely dawn. She cried aloud when she saw beside the sandbox four children, without clothes or skin! She stood there transfixed, her eyes involuntarily drinking in the hideous details. The skin of their hands had been torn away at the wrists and hung from their fingernails, looking like gloves turned inside out.

Feeling she was losing her reason, she dashed back into the shelter, accidentally brushing the two victims still squirming and moaning near the entrance. Their bodies felt like potatoes gone rotten. Their horrible animal croaking sound began again. She realized they were saying something. Mizu, mizu. Water, water. That cry was to run like a cracked record in the nightmares of Nagasaki survivors for years.

Michiko Ogino was ten years old and enjoying the summer holidays at home. Just after 11 A.M. she was terrified by a giant lightning flash, followed by a horrendous roar, and within seconds she was one of the thousands pinned under the roofs or walls of their homes. The blast of the bomb caused air to rush from the epicenter at over a mile a second, knocking houses flat. Almost immediately, an equally violent wind rushed back into the vacuum left at the epicenter.

Michiko was hopelessly pinned there, but her screaming brought a stranger who freed her. Outside, she was startled to see evil-looking clouds that twisted and writhed and blackened out the sun. What kind of new lightning had done this? Then she became conscious of a tiny voice becoming hysterical. It was her two-year-old sister trapped under a crossbeam. She turned for help and saw dashing toward them a naked woman, her body greasy, and purple like an eggplant, and her hair reddish brown and frizzled. Oh no! It was Mother! The speechless Michiko could only point to her sister under the beam. The mother looked wildly at the fires that had already started, dived into the rubble, put her shoulder under the beam and heaved. The two-year-old was free, and the mother, hugging her to her breast, collapsed onto the ground. There was no skin left on the shoulder that she had put under the beam, just raw bleeding meat. Michiko's father appeared, badly burnt too. He watched in dumb helplessness as his wife groaned and struggled to rise. Then all her strength ebbed away, and she collapsed, dead.

Nagasaki was now burning, and Sakue Kawasaki sat in disbelief inside the Aburagi air-raid shelter. He could see people staggering about outside, naked and swollen like pumpkins. Then came a babel of croaking voices piteously begging for mizu, mizu, but where could he get water? There was a puddle of dirty water outside the entrance to the shelter, and one of the victims crawled over, lowered his lips into it and drank with succulent noises. He tried to crawl to the shelter but collapsed and stopped moving. One by one, the others drank from the puddle and crumpled up motionless. What terrible thirst could drive men to act like demented lemmings?

The plutonium-239 bomb exploded in Nagasaki with the equivalent force of twenty-two thousand tons of conventional explosives but with vast differences. Setting aside for the moment the A-bomb's lethal radiation, there was its intense heat, which reached several million degrees centigrade at the explosion point. The whole mass of the huge bomb was ionized and a fireball created, making the air around it luminous, emitting ultraviolet rays and infrared rays and blistering roof tiles farther than half a mile from the epicenter. Exposed human skin was scorched up to two and a half miles away. Electric light poles, trees and houses within two miles were charred on the surface facing the blast. The velocity of the wind that rushed out from the epicenter was more than one mile per second, sixty times the velocity of a major cyclone. This caused a vacuum at the epicenter, and another cyclone rushed back in, picking up acres of dust, dirt, debris and smoke that darkened the writhing mushroom cloud.

Young Kato-san was walking his cow on a hillside outside Oyama, five miles south of the epicenter. He was startled by the flash and watched, rooted to the spot, as a huge white cloud rose up like a grotesque organism fattening itself by some weird magic. The cloud was white on the outside but fired by some hideous red energy within. Then came alternating flashes of red, yellow and purple. Gradually the cloud went into a mushroom shape, and a black stain grew on its stem. When the cloud reached a great height, it burst open and collapsed like an obscene grub that had gorged on more than its stomach could hold. The mountains all around were lit by the sun, but the area below the cloud was shrouded in darkness. Then came Kato's second shock, a roar of wind so strong that Kato mistook it for another bomb exploding nearby.

Section of a woodblock depicting the twenty-six martyrs of Nagasaki.

20

And the Rain Turned to Poison

Dr. Nagai had come out of the hospital air-raid shelter when the all-clear sounded at 10 A.M. on August 9. He doffed his steel helmet and heavy warden's gear, glad to breathe fresh air again and see sunlight. For a moment he paused and allowed his weary eyes to drink in the blood red of the oleander and canna in the hospital garden and the dark purple of the tiled roofs below him. He looked beyond to Nagasaki Bay, framed magnificently by the summer green of Mount Inasa and the sheer white clouds that floated across the bluest of skies. So peaceful, and what a contrast to our war-torn world, he thought, and with that, a saying of the ancient Chinese poet Toho came to mind: Kuni yaburete sanga ari. Though the nation be destroyed, the mountains and rivers remain. But he had work to do! Regretfully dragging his eyes from nature's ever-fresh beauty, he hurried back to the hospital. An hour later, he was seated in his office preparing a lecture.

"It was shortly after 11 A.M. when there was a flash of blinding light. I thought: A bomb has fallen right at the university entrance! I intended to throw myself to the floor immediately, but before I could do it, window-pane glass rushed in with a frightening noise. A giant hand seemed to grab me and hurl me ten feet. Fragments of glass flew about like leaves in a whirlwind. My eyes were open, and I had a glimpse of the outside—planks, beams, clothing were doing a weird dance in the air. All the objects in my own room had joined in, and I felt the end had come. My right side was cut by glass, and warm blood coursed down my cheek and neck. The giant invisible fist had gone beserk and was smashing everything in the office. Various objects fell on top of me while I listened to strange noises like mountains rumbling back and forth. Then came pitch darkness, as if the reinforced concrete hospital were an express train that had just rushed headlong into a tunnel. I had felt no pain as yet, but panic gripped my heart when I heard crackling flames and sniffed acrid smoke. I was conscious of my sins, especially three I had intended to confess that very afternoon, and directed my whole attention to the Lord our Judge and asked his forgiveness."

Nagai found himself muttering: "Midori, it's the end; I'm dying." But this hospital on train wheels shot out of the tunnel again, and he could see, at least out of his left eye. The flying glass had severed the artery on his right temple, and blood was spurting everywhere, filling his right eye. Nagai struggled to move, but he was held firmly by all the debris. The temperature dropped eerily, and an icicle of fear passed through his heart: Buried alive? What a grotesque death! He again tried to rise but discovered he was trapped in a pool of broken glass, some under his face, so he just lay there and called out: "Help, help!"

Nurse Hashimoto was next door in the x-ray room. Held fast against the wall and shielded by an anchored bookcase, she watched the weird dance of the room's movable objects. When everything stopped, she went and looked out a window and staggered. The sea of houses below was gone! The bright summer green had disappeared from Mount Inasa across the bay, leaving nothing but a red surface. Everywhere she looked was bare of grass and trees. The whole world seemed to be naked. She looked down to the front entrance and choked to see naked bodies tangled in debris on the devastated grounds. There was not a sound. Was all the world dead? She covered her eyes with her hands to block out the terror. "I'm seeing hell! Hell!" she screamed to herself. She opened her eyes again, but it was still like Dante's Inferno. Darkness began to descend as if to shroud all hope, and the seventeen-year-old nurse was sure her end had come. She began to tremble convulsively and whimper like a little child.

Then she heard words that came like two slaps in the face, reminding her she was an adult: "Help, help!" It was Dean Nagai! She tried to get into his room, but the way was hopelessly blocked by smashed equipment, and she knew she would need help. Feeling her way down the lightless corridor, she bumped into something soft. She bent down, and her hand became wet and sticky. She found an arm and felt for a pulse. There was none. Joining her hands in a brief prayer, she moved on. Suddenly the light of red flames pierced the gloom. Fierce crackling sounds told her she must hurry.

The atom bomb did not level this reinforced concrete hospital half a mile from the epicenter, but 80 percent of the patients and staff perished. The x-ray department was at the southeastern end and had maximum protection. Nurse Hashimoto found five of the x-ray staff and led them back. They formed a human chain, got through a window and freed Dr. Nagai. His war experiences in China stood him in good stead, and his calmness calmed them. He led them back to look for the rest of the x-ray staff, and they were shocked to find many of them dead, their bodies swollen and their skin peeled off as if they were overripe peaches. Others were beginning to move, and soon there was a piteous clamor: "Mizu, mizu! I'm burning. Give me water. Pour water over me. Mizu, mizu!"

Elsewhere on the campus, Nagai's students were faring badly. The heavy roof above his first-year students had come crashing down, pinning everyone like butterflies on a specimen board. No matter how he struggled, head student Fujimoto found it impossible to lift the masonry from his head and shoulders.

Several students began a strange conversation. It ended as the crackling fire closed in on them. One of them shouted, "Sayonara!" and gave a stirring rendition of the old war song:

> Whether we perish as bloated corpses in the sea,
> Or fall and rot in grass on the mountainside,
> If we die for you, O Emperor, we die without regret.

Fujimoto made one last effort to free himself, felt the floorboards move and slithered down, the only one of the whole class to escape.

The x-ray department did not have bed patients, so the dean said to his little band: "Quick, before the fires reach it, go and check on the equipment. See if we can move it to safety." As he waited, trying to plan, he thought: The Americans will land within a week of this. There will be shocking casualties among the citizens, so this is no time for wavering.

His group returned. The x-ray equipment was a write-off, with all valves destroyed, electric wires in tatters and the transformer under a mountain of debris. Nagai was at a loss for words or even thoughts and looked around at the faces. He said to himself: No, we can't panic. But if we do nothing, we'll be burned to death. Yet not a single practical idea came. Suddenly he broke into a nervous laugh. Everyone burst into laughter at the incongruity. It was unintended, but it relieved the tension.

Outside the hospital, the chaos was unnerving. Bodies hung upside down on stone walls and fences, heads or limbs missing. A wild-eyed mother ran by, clutching a decapitated child, and two children went dragging their father up the hill. Across the way, on the roof of a burning building, a man danced and sang, quite insane. A serene old couple, hand in hand, walked up the hill away from the roaring sea of flames below. Yet Nagai and his group could only stand there helpless as the fires spread all over the hospital.

More x-ray staff joined them, and one of them asked: "Shall we try to haul the equipment out?" "No," replied Nagai, "forget it. There are wards where patients will be burned alive. Go there first. Go!" He himself raced down to the underground emergency theater. Pipes had burst, and water had flooded everything. Instruments, medicine and stretchers were smashed and jumbled up in a desperate mess. "I felt like a mosquito whose legs had been plucked off." He knew they had reached rock bottom and thought: All we have left is our knowledge, our love and our bare hands. He came upstairs and looked uneasily at the strange mushroom cloud that glowered ominously over Nagasaki. Meanwhile, his nurses had tied wet hand towels around their faces, plunged into the smoke-filled wards and were dragging patients out.

It was now afternoon. Young Dr. Okura ran up to Nagai. "There's still an arthritis patient over in that ward. He refuses to leave unless I get a stretcher. There aren't any stretchers." Nagai looked at the thirty-three-foot-high flames fanned by the wind that now came in from the west. They were on the hospital's east side, on the slopes of Mount Konpira. For Okura to return to the ward looked suicidal. "Leave the patient. I take responsibility", said Nagai. It was just common sense, yet later Nagai and most of the survivors would be tormented by guilt, remembering this one and that one whom they might have saved, "had we not left them to perish while we saved our own skin."

When Nagai's temporal artery had been severed by flying glass, blood at first spurted out "like red ink from a water pistol". His staff had packed the wound and bound it heavily with bandages. This did not stop the bleeding, and now he was a man wearing a red turban. The west wind drove the fires closer to where rescued patients lay on the ground. Nagai shouted: "Quick, get them higher up the hill." He himself carried two of them to safety but then began to sway on his feet. Matron Hisamatsu grabbed his arm to take his pulse and gasped at the effects of the loss of blood and leukemia. His staff forced him to sit down while they completed the evacuation of patients.

When his chest stopped heaving, he looked around and saw all semblance of organization beginning to disintegrate. More people were pouring in from the city below, thinking they could get relief if they made it to the big hospital complex. Nothing was further from the truth—here the staff could scarcely touch their own patients, and panic was beginning to show in their faces. "Suddenly," said Matron [Head Nurse] Hisamatsu, who still lives in Nagasaki, "it all seemed utterly beyond us, and we started to lose our nerve." At that point, Nagai shouted: "Quick, find a Hi no Maru", which is the Japanese flag. He directed the command to young Dr. Okura, who could not think of anything as inconsequential right then as a flag! He went through the motions of looking for one in the few places not on fire and reported back: "It's impossible to find one." Nagai looked at a piece of white sheet as it blew toward him. He snatched it up, tore it into a square, pulled the blood-soaked bandage from his head and squeezed and dabbed blood into the center, making a rough circle of red. Matron Hisamatsu and several others added blood from their own wounds, and lo! The Japanese flag.

During the war in China, Nagai had witnessed how the centrifugal forces of shock and panic can sometimes be reversed by a bold action or a powerful symbol. For Japanese of 1945, the most powerful of symbols was the Hi no Maru, the national flag. For the past fifteen years, the militarists had made sure it flew prominently over all military headquarters and over every public building and important celebration. Nagai ordered Okura to tie the homemade flag to a thick bamboo pole lying nearby and drive it into a grassy spot a little distance above them. Matron Hisamatsu recalls it very vividly, forty-two years later:

"Suddenly we had a 'headquarters' to rally around, a center that put order back into the picture." Dr. Okura, who has since become a priest and (significantly) an expert on Saint John of the Cross, agrees: "It was so simple an act, and yet the psychological effect was profound."

In the past, when the going was tough, Nagai had always found comfort and encouragement in Mother Nature. Now he was horrified to discover that the bomb had deranged even her. Black rain began to fall, flat drops that left dark and evil stains. The air too had become foul. The wide-ranging fires, glutting themselves on oxygen, belched out so much carbon dioxide that Nagai and his co-workers panted like dogs and struggled for breath. It was now 4 P.M., five hours since the calamitous explosion, and the fires still burned fiercely. Patients moaned, some from pain, some from terror, but the medical staff could do little but take out splinters of glass or pieces of wood and cement, often with crude instruments, apply a little iodine and bandage the bigger wounds. They fetched great quantities of water from wells and a nearby mountain stream in their attempts to quench the cries of "Mizu, mizu!"

Tears glistened in Nagai's eyes when he found the university president lying sick in a field, his white coat smeared with black rain. He made a brief report to the listless president and turned to continue his work. Seeing x-ray technician Umezu-san crumpled up on the ground and soaked through, Nagai took off his coat and covered him.

Since about noon, when Nagai realized the whole suburb of Urakami was burning, he had experienced a great urge to rush down and search for Midori. But he knew that would be terribly wrong. He was one of the few authority figures on his feet, and the situation only worsened as more people came staggering up from the suburbs below. He kept taking furtive glances, hoping and praying to see her among the refugees. But 4 P.M. came with no sight of Midori, and a terrible depression settled on him. He stopped what he was doing and looked down on the suburb of Urakami. All that stood now were jagged remnants of the cathedral walls and black concrete shells of a few public buildings. The whole area around his home was a flat, smoking desert of ash. At that moment, the certainty of her death struck him like a body blow. His mind and body had already been driven beyond normal endurance. Suddenly his legs went rubbery and buckled, and as he sank to the earth, a colleague heard him mutter: "She would have come by now. She's dead, she's dead. Midori!" One hand meaninglessly crushed a handful of dirt, and then he fainted, mainly from loss of blood.

He regained consciousness with Professor Fuse shouting anxiously: "Thread. Forceps. Gauze, gauze. Press down ... the end of the artery has slipped behind the bone!" Nagai fell unconscious again, but the bleeding had been stopped. When he next opened his eyes, he was looking at a sliver of moon above poor denuded Mount Inasa. The nurses had collected pumpkins from the surrounding fields and were boiling them in air-raid helmets while the men were making lean-to shelters for the patients and injured. Nagai's eyes fell on two diminutive, youthful nurses working industriously. They were in his department and were affectionately nicknamed "Little Bean" and "Little Barrel". "Little Octopus" made the trio, but she was dead. So was their friend, magnificent young Hamazaki, a nurse he had been with as she expired. In Nagai's pocket was a snippet of her hair. He would give it to her family, and they would place it in a small urn on the family altar. He grew gloomy as he thought of all the families who would not have even that consolation as they prayed for their dead.

Dr. Nagai got up and joined the little circle of his colleagues, nurses, doctors and x-ray technicians. He writes: "As we looked at one another, we sensed that we were bound together by some incomprehensible fate. Grasping one another's hands and holding them tightly, we just sat there in silence."

Photo of the destroyed Urakami Cathedral soon after the A-bomb.

Sketch by Nagai of the cathedral four months later.

21

The Last Black Hole in the Universe?

The sun had long gone down, but great fires still raged below as doctors and nurses continued searching for the living in the surrounding fields. Many of the injured struggling up from the city to the hospital hill did not make it all the way, and doctors and nurses kept going out looking for them in the dark. Often the rescuers fell and gashed themselves on broken glass or fell headlong into culverts, ignorant that a bridge had disappeared, as they staggered along carrying the injured. Boards with protruding nails had been flung in all directions and left wounds in many feet. It was now about midnight, and the fires below were dying down when Matron Hisamatsu said agitatedly: "Doctor, the cathedral is going up in flames." Built so that it stood alone on a hill, it had been demolished by the initial blast but had not caught fire with the rest of wooden Urakami. However, flying sparks finally ignited its smashed timbers, and now great red flames shot up like players in a danse macabre. He watched, transfixed, until a great crash of timbers and bricks sounded the cathedral's death rattle. That moment was forever burned into Nagai's memory.

The classic Greek tragedy of World War II, he reflected, seemed to be coming to a cataclysmic close. A deus ex machina had appeared, carried to center stage by a lumbering B-29. This deus, this new god, was some weird bomb created by the scientific age of enlightenment! Nagai the believer could only think of the horror and yet the magnificence of the Book of

Revelation. The broken cathedral lay like the Lamb that was slain. Nagai the scientist cocked his eye at the strange cloud that seemed somehow to be drawing energy from the fires below. What was it, and what was the new bomb that exploded like black magic?

With the dawn, the doctor and his staff rose from fitful sleep and were struck speechless by the nuclear ashscape below and around them. Nothing alive, nothing green. No summer sounds of cicadas, just nothing. They dragged themselves back to the gutted hospital, hoping to find some instruments and medicine. Skeletons and charred bodies were everywhere. They went to the rooms where friends had been at 11:02 A.M. the day before and found them—professors, students, doctors, nurses, technicians and patients—reduced to charred lumps. Some were huddled in a row; others lay with their hands raised above their heads. Nagai lowered his eyes and prayed briefly.

Matron Hisamatsu came running up to Nagai, waving a leaflet dropped by a U.S. plane warning the citizens to leave the city before it was too late. Nagai, after a quick glance at the letter, shouted involuntarily: "The atom bomb! Yes, it had to be that!" The mind-boggling destruction in Nagasaki, tallied with all the details long speculated from atomic fission, made it clear. "Conflicting emotions churned within me at that moment: the victory of science and the defeat of my country; a triumph for physics and a tragedy for Japan." A bamboo spear lay at his feet, one of the weapons women had been training with since August 14, 1944, when the General Mobilization Ordinance was passed requiring regular bamboo spear practice for all females between thirteen and sixty years. They were to fight invading Americans like the wives, children and grandmothers of samurai of old who took to the field of battle with such weapons when their castle was threatened. Bamboo spears against atom bombs! Nagai kicked the flimsy weapon in anger and in despair while thinking: "Will we Japanese be now forced to stand on our shores and be annihilated without a protest?"

He took the leaflet down to a great scientist, Professor Seiki, who lay on the bare ground in a makeshift air-raid shelter. Seiki read it, groaned and just gazed at the empty sky for a long time. Then, in his inimitable brilliant way, he began a discussion with the physicists around him. "Strange though it seems," writes Nagai, "we became totally absorbed, oblivious of everything else." Japanese scientists had been working on uranium-235, but the army had stopped the costly research. Who had made the breakthrough in the West? They proposed a number of prewar front-runners: Einstein, Dohr, Fermi, Chadwick, the Joliot-Curies, Madame Meitner, Hahn. Then Seiki brought up the moot question of the radiation that follows the splitting of the atom.

Nagai had been blessed with a sense of wonder. He could be swept off his feet on a clear night when he looked up at old friends like the Great Bear constellation or the North Star—"they evoked a sense of intimate kinship in my heart." Now, squatting on the bare earth beside illustrious Professor Seiki, he animatedly discussed radiation as if it were of no personal concern, conscious only of the opportunity of "participating in a precious scientific experience". This hillside was now an experimentation table where he and his colleagues would discover what happens to humans, insects and plants after the much-debated atomic fission. Yesterday, they were crushed with grief and consumed with anger at what had happened to their people. Today, there stirred within them "a new dynamism and motivation in our quest for truth. On this devastated nuclear wilderness, something was already growing, the vigorous seedlings of new scientific data."

Nagai dragged himself away from the fascinating discussion to attend to the victims. The devastating force of the wind created by the atomic fission was now more evident in the daylight. He found, for instance, heads taken off at the neck as if by a giant sword. The terrific heat of fission-released infrared rays was terribly obvious too. The incidence of gamma-ray sickness increased dramatically. Some said they felt as if they had inhaled town gas;[1] others said it was like a really bad hangover or seasickness. People who thought they had escaped unscathed began flopping down lethargically in the nearest shade, too sick to move. Nagai was now feeling ill himself. This double dose of gamma radiation was very distressing, but it put him in a unique position to observe scientifically and experientially the effects of A-bomb radiation.

U.S. planes kept flying overhead on August 10, which terrified Nagai and his companions. They had no way of knowing if these planes carried more A-bombs. Moving as systematically as possible among the fallen to find if any were living, they would frantically dive for cover when they heard a plane. A certain neurosis began to set in as they gazed on the sickening sights of people who had been skinned alive or turned into big sticks of charcoal. Each sound of an enemy plane came like an electric prodder on exposed nerves. A kind of psychological vertigo took over as limbs grew more leaden and their task looked more hopeless. When darkness came on the tenth, they collapsed onto the earthen floor of their shelter, sick with despair and radiation nausea. Was it really a shelter? Or was it the last black hole in a universe collapsing in on itself? The shelter floor was jam-packed with groaning, restless bodies. Before long some of them were corpses, but no one had the energy to remove them. About midnight, someone in a nightmare grabbed Nagai's shoulders, shrieking the name of Oyanagi-san, a nurse who had died the previous day.

[1] A synthetic fuel made from coal; it is similar to natural gas.

22

Talking Bones and a New Mantra

When August 11 dawned, the medical staff dragged themselves up and began carrying patients to the pickup place for doctors and nurses from a military hospital. It was high summer and the dead were beginning to smell, so they started building cremation pyres. Wood lay in all directions, as if a great tidal wave had thrown driftwood as far up as the mountains. If they recognized a body, they would write the name on a wooden slat, pushing it into the ground before lighting the pyre. Relatives were moving about too, searching for kin. In the communal nervous breakdown, ordinary decency fled. Searchers would come up to a group of injured, look rudely at their faces and say, "No, no one among this lot."

When the army doctors and nurses arrived to take responsibility, Nagai was at last free to think of his own family. His children and Gran were safe four miles away in the mountains. But Midori! As he stumbled down the slope toward the desert of ash that had once been Urakami, remorse flooded his soul for not going to her aid as soon as he was rescued from the debris in his office. He had now reached the neighborhood of his home, where radiation could be much worse, but he was determined at least to give her a decent burial, beneath a cross in their family plot.

With difficulty he found their home in an area that was now nothing but broken roof tiles and white ash. What was that black lump over there? It was Midori! There was little more than the charred remains of her skull, hips and back-bone. He could see she died in the kitchen that she loved. Sobbing, he picked up a heat-buckled pail and knelt to gather her bones. What was the dull glint among the powdered bones of her right hand? Though the beads were melted into a blob, the chain and cross identified it as the Rosary he had seen slipping through her fingers so often. He bowed his head and sobbed: "Dearest God, thank you for allowing her to die praying. Mother of Sorrows, thank you for being with faithful Midori at the hour of her death." As he carefully scooped the bones into the pail, he murmured: "Ah, gracious Jesus our Savior, you once sweat blood and bore the heavy Cross to your crucifixion. And now you have shed peaceful light on the mystery of suffering and death, on Midori's and my own."

He stood up and began walking slowly to Akagi Cemetery. Suddenly emotion overwhelmed him, and he stopped and looked down at the pathetic burden in the bucket: "Midori, those secret pilgrimages you used to make early in the morning to Hongochi Monastery, praying for me, they are over now. Thank you for that and for your countless acts of kindness. Forgive me! Forgive me for taking you for granted. You remained at home while I selfishly pursued my studies and got promoted. Forgive me for not going straight to you when you were dying. Please forgive me." He began walking again, but he stumbled over debris, and the bones rattled in the bucket. He had the extraordinary impression that the sound of the bones formed the words: "No, forgive me. It is I who should ask forgiveness." He knew it was an illusion, but his vivid memories of her habitual generosity and readiness to go more than halfway made it almost believable that she had spoken in reply.

The story continues in his book *Horobinu Mono Wo*. He buried her bones in their plot at Akagi Bochi, "the cemetery by the red tree". Finishing his prayer, he made his way distractedly back to the ruins of his house and began poking in the charred rubble with his stick. What was that metal lump? His medals! Midori had been so proud of his university and army medals, especially the Order of the Rising Sun, keeping them polished and carefully placed in a cedar box. Now they were just a formless black lump of metal. The fine cloisonné work on the Rising Sun medal had disappeared entirely. Was this a sign of things to come in what *was* the Land of the Rising Sun? All his scientific textbooks, notes, case histories and x-rays had gone up in the hospital flames. The fire here had devoured all his precious classical literature. He gazed sadly at a carbonized heap of books and noticed that the metallic print was faintly legible on the top page. Peering closely, he discovered that it was a poem he had loved since schooldays, composed by "the saint of Japanese poets", Kakinomoto. Kakinomoto was a court official in seventh-century Nara and wrote this poem while banished to distant Shimane Prefecture, languishing for home and above all for his wife. "The whole hillside is astir with the rustling of bamboo grass. . . . But I have thoughts only for the one I have left behind, my little sister." "Little sister" was a term of affection a husband sometimes used for his wife. Nagai stopped, unable to continue as the full realization came that he had lost everything of value, his books, his research data, his home, the cathedral he loved, his best friends. But above all, his little sister Midori, totally lovable and utterly dependable. Emotions he had dammed back for days burst out in full flood, and he wept uncontrollably. His physical stamina too, sapped by leukemia, loss of blood, radiation and lack of proper food and sleep, now gave out. Once again his knees buckled beneath him, and he fell on his back in the ashes of his home, where he lay unconscious for hours.

He came to his senses the next morning just before the dawn, conscious of a fresh breeze from the bay playing on his face. He opened his eyes and found himself gazing into a bright light.

What was it? A streetlight? Making a great effort to focus his eyes and mind, he realized he was looking up at Venus, the morning star! "Morning Star, pray for us", he murmured automatically. "Morning Star" was a title of Mary in one of his favorite prayers, the Litany of Loreto. He felt a great need to pray to Mary and, moving stiffly onto his knees, slowly recited the Rosary. He rose up from that prayer, he says, refreshed in spirit and ready to finish whatever God planned for him before he went to join Midori.

The serene light of morning was flooding into the Urakami valley as he set out for Koba, where Gran and his children were. Soon he had left the devastated city behind and was on a tiny mountain road skirting a clear stream. He washed his face and hands in the cool mountain water, drank deeply and set off again, wondering how he would break the news to his children and Gran. After the carnage, smoke and ash of the last few days, the mountains had never looked so beautiful and dependable. That Chinese poet had expressed it well: Though the nation go under, the mountains and streams remain. Though men explode atom bombs, God's sunlight never fails. Scientist Nagai corrected that thought: "The sun's fuel is already half spent, and one day sunlight will disappear and the green mountains around me will die, just as surely as my wife died and my books and medals turned to ash." His copy of the New Testament had also turned to ash, but as he walked, a verse from it took hold of his heart: "The heavens and the earth will pass away, but my words will never pass away." There it was, the truth more reliable than mountains and sunlight and the answer to the horror and sadness of August 9! He repeated the verse again and again, in rhythm with his walking, just as he had prayed Scripture verses on lonely marches in China. He felt his new mantra flood his body, soul and spirit, and with it came a consciousness that everything was all right. Midori had merely finished her work early and gone home to God. His own future? The war might end it soon—or peace might come, and he would have to find a home for his children and Gran, work hard to rebuild the university and cathedral, and meet a painful death from leukemia in two or three years' time. Meeting that manfully, with Christ's word as his North Star, was his way home to God and Midori—a way as simple and sure as the little mountain road that now led his feet to the remnant of his family. An extraordinary sense of gratitude possessed him as he marched along to the beat of his new mantra.

The Shokado, *woodblock print, 1799. Shojo, one of the most prolific of Japanese artists and also a calligrapher and* chajin *(tea master), built this hut as a retirement cottage. He named his hut Shokado, "pine flower hall". Here he welcomes a visitor.*

23

High Noon, and a Nation Wept

On the day after the A-bomb fell, Grandma Moriyama made the heartbreaking journey to Urakami and brought back some fragments of Midori's bones in a small metal container. She told Makoto he must not look into it, but the reverent way she treated it and her continual tears aroused his suspicions, and when she was out for a moment he crept over, trembling, and opened it. He was instinctively certain it was his mother's bones. Several days later, as the boy and his grandmother sat gloomy and silent at a frugal table, the sliding door clattered back without warning. At first they did not recognize the emaciated, unshaven man who stood there with a blood-caked bandage covering most of his head, clothes torn and filthy. When he entered and tried to pick up little Kayano, she screamed and ran in terror behind Gran. It was a sad homecoming.

Nagai soon discovered that great numbers of A-bomb victims had been carried or carted or had stumbled to this cool mountain valley with its clear stream and its mineral spring, which had a reputation for helping burns heal. The local farmers had been very generous in welcoming the pitiful casualties. One neighbor, Takami-san, was sheltering over a hundred. Many were grotesquely swollen and dying, but others, with glass, concrete and wooden splinters embedded in them, could be helped. His little band of survivors from the x-ray department kept their appointment with him the next day and decided to begin a mobile medical unit there in Koba, grossly lacking in medicine and instruments though they were. They set out early each morning, treating people throughout the whole valley, pulling out splinters of glass and other materials and treating festering wounds. They discovered that the mineral spring water helped burns, but they could do almost nothing for the many victims of radiation sickness. There were always too many patients, and they would return home late every night, exhausted.

It was not all hard work. City dweller Nagai speaks of the nostalgic experience of "inhaling the fragrance of summer grasses and washing away our grime and weariness in swift mountain streams." Walking the unspoiled country roads, he saw symbols of his new mantra everywhere. The mountains that stood unmoved before the onslaught of high winds, mist and rain were fingerprints of the ever-faithful God. On clear mountain nights, he would gaze up spellbound at the dark fields laden with astral grain. The constellation Virgo set him thinking. According to the old Greek legend, Virgo was so distressed by the evil ways of men that she fled earth to find a chaste place in the heavens. Virgo was like Hamazaki and all those nurses in his department who died because of the evil ways of military men. How sad that these young women would never know the embrace of a husband or the smile of children!

Well before August, Japan's navy and air force had been crippled, effectively neutralizing the Imperial Army units stationed on the Asian mainland and in Japan proper. U.S. planes bombed factories and ports almost at will, and sensible Japanese leaders knew the war was lost and were ready for peace. Prime Minister Suzuki despatched Foreign Minister Togo to Moscow, seeking to enlist Russia as a peace negotiator with the West, but Russia was waiting until Japan was weak enough to be attacked with impunity. An influential group of Americans was trying to convince the White House that "unconditional surrender" had little chance of Japanese acceptance because it did not recognize the sacred position of the Emperor. Leading this group was Joseph Grew, who had been the U.S. ambassador in Tokyo until the war in the Pacific broke out. Historian Toland writes that Grew "had a rare understanding and affection for Japan and all things Japanese". Citing ten years' experience in Japan and his inside view of the genesis of the war, Grew insisted that the Emperor was not a war criminal and had tried to prevent the war. Most Japanese, he continued, would resist a surrender that might mean the Emperor's trial as a war criminal and would not cooperate with an occupation that sanctioned such a sacrilege. Grew was strongly supported by some Far Eastern experts in the State Department—Dooman, Ballantine and Professor Blakeslee—and by Assistant Secretary of War McCloy. Their argument was rejected, and the Allies broadcast the Potsdam Proclamation for unconditional surrender on July 27, 1945.[1] Seventy-eight-year-old Prime Minister Suzuki was desperate for peace, but peace that would protect the Emperor. On July 28 he replied to the Allies with the word *mokusatsu*, meaning "rejection". The Japanese people accepted that decision and gritted their teeth for the hard battles when the Americans would land. The Japanese media did not carry news of the August 6 A-bombing of Hiroshima.

At 11 A.M. on August 9, the Supreme Council of War sat down to discuss the Potsdam demand in view of the new development in Hiroshima. The Emperor, as tradition demanded, attended the meeting as a passive onlooker. Three of the six council members were for unconditional surrender—Prime Minister Suzuki, Foreign Minister Togo and Navy Minister Admiral Yonai. The other three were adamantly against it—War Minister General Anami, Army Chief General Umezu

---

[1] The Potsdam Conference was the last meeting among the Allied Forces during World War II. Potsdam is a city near Berlin, Germany.

and Navy Chief Admiral Toyoda. The deadlock was hopeless, and the meeting was abandoned.

Some hours later, the Emperor heard of the second A-bomb
on Nagasaki and was deeply depressed. If he continued to
"reign" passively, would he be guilty if his people were wiped
out? He came to a lonely decision and requested that the
Supreme War Council, all cabinet ministers and high imperial
officials meet with him that midnight in his air raid bunker.
When they humored him and had gathered in his bunker, he
announced without ado that Japan would accept Potsdam's
terms. The audience was as stunned as if a two-thousand-year-
old stone crane had suddenly spoken! Most of his listeners
sobbed, and some wept openly. The Emperor said he himself
would broadcast this to the nation, again breaking all precedent.

When Nagai and the rest of Japan were told to stand by
their radio sets at 12 noon on August 15, they presumed they
would hear an exhortation to repel the Americans just as their
ancestors had repelled the Mongol horde in the thirteenth century. They were stunned when the high-pitched voice from
the Chrysanthemum Throne came over the airwaves telling
them they "must bear the unbearable and suffer the insuffer-
able". That meant unconditional surrender. People all over Japan
burst into tears, many kneeling in grief facing toward the
Emperor, their foreheads on the ground. Nagai writes of the
shock "unconditional surrender" was to him: "Our Japan, sym-
bolized by Mount Fuji rising up through the clouds, the first
mountain to be touched by the rays of the sun when it rises
in the East, our Japan was dead! Our race was hurtling into an
abyss!"

Wild rumors flew: The Americans would kill all Japanese
men and rape the women to create a bastard race. Nagai and
his team did not know what would happen, but they feared
that unconditional surrender meant the dismantling of Japan
and the end of her culture. She would be a helpless colony

like India. They lost all will to continue their mercy mission, sitting listlessly at home all day and touching no food that night.

The next morning, having eaten little breakfast and in almost total silence, they just continued to sit, making no attempt to wash the dishes. A man appeared at the door asking for a doctor to come and see a sick friend. Nagai snapped angrily at him: "One sick man makes no difference when the whole nation is doomed." The startled man left, dejected, and they watched him returning across the fields. Suddenly Nagai had a change of heart and sent Little Bean scurrying after him. The tired band followed Nagai and recommenced their medical rounds. However, their stamina had noticeably lessened, and they too were now coming down with radiation symptoms—fever, an abnormal white blood cell count, hair loss, bleeding gums, exhaustion. On September 8, 1945, Nagai manifested severe symptoms of A-bomb sickness. His temperature rose to 104 degrees and stayed there for a week. His whole body had swollen, his face like a soccer ball. The flesh around his temporal wound rotted, leaving a gaping wound, and bleeding began again. Dr. Tomita and Nurse Morita took turns pressing down on the temporal artery, day and night. Otherwise he would bleed to death within three hours. He had already lost a lot of blood, and his pulse and heartbeat began showing unmistakable signs of giving out. Someone gave him an injection. Ah, nikethamide,[2] Nagai thought, judging by the pain. Father Tagawa came, and Nagai said he wanted to make a general confession. After that, he received the Eucharist, and "experiencing great peace, I was ready to die." He asked for a brush and Chinese ink for his *jisei no uta*, the traditional farewell song. From ancient times, in the code of *bushido*, the true samurai dies calm and self-possessed, leaving a farewell poem

[2] A respiratory stimulant.

for his family and friends, often saluting the beauties of nature around him.

Nagai took inspiration for his farewell song from the clear autumn sky he could see through the window. Writing with weak brush strokes, he bid sayonara to a world that had given him much pleasure:

Hikari tsu tsu Aki-zora takaku ... Kie ni Keri.

A high and shining autumn sky ... I take my leave.

Soon after writing his poem, he lapsed into unconsciousness. When his eyes opened again, he noticed his breathing had deteriorated, and he calculated he was several hours from death. Gazing at Dr. Tomita pressing on his temporal artery, he murmured: "Cheyne-Stokes breathing", and Tomita answered, "Yes". Nagai's chest now felt "as if an empty automobile were lurching around inside." Dr. Fuse had gone to Nagasaki, hoping some university colleague might have advice or medicine to help pull Nagai through. He managed to find three professors from the medical university, Doctors Cho, Kageura and Koyano. When Fuse described the symptoms, each gave the same reply: Nagai is dying, and nothing can be done.

Nagai, slipping in and out of a coma, now realized he could not move his head or open his eyes, and he thought: Convulsions will soon begin. He could hear the prayers and his son's voice. That made him want to live. He heard a woman's voice speaking reassuringly. Ah, that's Gran. "This is water from our Lady's grotto at Hongochi Monastery", she murmured gently, and her words evoked a very clear image of the Lourdes Grotto and the encouraging face of Mary the Mother of God. Nagai continued: "I heard—how, I don't know, but I alone heard it, and heard it clearly—a voice telling me to ask Father Maximilian Kolbe to pray for me. I did as I was told, begging Father

Kolbe's prayers. Then I turned to Christ and said: 'Lord, I leave myself in your divine hands.'"

Nurse Morita, who had been pressing the broken artery, suddenly faced Dr. Tomita and said: "The bleeding has stopped!" The large wound, which had resisted medication, had healed without medical help. Nagai wrote of the experience in detail in one of his later books. While noting that it is always possible to be mistaken in the matter of miraculous cures, he said that he and the attending doctors believed his recovery was miraculous. He quickly added that miracle cures are not signs of holiness, pointing out that at places like Lourdes, people of little faith or of none at all are among the cases that panels of doctors have declared medically inexplicable.

Nagai credited Father Kolbe with his recovery. Kolbe was a Polish Franciscan who came to Japan in 1930. He founded a monastery in Nagasaki and built behind it a Lourdes grotto that has now become a national place of pilgrimage. The Marian monthly he started was still Catholic Japan's most-read magazine. Nagai knew him well and on one occasion x-rayed him for tuberculosis. In 1936 Kolbe was recalled to Poland as prior of a very large monastery. Under him, the monastery began putting out Catholic newspapers that sold millions of copies weekly. His influence soon attracted the attention of the Nazi occupation, intent on crushing any form of "resistance". In May 1941 he was arrested and became Number 16670 in Auschwitz. In July, when a prisoner escaped, Commandant Fritsch lined up the whole block and chose ten prisoners at random to be executed in retaliation for the escapee. They were ordered into a bunker to be left without food or water until they "dried up like tulip bulbs", as Fritsch put it. Sergeant Francis Gajown-iczek was one of the doomed men and muttered, to no one in particular: "My poor wife and children." Kolbe stepped forward, said he had no family and asked to take the sergeant's place. Kolbe and the other nine were incarcerated on July 31, and by August 14 all had died except Kolbe and three other unconscious prisoners . An orderly was sent to finish them off with an injection of carbolic acid.

The news blackout prevented the Nagais from knowing any of this. However, Midori would sometimes think of Kolbe when she made her pilgrimage to the Lourdes Grotto he built. Gran used water from that shrine to moisten the dying doctor's lips but made no mention of Kolbe. Nor did anyone else in the room. Nagai himself had no doubt that Kolbe's prayers were responsible for the cure. Kolbe was not a famous canonized saint at the time. Today, however, most Christians who come on pilgrimage to Nagasaki visit both Kolbe's shrine and Nagai's hut. It is appropriate, for somehow the lurid colors of the flames of Auschwitz and Nagasaki were regathered and transformed into clear light when passing through the hearts of these two men.

Sketch by Nagai of the statue of the Sorrowful Mother left standing at the enrance of the ruined Urakami Cathedral.

24

Not from Chance Our Comfort Springs[1]

Nagai's remarkable recovery occurred on October 5, by which time government medical teams were taking over and Nagai's band could return to their own homes. Nagai spent a period of mourning, praying for Midori and the other dead from the university hospital. During that time, he followed an old Eastern tradition of cutting neither hair nor beard and living as penitentially as he could. During this period, he also returned to Urakami and tackled the problem of residual radiation. He had no instruments, but when he discovered live ants and then earthworms, he was convinced the autumn rains had washed most of the fallout away. The wild rumors that all life would be impossible for seventy years were wrong. Like the ants, back to work! Helped by some friends, he built a small hut by leaning charred beams against the stone retaining wall of his home and roofing the structure with pieces of heat-buckled tin. His children demanded they join their father, and they and Gran moved in. Eight thousand Catholics died in Urakami, but others were out of town or overseas in the army or Japanese colonies when the bomb fell. Many heeded Nagai's call to rebuild the suburb, and they put up huts around his. The remnants of the university staff set about planning a new university, and Nagai joined in energetically.

[1] Roman breviary hymn.

185

Nagai returned to live where Midori and eight thousand Christians died "so that I could contemplate the meaning of the event." Some people were muttering that the A-bomb was obviously *tenbatsu*, heaven's punishment. At this juncture the bishop announced plans for an open-air Mass for the dead and asked Nagai to speak on behalf of the laity. Nagai intensified his efforts to find meaning in the A-bomb. Reflecting on two events led him to an insight that was startling. Nurse Kosasa and some others from radiology heard women singing Latin hymns about midnight after the bomb dropped. They were too exhausted to think much of it, but they passed the place the next morning and discovered the near-naked bodies of twenty-seven nuns from Josei Convent. The explosion had demolished the convent, killed some nuns outright and left some others horribly burned. These latter obviously died in agony clustered around a little stream nearby, yet they died singing!

The other incident concerned girls from Junshin, a school where Midori had taught, run by nuns well known to Nagai. As the air raids intensified, the principal, Sister Ezumi, had the whole school sing a hymn every day for God's protection. The opening line was: "Mary, Mother! I offer myself to you, body, soul and spirit." In the very dark days of 1945, the girls came to sing it very earnestly. On the morning of August 9, many Junshin girls were at work in factories at Tokitsu and Michino. Some were killed instantly, while others were cut by flying glass or roofing iron and were badly burned by infrared rays and suffered that terrible thirst that characterizes A-bomb victims. Over the next days and weeks, Nagai heard a number of stories about little groups of Junshin girls gathered in a field, in a makeshift dispensary or down by the river. Most were badly injured and many would be dead within days, but they kept encouraging each other, singing verses of their hymn, "Mother Mary, I offer myself to you."

Nagai was sitting on a pile of rubble inside the remains of the cathedral, thinking of his talk at the open-air Mass. In the fading light, charred timbers lying in crisscross fashion took on the appearance of the black limbs of plum trees in winter— black, like the rain and the sun on August 9 and like the sun in the Book of Revelation! He gazed at the broken altar ... the Lamb that was slain! The Lamb of Revelation was followed wherever he went "by a white-robed choir of virgins singing". Suddenly a vision came into focus. The small group of Josei nuns and the girls from Junshin had died singing "the new song" learned from the Lamb. It was the song of the redemptive dimension of suffering and death. The holocaust of Calvary gave meaning and beauty to the holocaust of Nagasaki. He took a pencil and jotted down a tanka poem:

> Hansai no hono no naka ni utai tsutsu
> Shira yuri otome moe ni keru kamo.
>
> Maidens like white lilies
> Consumed in the burning flames
> As a whole burnt sacrifice
> And they were singing.

On November 23, 1945, Nagai knew what to say to bandaged, limping, burn-disfigured and demoralized Catholics who gathered beside the shattered cathedral to assist at a Requiem Mass for their dead. When his turn came to speak, he rose a little unsteadily, looking like a *sennin*, an ancient mountain shaman, with his emaciated features and uncut hair and beard.

With a slow bow to the robed priests and another to the congregation, he began: "On the morning of August 9, a meeting of the Supreme Council of War was in session at Imperial Headquarters, Tokyo, to decide whether Japan would surrender or continue to wage war. At that moment the world stood at a crossroads. A decision had to be made ... peace or further cruel bloodshed and carnage.

"And just then, at 11:02 A.M., an atom bomb exploded over our suburb. In an instant, eight thousand Christians were called to God, and in a few hours flames turned to ash this venerable Far Eastern holy place.

"At midnight that night, our cathedral suddenly burst into flames and was consumed. At exactly that same time in the Imperial Palace, His Majesty the Emperor made known his sacred decision to end the war. On August 15 the Imperial Rescript, which put an end to the fighting, was formally promulgated, and the whole world saw the light of peace. August 15 is also the great feast of the Assumption of the Virgin Mary. It is significant, I believe, that the Urakami Cathedral was dedicated to her. We must ask: Was this convergence of events, the end of the war and the celebration of her feast day, merely coincidental, or was it the mysterious Providence of God?

"I have heard that the atom bomb ... was destined for another city. Heavy clouds rendered that target impossible, and the American crew headed for the secondary target, Nagasaki. Then a mechanical problem arose, and the bomb was dropped further north than planned and burst right above the cathedral. . . . It was not the American crew, I believe, who chose our suburb. God's Providence chose Urakami and carried the bomb right above our homes. Is there not a profound relationship between the annihilation of Nagasaki and the end of the war? Was not Nagasaki the chosen victim, the lamb without blemish, slain as a whole burnt offering on an altar of sacrifice, atoning for the sins of all the nations during World War II?"

Nagai used *hansai*, the Japanese word for the Bible's "holocaust", or whole burnt offering. The angry reaction of some mourners is well captured by famous director Keisuke Kinoshita in *Children of Nagasaki*, the most recent movie on Nagai's life. Some of the congregation stood up and shouted in protest that Nagai should try to dignify with pious words the atrocity perpetrated on their families! Nagai showed neither anger nor surprise. Having traveled through the dark valley they were in, he was sympathetic to their response. He continued with a quiet authority that compelled silence.

"We are inheritors of Adam's sin . . . of Cain's sin. He killed his brother. Yes, we have forgotten we are God's children. We have turned to idols and forgotten love. Hating one another, killing one another, joyfully killing one another! At last the evil and horrific conflict came to an end, but mere repentance was not enough for peace. . . . We had to offer a stupendous sacrifice. . . . Cities had been leveled, but even that was not enough. . . . Only this *hansai* in Nagasaki sufficed, and at that moment God inspired the Emperor to issue the sacred proclamation that ended the war. The Christian flock of Nagasaki was true to the Faith through three centuries of persecution. During the recent war, it prayed ceaselessly for a lasting peace. Here was the one pure lamb that had to be sacrificed as *hansai* on His altar . . . so that many millions of lives might be saved."

Nagai turned to the poetry of the Easter Vigil, in which the tall Paschal Candle is lit in the predawn darkness, a ceremony performed in the cathedral every year. "How noble, how splendid, was that holocaust of midnight August 9, when flames soared up from the cathedral, dispelling darkness and bringing the light of peace. In the very depths of our grief, we were able to gaze up to something *beautiful, pure and sublime!*"

By way of conclusion, Nagai turned to the Mount of the Beatitudes and to the skull-shaped hill outside Jerusalem: "Happy are those who weep; they shall be comforted. We must walk the way of reparation . . . ridiculed, whipped, punished for our crimes, sweaty and bloody. But we can turn our minds' eyes to Jesus carrying his Cross up the hill of Calvary. . . . The Lord has given; the Lord has taken away. Blessed be the name of the Lord. Let us be *thankful* that Nagasaki was chosen for the whole burnt sacrifice! Let us be thankful that through this

sacrifice, peace was granted to the world and religious freedom to Japan." When Nagai finished and sat down, the silence
was deep. His finding of God's Providence at work even in
the horrors of August 9 had a profound effect on the listeners
and, when repeated later in his books, on non-Christians in
Nagasaki and throughout Japan.

Nagai settled down in his little hut, which was neither wind-
proof, rainproof nor, as the winter soon proved, snowproof.
The most recent medical opinion gave him a life expectancy
of two to three years. His first concern was his children, a
daughter four years old and a boy ten. He was determined to
spend as much time with them as possible, hoping to "edu-
cate them in self-reliance." In a society and economy fractured by the disastrous war, only the self-reliant would make
it. This primitive hut would be their classroom. He had told
Gran of his plans, and she, still too numb to argue, simply
accepted them. Their first kitchen was a fireplace in the open,
their utensils an iron pot with no handle and an earthenware
jar with a broken neck.

Two relatives with nowhere else to go joined them. To fit
the six inside, they had to alternate positions in "bed" at
night, with the first head at the north end, the second at the
south and so on. Incidentally, they had only a blanket each,
and sleeping like this conserved warmth. Most of their clothes
and all of their bedding had disappeared with the bomb. Winter came, rain and snow blew in, and yet they did not catch
colds. Nagai thought this was an unexpected benefit of Urakami's dose of radiation. He had noted that wheat exposed to
radiation was quickly sprouting everywhere. Corn also began
to sprout but gave no grain. Morning glories put out new
tendrils immediately after the bomb, but the flowers were
small and the leaves deformed. Green vegetables thrived, while
sweet potatoes sprouted almost immediately but produced no
crop.

Professor Suetsugu, now in the x-ray department at prestigious Kyoto University, came down to see his old colleague, who had taken over his deanship at Nagasaki. Nagai had nowhere to meet him but in the hut. Any cultured householder in Japan brings guests to the room with the *tokonoma*. This is a tall but shallow alcove above a barely raised pedestal, half-framed by a cypress beam that is unpainted to display its natural grain. Inside the alcove is usually a hanging scroll with some calligraphy or a short poem from classical Chinese literature. Nagai's one-room hut had no floor, let alone a *tokonoma*, but Suetsugu took out a brush and wrote a classical Chinese poem on a strip of white paper: Mu ichi butsu dokoro mu jin zo! Not a single object here, and yet it is a limitless treasury! Nagai was delighted. It was the very thing he had been telling his children. He stuck the poem on the wall, and it meant more to him than the beautiful *tokonoma* and classical scrolls in their old home.

An old man was getting water from a nearby well. The bomb had hurled in a lot of rubble, and he had to drop the bucket to the very bottom and work hard to get water. "See that, son", Nagai said to Makoto his son. "Our life is now like that. We're scraping the very bottom. We have to begin from almost nothing and dig foundations down in the dark. But we can do it with patience and faith, lad. God is with us."

A little later, Nagai saw a young acquaintance looking aimlessly at the nuclear wasteland. He was one of the youngest Saint Vincent de Paul members when drafted into the marines some years before. He ended the war fighting a rearguard action in South Pacific jungles, in a ragtag remnant long out of food and medicine. Shaking with malaria, he had to use every fiber of willpower not to lie down in the jungle mud and let the fever take him into merciful unconsciousness. The thought of his parents needing him kept him going. Now, back in Urakami, he discovered his parents had died without a trace on August 9.

He sat on a blackened rock near the site of his home and suddenly broke down and wept like a child. Nagai, who had been watching him, went to his side and put an arm around him without speaking. The shoulders stopped shaking, and the gaunt ex-soldier said: "I went through hell in the jungle, but I kept going for them. They're dead, and all I went through has no meaning! I want to get away from here, to go so far away that nothing will remind me of Urakami again." "Yes," said Nagai, "I can understand that feeling. But if you go away and forget, their deaths and all your pain will have little meaning for you. If you stay here in Urakami and build a hut like ours, you keep their names alive and you give your sufferings tremendous meaning." The young man stayed and built a hut where the old home had been and a year later bowed low to Nagai as he introduced his bride-to-be.

Pen and ink were hard to obtain, and Nagai began his first book in pencil. It was a hundred-page medical report on his experiences and observations treating A-bomb victims during the month after August 9. His purpose in writing the world's first scientific account of the effects of an A-bomb was to help doctors treat the many victims languishing in Nagasaki and Hiroshima. His treatise had the advantage of coming from a specialist in radiation who had suffered a double dose himself, and the book proved to be a real contribution to medical science.

Several friends came and told Nagai they could find him a good wife from among the many war widows to help him and his children. Nagai gave this serious thought but refused. He wrote his reasons: "It is a terrible thing for a child to lose a mother, far worse than losing a father. My two children have beautiful memories of Midori. To introduce a stepmother into their lives would only confuse them more." There was also a personal consideration. His children looked very much like their mother, especially his daughter. While Kayano was beside him, he wrote, he could never forget Midori nor entertain the idea of choosing another Mrs. Nagai.

He decided Japan needed a popular book about the A-bomb. The central idea and the title came to him on Christmas Eve 1945, with the help of a friend, Ichitaro Yamada. Before August, the Urakami Cathedral had two bell towers, with matching cupolas that housed two big bells. The cupola on the north, or left-hand, side was hurled scores of yards away by the A-bomb. Part of it is still visible, embedded in the bank of the small watercourse beside the cathedral. Its bell was cracked beyond repair. The southern cupola dropped straight down, the bell with it, and was covered by tons of brick, masonry, charred girders and ash.

Yamada was a soldier stationed on a nearby island when the A-bomb was dropped. He had returned quickly to Urakami to discover the bomb had literally vaporized his wife, his five children and his parents. Near despair, he went to see his friend Nagai. He had to shout out his anger to someone. Nagai listened to Yamada, and after his outburst, Yamada listened to Nagai, for he knew how deep was the wound left by Midori's death. Nagai suggested that the only way open to anyone who believed the Gospel was to see the A-bomb as part of God's Providence, which always brings good from evil. Yamada means "mountain field", and Nagai said with a smile: "Let's climb the Mount of the Beatitudes together." The broken Yamada became Nagai's disciple. When December came around, the two decided it might be worthwhile digging for the buried bell. Yamada and several young men went to work clearing the mountain of rubble, and by late morning on December 24, they could see the top of the bell. They had lunch, and Nagai led them in the Rosary. Then they set to with a will, cleared the sides of the bell and found no cracks. Yamada set up block and tackle and lifted the bell, and it seemed sound. By the time they had the bell hanging securely on a tripod of cypress logs, it was dark and almost 6 P.M., and they decided to ring the Angelus.

Nagai, Yamada and their helpers, not knowing if the buried bell would ring, had not advertised their project to the Urakami Christians. At that moment, the latter were sitting down in drafty huts for skimpy suppers, with nothing to look forward to but the drabbest-ever midnight Mass in a burnt-out hall of Saint Francis Hospital. Then suddenly a real miracle transformed the winter darkness. The nostalgic Angelus! The peals were all the clearer for the absence of any tall buildings in the suburb of huts. It seemed to them that the cathedral had risen from the ashes to herald Christ's birth. They listened in awe like the shepherds when singing came from the dark sky above Bethlehem. That night the title of Nagai's book was born— *The Bells of Nagasaki*. Its message would be that not even an A-bomb can silence the bells of God.

Paper was scarce and suitable places to write even more so, but the book gradually took shape. As he wrote, he began to see himself as spokesman for Nagasaki's seventy-two thousand dead and for the orphans, widows and widowers they left behind. The book is an objective scientific account of the A-bomb but is written in layman's language. He employs an abundance of simple but telling anecdotes, for example: "It is nighttime, and I am in bed in the hut with four-year-old Kayano in my arms. She is drowsy and almost asleep but instinctively reaches under my shirt and takes hold of my nipple. With a shudder, she realizes it is not her mother's breast and that her mother has disappeared. Suddenly she is awake and sobbing."

In later books, he would go more deeply into the difficult question of atomic energy. In this book, he simply poses the question: "Atomic energy is a secret that God placed within the universe. Scientists have unlocked this secret. Will this result in a tremendous leap forward for civilization, or will it destroy our earth? Is atomic energy a key for survival or for total destruction? I find the only guide to using this key is authentic religion."

Authentic religion? How do you find it? Nagai relates how he and his little community found religious hope in the nuclear wilderness. On the last page of his book, music from the cathedral bell floods the valley of ashes, and he kneels with his children to say the Angelus. Despite their poverty and loss, they know that God is love, that suffering and the effort to keep on loving are worthwhile. "The people without a vision perish." Nagai has come to see it is prayer that gives the vision.

The very *Nihon-teki* Nagai, descendant of samurai and lover of the classics of the Far East, has become one in heart with the very French Pascal—one in their love of science and literature, of course, but above all one in their vision of prayer. Psalm 36 expressed it for both of them: "In your light we see light."

Mu, *famous Far Eastern word translated as "No Thing", "the Void".*

25

The Parable of the Bare Hut

Nagai made a concrete suggestion to his old Urakami friends who had returned: Let us put up simple huts to live in and then spend our energies rebuilding Saint Francis Hospital, the sisters' orphanage, the schools and a wooden church beside the old cathedral. Father Nakata, who became parish priest after Father Nishida died in the cathedral on August 9, called a general meeting. He said a man who had timber growing on a nearby mountain would donate enough for a new church. Nagai spoke: "As citizens of Christian Urakami, let us declare our priorities by building the church first. A wooden one will have to do until we can rebuild the cathedral again." The motion was passed, and the able-bodied among them, women and girls included, went to work with a will. Some felled and dragged the timber from the mountain. Others cut and dressed it and built the church under the direction of Yamada, the head of Urakami's Christian carpenters' guild. This church was the first public building to be built in the devastated suburb.

Nagai was again teaching radiology in a struggling university temporarily housed in three neighboring towns. Junshin Girls' School had moved too, utilizing old military barracks in the neighboring town of Omura. He wrote their 1945 Christmas play and painted most of the stage settings. In March 1946 Junshin's principal, Sister Ezumi, asked Nagai to give the address at what promised to be a very sad graduation ceremony. The mood was subdued when he rose to speak. There were

131 girls in the class before August 9, but now there were 31. All of these had lost friends and many of them parents too. The principal was still shaky on her feet, and many of her teaching sisters were bedridden or lay beneath the pines of Akagi Cemetery. Nagai said what you would expect him to say about the need for courage and faith. "All of us must forget personal comfort and must work until our city and our nation can rise again." What was unique, however, was the humor he gradually introduced. Nagai's refusal to become pessimistic about *any* human situation was a trait that his widening circle of admirers found very attractive. When he began the graduation address at Junshin, there was hardly a listener who was not red-eyed. Many just sat glumly with bowed heads, thinking of students who were dead. By the time he ended, however, real laughter had returned to the hall.

He completed his book *The Bells of Nagasaki* by the anniversary of Midori's death, August 9, 1946. Three years later, it would become a best seller and a top box-office movie. But in 1946 no publisher was interested in it. Every major city in Japan had been bombed. Who would want to be reminded of that or of the grotesque fate of A-bomb victims? Nagai was not unduly upset by this initial reaction from publishers. He began two more books. One was a translation of Bruce Marshall's little classic, *The World, the Flesh and Father Smith*. The other is the book where he most reveals himself, *Horobinu Mono Wo* (What does not pass away), where he writes autobiographically in the third person, calling himself Ryukichi. It is a name of two ideographs, one of them the ideograph for his real name, Takashi. Midori is called Haruno, which means "springtime field".

In July 1946 Nagai collapsed at the Nagasaki railway station. He had deteriorated badly, his white blood cell count being 180,000 per cubic millimeter and his red, 2,290,000. [Normal counts would be 5–10,000 white cells per cubic mm.

and about 5 million red cells per cubic mm.] He was carried to the university hospital, where his colleagues examined him and told him it would be suicide unless he took to bed. His condition worsened, and from November of that year until his death, he was permanently bedridden. He had told the 1946 graduation day audience at Junshin that "we A-bomb sufferers must not feel sorry for ourselves. We have work to do, each doing what he can. Every one of us, even the sick, can do something." Now bedridden himself, he devoted more and more time to writing. His swollen spleen meant he had to lie on his back, so he set up a wooden page holder above his head and did his writing in pencil—ink was quite impractical. Bedsores were to become a problem, and his weakening hand is reflected in the progressively softer lead pencils he used for his successive books.

A monetary windfall came when the prestigious women's monthly *Shufu no Tomo* serialized Nagai's translation of Bruce Marshall's novel. After that, other magazines began asking him for articles. Some struggling editors told him they had no money, and they were telling the truth. Believing it was the duty of every Japanese to work selflessly to remedy the depressed economy, he wrote articles for such magazines for nothing.

In 1947 a carpenter relative of Midori returned to Urakami and built the Nagais a more substantial hut. It was larger and much better but was still a one-room hut where the bedridden doctor, Gran and the two children ate, lived and slept. The size was six tatami mats—which is roughly nine feet by twelve feet. Money was beginning to come in from articles, but he refused to build a proper house, telling Gran he would be a poor citizen and Christian if he lived well while the people of Urakami lived in poverty. After taking money for essentials, he gave the rest to needs like the rebuilding of the hospital. Sometimes there were projects of which one with less of a poet's heart might disapprove. For instance, he received a substantial sum of money from the newspaper the *Kysushu Times* as the 1948 winner of their annual culture award. Though he and Urakami were still poverty-ridden, he used a very large part of the money to have one thousand cherry blossom trees planted—around the cathedral ruins, in school yards and along streets. It would seem Urakami residents had poets' hearts, as there is no record of anyone disapproving.

In December 1947 the Saint Vincent de Paul men called on Father Nakata, the parish priest, and said: "We owe it to Dr. Nagai to build him a decent house, with the privacy and quiet a writer needs." The pastor agreed, so they came and told Nagai it was decided. All he had to do was give them the specifications for an ideal house for himself and his family.

Nagai had a younger brother, Hajime, who before his call up to the army had married and was employed at a university in Manchuria. The Russians attacked Manchuria after the Hiroshima A-bomb fell, and Hajime was captured and sent to one of the infamous labor camps in Siberia. His wife and three children returned to Japan with all their possessions in one knapsack and lived with relatives. Now, early in 1948, Hajime had been repatriated to Japan and was looking for a home for his family. He was, however, penniless. Nagai decided that if he moved out and the six-mat hut was extended a little, Hajime and his family could move in with Gran and his two children. He therefore agreed to the Vincentians' offer and drew a simple sketch of his ideal house. It was a one-room house, approximately six and a half feet by six and a half feet! Nagai chose such a hut because of his love for an ancient Oriental tradition. The hut assumes a central role in the rest of his life and demands some explanation.

The wisdom of the East had long seen the value and even the necessity of certain mature individuals withdrawing to live alone in a prayerful, ascetic atmosphere. They are hermits, but hermits very ready to listen to, counsel and pray for the distracted citizens of the marketplace. This ideal entered Japan with Buddhism in the sixth century A.D. and appears here and there in literature. For instance, *The Tales of Heike* describes how the empress dowager Kenrei-mon-in embraced such a life in 1185. She lived alone in a ten-foot-square hut at Ohara. Most famous of all the pilgrim hermits is thirteenth-century Kamono Chomei, whose book *The Ten Foot Square Hut* is a twenty-one-page literary gem and among the most influential books in Japanese history. In the same thirteenth century, Zen Buddhist monasteries attracted many communities of monks who lived together but spent much time in solitary meditation like hermits. Laymen came for spiritual guidance and even secular advice, and the monasteries profoundly affected Japanese art, culture and history. Zen monks had turned green-tea drinking into a spiritual discipline, and the practice flowed on to the secular world. It became one of the famous Japanese "ways", highly appreciated by nobility and samurai at first, and then by commoners. Special tea huts were built, simple, rustic places modeled on hermit Kamono's ten-foot-square hut. These austerely beautiful huts still stand all over Japan, places where busy industrialists or housewives gather for an hour of *wa-kei-sei-jaku*—peace, mutual respect, purity of heart and solitude.

In the sixteenth century, the Christian baron Lord Takayama built such a tea hut as his private chapel where he performed the tea ceremony as preparation for prayer. It quieted his mind so that he could forget the affairs of state "and become like a child" as he contemplated the Gospels. Nagai greatly admired Lord Takayama and, like him, brought his Japanese culture into his Christianity. He asked the Urakami carpenters to build him a house like the hermit tea hut. The floor space was to be two tatami mats. A tatami mat is approximately six feet by three feet, enough for a person to sleep on. One tatami was for himself, the other for his small children to sleep on when they stayed with him occasionally. Normally they would live with Gran and his brother's family next door. The carpenters put a narrow ledge on the western side where callers could sit and talk to him. The furnishings were one naked electric light; shelves for his Bible, books and writing materials; a crucifix; and a statue of Maria-sama.

A pilgrim hut has a name, and Nagai called his hut Nyokodo. *Do* means "shrine", *ko* means "yourself" and *nyo* means "just as", an example of the haiku-like suggestiveness that Japanese love. His Christian friends immediately saw the reference to the Gospel dictum to love others "just as yourself". He said he chose this name to honor the unselfish carpenters who built this hut because they were men of Gospel love.

It was not a hut designed for comfort. Nagasaki can be blazing hot, but he had no electric fan. Squadrons of mosquitoes came in summer, and chill Siberian winds had no trouble penetrating the sliding doors in winter. His books speak of none of these discomforts but only of his good fortune in having such a fine hut, waxing eloquent on the advantages: "Even a garden designed by Professor Kataoka. Just look at those roses!" Roses were his favorites, and one of his delights was to find a new species and study all about it. He loved everything about roses, the ancient Christian symbol of love.

He moved into Nyokodo in the spring of 1948, emaciated but thirty-eight inches around the waist because of his swollen spleen. Gandhi had been much in the news at the time, and the Japanese people had a profound respect and affection for him. Gandhi himself had marched to the drum beat of the semirecluse when he said good-bye to his wife, family and home and went to live in a little room in New Delhi. Japanese newspapers often ran articles on the poor man in the loincloth who shared all he had with the poor of India. When Gandhi was assassinated in January 1948, they began to call Nagai "the Gandhi of Nyokodo".

This invocation of Gandhi was not simply journalistic flourish but something particularly appropriate. The origins of the hermit hut, and therefore of the tea hut and Nagai's Nyokodo, are in the Indian Yuima sutra. This piece of Buddhist holy writ tells the parable of the bare hut: you best meet the Supernatural if you make your heart like a hut that is empty of everything but the bare essentials.

Haiku poet and Zen devotee Basho, in a pilgrim hut.

26

The Little Girl Who Could Not Cry

Nagai's tiny daughter Kayano was a spirited girl who unconsciously sought to assuage the anxiety and emptiness of a motherless child. She showed great affection for her father, and this was a problem. Nagai's doctor one day said: "Look, she will only have to come running in and jump on you, and your spleen will rupture. That would kill you, as you know. You must stop her from being too affectionate!" Nagai sadly erected a little barricade beside his bed in Nyokodo. One day he was asleep, and she tiptoed in right beside him, bent over and laid her cheek on his. He was now awake but feigned sleep and heard her whisper: "Ah! The lovely smell of my daddy." Nagai goes on: "You might suppose that a man with leukemia is cold-blooded, but my blood coursed hot through my veins when I heard that pathetic cry. I knew my death couldn't be far off, and I saw little Kayano in my fantasy coming home from my funeral, now fatherless and motherless . . . and burying her face in my mattress for one last 'smell of my daddy'."

Nagai was getting busier during the day as visitors increased. People would read an article by him or about him and come with some personal problem to seek this holy man's counsel. Some came from as far as Tokyo and beyond, and many were non-Christians. Despite days that were progressively busier, he was waking regularly about 2 A.M., worried. The doctors had given him two or three years, and that time was almost up.

How would his children be affected by his death? He decided to write down all the things he wanted to tell them in the hope that it would help them when they could understand. These jottings were to become two best-selling books. A brief summary provides some clues to the thought patterns of the forty-year-old Nagai.

He wrote: "You are small children and have already lost your mother. That is an irreplaceable loss. A father's death is not anywhere near the loss of a mother. My death will leave you orphans, vulnerable and alone in the world. You will weep. Yes, you might even weep your hearts out, and that will be good—provided you weep before your Father in heaven. We have it on the authority of his Son, and I have experienced the truth of it personally: 'Happy are those who weep, for they shall be comforted.' Spill your tears before him, and he will always dry them. That is the Sermon on the Mount, the place where you can find all the answers. Climbing this mountain can be hard-going, and at times through mists, rain and snow. But when the mists and clouds lift, what a vista of beauty, peace and love! Yes, a vista of the values that last and give meaning to our lives and worth to our struggles. Right now, all I have to leave you in the way of possessions is this hut, Nyokodo. Ah! But Jesus tells us to love our eternal selves rather than our material possessions. Yes, each of us is a child of the heavenly Father! That gives us tremendous worth. Do you realize that you are of more worth in your Father's eyes than that beautiful bright star that keeps our earth alive, the sun? You are his very own son and daughter, and so are all the people around you. Love everyone and trust his Providence, and you will find peace. I have tried it and can assure you it is so.

"I must be honest with you, my children. You will drink a bitter chalice as orphans. You will have to struggle against the temptation of resentment toward your school friends who have mother and father and against the subtle temptation of coldly resigning yourselves, with a mistaken sense of independence, to that dark and dismal unbelief called fatalism. Don't live negatively by blind fate but live meaningfully and lovingly and experience the Father's personal Providence. He has asked the three of us to accept a bitter drink. This is our 'way' to peace and to participation in his great plan, the one Jesus saw when he spoke of the lilies of the field and of the sparrows that are precious in the eyes of the Father. As a doctor, I sometimes had to give bitter medicine. I didn't say: Poor child, suffering so! Let's give him some sweet juice! You understand that, don't you? We believe in a great God who doesn't dole out cheap syrup but gives us the cleansing, healing, nourishing waters of life. Sometimes they seem bitter because our taste is sick. But persevere! He is fitting us for eternal companionship with him and our loved ones in heaven. I'm sure you remember the fairy tale about the bluebird of happiness. When your mother died, your bluebird, alas, flew away. You will not find your bluebird again except in heaven."

In a later book, *Rozario No Kusari* (The Chain of the Rosary), Nagai described how evening would fall over Urakami's devastated moonscape. Lamps would glimmer from the huts, and smoke would curl up from rough-and-ready fireplaces. That would be when he would find himself thinking of Midori. He would feel so miserable that he would want to cry. But his little daughter Kayano never cried! He would see her, at the time when the sun sank and darkness began to fall, just staring out at the nuclear desolation, biting her bottom lip. On one later occasion, his brother Hajime's tiny daughter came in, having just woken up from an afternoon nap, looking lost, and demanding: "Where's *kaa-chan* [Mommy]?" "In heaven", replied Kayano ingenuously. At that moment, Hajime's wife came in, and the bewildered tot ran into her apron, crying, "Kaachan." Nagai watched Kayano's face cloud over. She went over to the *shoji*, the sliding paper door, and just stood there, rubbing her finger up and down the panel frame. A meaningless action but meaning much to him.

All around their hut was a desolate waste littered with smashed roof tiles and rubble. Nagai saw Kayano stumble a number of times and cut her knees. She would slowly rub the blood off with her finger but never cry. Once, an overplayful dog chased her, and she ran terrified into Nagai's room—but uttering not a single cry, not as much as a whimper. She worried him, this daughter who could not cry. It made his hatred of World War II and the A-bomb all the more intense and personal. It led to a written reflection in another book that he hoped she would read when she was older: "Our childhood is happy because we can cry. We know that if we cry, our mother will come and comfort us. At times since your mother died, Kayano, I wanted to bawl my eyes out. But an adult cannot do that; only a child who has a mother can." He had worked, he continues, in an orphanage and noticed that an orphan who cries is laughed at by the others and learns the art of clamping back tears. He concludes: "The only one who has the whole answer said, 'Happy are those who weep, for they shall be comforted.' You are always able to weep before him, and your tears will be heeded."

Nagai had some favorite scientists mentioned in references scattered through his books—Pascal, Copernicus, Mendel, Pasteur, Ampère, Marconi. "These", he wrote, "were the free men, who gazed at creation with humility and understanding." It annoyed him to no end to read that science and faith were opposed to each other. He writes: "If you read what the great scientists actually said, it is not so. Social and literary critics, that is, men who have held pens but never test tubes, are the ones who make that claim." A little further on in the book, he added: "One must approach the study of any part of God's creation with profound respect and a certain chastity. A real scientist experimenting in his laboratory is really at one with a monk in his cell. Yes, experiments become prayers!"

"A certain chastity." Nagai loved science, especially radiology and the study of atoms and radiation, but with a chaste passion. The proof came when he let go of his university and laboratory without resentment and cheerfully said good-bye to the lecture halls where he had enjoyed his star role. He said good-bye to Midori too, without resentment for the Americans or God. Sadness and tears, yes, but resentment, no. This becomes abundantly clear if you read his books or speak with the people who knew him intimately. They portray a man who "cared and did not care".

Nagai often wrote of the stars and constellations. His eyes never tired of their beauty nor his mind of the order and reliability that made them indispensable friends of ancient travelers across land and sea. The mountains were another lifelong love. Come autumn typhoon, winter snow or summer heat, they stood firm, guarding their great stands of cedar and cypress. He had always found himself at peace in the mountains, the traditional places where his people had discovered great spiritual ideas, mountains like Fuji, Yakumo, Hiei, Koya. There is one mountain, however, that becomes progessively central in his writing, the Mount of the Beatitudes. In one book, he wrote for his children: "Being poor in spirit and pure in heart might not win you a lot of money, but it will give you something even more precious, peace of heart." He would repeat this to them when gifts came pouring in from his readers, and he shared those gifts with the whole poverty-ridden neighborhood.

He writes of one experience with six-year-old Kayano that gave him much encouragement. She had just started going to Yamazato Primary School, which was only about 100 yards from home. One afternoon she had not yet come home, although classes had been finished for nearly half an hour. He was beginning to worry when he heard tiny shuffling sounds. She appeared before him carrying a cup, both hands holding it as if it contained a precious flame that must not go out. She kicked her shoes off as if they were of no consequence and stepped up onto his tatami floor. Her eyes never left the cup until she put it down on a shelf. Then she exhaled noisily in relief. Intrigued, he asked her what it was. A big smile, and the child explained. Nagai recounts: "That day at school, everyone was given a cup of something new called pineapple juice. It tasted so nice when she sipped it that she decided it would do her sick daddy good. She guarded it from lunchtime until school ended and was coming out when a seven-year-old ran into her, causing her to spill some. But she didn't lose another drop after that." His eyes moistened as she solemnly carried him the cup with the remaining juice.

Their early days in the hut were physically miserable. When it rained, water seeped in, and lighting a fire outside and cooking on it became quite a problem. Later in the year, snow came in to join them with the raw north wind. Hunger was usually an unwelcome guest at their makeshift table. Nagai caught a rat one night, and knowing it would be a source of protein, he cleaned and cooked it. He discovered the truth of the old Japanese proverb: To an empty stomach, all food is tasty. However, things gradually improved, especially when the carpenters built his new home, Nyokodo.

American shogun MacArthur was masterminding a military occupation that will go down as one of the most peaceful in history, the friendship between the general and the Emperor being a big factor in it. MacArthur's reforms—designed to root democracy deep into Japanese life, make a return to militarism impossible and restore a shattered economy—won the Japanese people's support. However, he still held a heavy hand over the media. When a publisher accepted *The Bells of Nagasaki* and applied for permission to print it, MacArthur's censorship office refused. The Americans were now sensitive about the A-bomb. Around the world, a question was beginning to be raised: If Nazis and Japanese generals were executed for war atrocities, should there not be some accounting for Allied atrocities like the A-bomb? Eventually, early in 1949, permission was given for publishing *The Bells of Nagasaki*, provided that the book carried an equal number of pages from the U.S. military court's documentation of Japanese atrocities in the Philippines. Nagai accepted this provision, and the book was released on April 1, 1949, as a tandem edition.

The Bells of Nagasaki was an immediate success, and a year later a top-ranking movie company, Shochiku, began production of a movie version that was to enjoy great popularity all over Japan. The Japanese were psychologically ready for a story about a man who had lost everything in the war and yet entertained hope and even enthusiasm for the future. A very many people could identify with Nagai's painful experiences. From the time that all-out war began in China in 1937 until peace came on August 15, 1945, a total of 2,470,000 Japanese had died—1,672,000 in the armed services; 289,000 Japanese civilians in Manchuria, Korea, Okinawa and so forth; and 509,000 in the air raids on Japan proper. Two and a half million dead! Most Japanese had suffered the death of a family member, relative or friend—not to mention the injured and the destruction of homes, possessions and livelihood. The future looked bleak, and morale was low. Yet here was Nagai, positively optimistic about life even though he had lost almost everything.

The Shochiku Movie Company sent producer Hideo Oba and the two lead actors, Masao Wakahara and Yumeji Tsukioka, to interview bedridden Nagai in Nyokodo, hoping to capture the spirit of the man and his wife Midori. They called the movie *The Bells of Nagasaki*. A song with the same title was written for the movie by Hachiro Sato and became one of the most enduring hits of the decade. Many popular songbooks still carry it. The Japanese are a deeply emotional people, agreeing with Ignatius of Loyola that tears are a gift. On this score, the huge crowds that saw *The Bells of Nagasaki* were very gifted!

From the end of the war in 1945 until his death in 1951, Nagai wrote twenty books, a number of them best sellers. Among the latter was *Nyokodo Zuihitsu* (Reflections from Nyokodo). There is more sadness in this book and more about peace and the nuclear threat because he wrote it in response to the war that broke out in 1950 between North and South Korea and involving United Nations troops. He had written much about war and peace before 1950, but the Korean conflict brought a note of crisis to this book. Nagai died eighteen months before the H-bomb was exploded, triggering the great debate over nuclear weapons. He did write, however, about the possibilities of atomic energy, together with the horrific scale of nuclear war. His ideas are worth recalling.

First, he never regarded the discovery of atomic energy as the fatal opening of a Pandora's box. He viewed the whole universe as good and saw atomic energy as one dimension of its magnificent dynamism. Atomic energy brought the sun's light and warmth to the earth, for instance. Our remote ancestors used their intelligence to wrest the secret of fire from flint and sticks. Atomic energy was a "providential" breakthrough at a time when the days of the world's oil resources were numbered. Human responsibility, of course, was demanded, as it was with fire, petroleum, electricity and dynamite. Atomic energy increased the dangers immensely and sharpened the pain of living with risk and uncertainty, but these latter have been constant companions of our race in its pilgrimage through history. Pain and risk even seem to play an indispensable part in our becoming truly human, that is, people of maturity, depth and compassion.

Nagai was particularly conscious of Japan's total lack of oil because that was the reason his country went to war with America. He saw atomic energy as the possible solution to Japan's chronic energy problem. He died before this became anything of a reality, but soon an ever-increasing number of nuclear power stations were operating throughout the land. The Japanese understand the risks of nuclear power, but most believe the 1941 situation of relying on imported petroleum is even riskier.

Until the outbreak of the Korean War in 1950, Nagai entertained the fond hope that the horrendous nature of A-bombs would keep the superpowers from going to war with each other. The Korean conflict destroyed that illusion, coming as such a shock and disappointment that he felt compelled to begin another major book, despite his terrible physical condition. He was now running high fevers, his swollen spleen was pushing his heart out of position and he had constant pain in his bones. This latter was a very painful aspect of his worsening leukemia.

Vis-à-vis the confrontation between the West and Communism that fueled the Korean War, Nagai begins his new book by stating some historical facts. In the lands occupied by the Soviet and Chinese armies after World War II, people's courts tried opponents of Communism as "enemies of mankind" and executed, imprisoned or sent many to concentration camps. This was in stark contrast to the Western Allies' occupation of Japan under MacArthur. Japan had been a totally crippled nation, which surrendered unconditionally before poised American forces. The United States set about channeling vast resources into Japan, staving off starvation in the winter of 1945–1946 and rehabilitating the economy. MacArthur understood and accepted the unique role of the Emperor and respected, in most cases, the Japanese way of life.

The Soviet army came into the war only after the Hiroshima A-bomb, which was nine days before Japan's surrender. The Russians rounded up all the Japanese soldiers they could lay hands on in Manchuria and China and put them to work in Siberian labor camps. Nagai's younger brother Hajime, who was held in one of these camps for thirty months, gave Nagai harrowing descriptions of the treatment they received and the death toll. In striking contrast, the Western Allies sent Japanese soldiers back home to civilian life. The only exceptions were the small percentage of accused war criminals who were tried in public courts of law and provided with defense lawyers. Nagai challenged readers who were attracted by the fine theories of Communism to study recent world history and "judge the tree by its fruits". Nagai, in his antiwar writing, never displayed that anti-American or anti-Western element that was to become such a contentious characteristic of many "peace movements".

Nagai had sobering memories of Japanese mobs manipulated by fascist slogans during the decade before the war in the Pacific. He had an intense distaste for slogan-shouting mobs, whom he saw as shallow people who shirked the hard work required to understand the issues about which they were demonstrating. He also wrote trenchant words against political and religious people who "used" the common citizen's yearning for peace. He regarded world peace as something most noble but also most arduous; it was irresponsible for politicians or ideologues to promise cheap and simple solutions.

He expressed grave suspicions about "angry people" in peace movements. There is a great need for peace movements, he wrote, but only if made up of people with hearts that are at peace. He warned of any peace movement that was "merely political" or ideological and not dedicated to justice, love and patient hard work. Angry shouting in the streets about peace often cloaked very unpeaceful hearts, he commented. Such writing did not endear him to everyone!

There is nothing particularly remarkable in the foregoing, but he was remarkable in promoting the Sermon on the Mount as the practical charter for world peace. If one is a Christian, he writes, one will not demand that the Communist lay down his sickle before going to make peace with him. The Christian will go weaponless and embrace the Communist, even at the risk of being pierced by that sickle. Utterly impracticable? Yes, unless you know how to pray, he replies. Not any kind of prayer, though, for some prayer is "plain superstition" or "no different from purchasing a lottery ticket". Real prayer does not make terribly difficult demands "like going off to mountains alone and becoming ascetics". No, we can pray as soon as we can speak with the loving Person who is the source of all dynamism in the universe. In one place, Nagai says that all of us are called to contemplation, "which is not difficult. You see children praying this way, for instance, before the crib at Christmastime." He quotes the Gospel: "I thank you, Father, for hiding these things from the clever and revealing them to little ones." Little ones can discover the delightful wellsprings of contemplation, he adds, and all of us are called to become little ones! The Gospel invitation is contemplation for everyman.

One famous book on Christian contemplation is *The Cloud of Unknowing* by an English mystic of the fourteenth century. The title refers to Moses climbing into the darkness of cloud-shrouded Mount Sinai to meet the God of revelation. It was precisely in a nuclear desert, darkened by a mushroom cloud, that Nagai tasted contemplation. He wrote: "Walking with God through Urakami's nuclear wasteland has taught me the depths of his friendship." To many, the mushroom cloud is a sign of despair, heralding the end. Nagai's faith transformed it into the cloud of another Exodus, leading the people away from the scientific slavery of a new Egypt. Only when Jerusalem was devastated and the people led away captive into Babylon did they understand the beauty of Zion. Looking out at the nuclear wasteland, Nagai said with the faith of Isaiah: "God will turn [Jerusalem's] desolation into Eden, and the wasteland into a garden of Yahweh."

William Johnston, a specialist in Japanese Zen, has had a profound impact on the dialogue between Buddhist Japan and the (sometimes) Christian West. His special field is Buddhist and Christian prayer experience, and he believes Nagai made a unique contribution. Johnston translated Nagai's first popular book, *The Bells of Nagasaki*, into English and writes in the preface: "Nagai the scientist, Nagai the patriot, Nagai the humanist became Nagai the mystic. He is a mystic of peace for our times. In the vast quantity of atomic literature he has a unique place.... He attempts a theology born of cruel suffering and painful conversion of heart.... With his message of love he takes an honoured place beside ... great prophets."

The blasphemous mushroom cloud turned the woman he loved into charred bones. Yet his faith in God's Providence changed the evil flames of fission into Elijah's mysterious chariot. You see this clearly in two Chinese ink paintings he did while lying in Nyokodo. They are on display in the small Nagai Museum that now stands beside the hut.

The first painting is of Mary and is unmistakably patterned on Murillo's painting of the Blessed Virgin Mary assumed into heaven on a cloud. The second is similar, but the woman standing on the cloud is Midori. She is not attired beautifully like Mary but is dressed in the baggy wartime *monpe* and blouse she was wearing when the A-bomb exploded over Urakami. There is another difference: Midori is standing on a mushroom cloud.

Sketch by Nagai of his daughter Kayano.

27

The Song of a Tokyo Leper

By the end of 1948, people all over Japan were reading Nagai.
On May 25, 1949, the National Welfare Ministry gave special
commendation to his book *Kono Ko wo Nokoshite* (Children
of Nagasaki). When *The Bells of Nagasaki* came out as a movie,
the National Education Ministry recommended it for all schools
and inserted sections about Nagai into syllabus textbooks. He
had become known overseas too. Nagai's collection of stories
under the title *We of Nagasaki* was the first book in English
by a survivor of nuclear bombing. Readers from North and
South America began sending him gifts. More periodicals ran
articles about the dying scientist who kept on working and
writing, and four new Nagai books were published in quick
succession.

In September 1949 a rather extraordinary bill was tabled in
the Lower House of the Japanese National Diet. It proposed the honoring of two Japanese who had done much to
rally the demoralized nation: Japan's first Nobel Prize winner,
physicist Hideki Yukawa, and the scientist–holy man of
Nagasaki, Takashi Nagai. Communist and left-socialist Diet
members opposed the bill. They accepted Yukawa's creden-
tials but stridently opposed any Diet commendation of the
"religious sentimentalist" Nagai. The campaign turned to vil-
ification: Nagai was not even a victim of the A-bomb, nor did
he have real radiation disease! He did not write the books and
articles coming out in his name but was using a ghostwriter,

playing on people's sympathy in his quest for a quick yen. Anti-Nagai politicians had access to media channels, and they used them unscrupulously to stop the Christian Nagai from being acclaimed as a national hero.

A Dr. Shimizu, for instance, wrote an article in the newspaper *Nihon Dokusho* arguing that a man in Nagai's (reported) physical condition would find it utterly impossible to produce the material coming out under his name. Nagai's friends, like the historian Kataoka, were furious and begged him to counter the public accusations. For reasons incomprehensible to them, Nagai refused. He was hurt, that is certain, but said: "Let it be. They say I haven't written the books, and essentially they are right because all the ideas in my writings are from the Bible or other people. Nor do I have illusions about my literary prowess. God's grace is the source of any inspiration in my writings." But Japan had a prime minister who did not possess Nagai's patience and humility. This was Shigeru Yoshida, who had distinguished himself as a foreign diplomat before the war. As prewar ambassador to Great Britain, for whose traditions and system of justice he had great respect, he adamantly opposed Japan's new militarists. He was forced by the latter to resign his post, sat out the war in Japan and was in a Tokyo prison before hostilities ended. Prime minister for seven years after the war, he was outspokenly liberal and pro-Western. He had a loathing for Japanese Communists, who were, he said, out to wreck Japan for the sake of a foreign ideology. He suspected that the Communists attacked Nagai only because of his Christian faith. Yoshida was not a Christian but had high regard for the Sacred Heart nuns who educated his daughter and the daughters of a number of diplomat friends in Japan and overseas. Yoshida appointed a Diet committee to investigate the charges against Nagai.

The committee chairman went to Nagasaki and interviewed city officials, university staff, doctors and Nagai's publishers. He even studied book manuscripts penciled laboriously in Nagai's hand. Magazine editors came forward, showing the chairman articles Nagai had written for nothing. Assistant Professor Asanaga of Nagasaki Medical University documented the case history of Nagai's leukemia, first, of Nagai the radiologist: From 1932 Nagai had worked for twelve months as a pioneer with an x-ray plant that had no shield against radiation. From 1934 to 1937, a time when doctors were as yet uncertain about how much radiation they could absorb without danger of leukemia, Nagai x-rayed for eight hours a day and more. From 1940 to 1945 he pioneered and kept running the hospital's tuberculosis detection unit, x-raying great numbers of people when the war had reduced the radiology staff—and this in addition to his heavy x-ray schedule with hospital patients and medical students. Asanaga, concluding that Nagai was almost certain to contract radiation cancer, added a detailed diagnosis of Nagai's chronic leukemia since exposure to radiation after the A-bomb.

Common folk began defending Nagai too, telling of his heartening replies to their troubled letters. Bundles of this correspondence can still be seen in the Nyokodo museum. I came across one of Nagai's "pen pals" when I was visiting a sick friend in the western district of Tokyo in 1985. He was in an institution for patients with stabilized Hansen's disease. Matron Koseki came into the room while we were chatting and asked what I was doing in Tokyo. She reacted immediately when I told her I was gathering material on Dr. Nagai. "Dr. Nagai? Really? Oh, wait a moment."

She dashed off, leaving me mystified, but soon returned waving a letter. "Look, this is a reply from Dr. Nagai to a letter I wrote", she said, and she told me the story. In 1949 she was working as a nurse in a government leprosarium. In those days patients with Hansen's disease often lost their sight, and a nurse's duties included reading books to them. Somehow a Nagai book came into her hands. After reading it to her patients, she wrote to the author telling him "how beautiful it was to see hot tears running from their sightless eyes." He replied with the letter she held in her hand. It contained a *waka* poem[1] that might have caused deep resentment had it come from some-one else: "Hito ni torite totoki mono wa tamashi to Shirash-imen tame ni rai wa aru nari." (Leprosy taught them that man's priceless possession is his spirit.)

My blind friend, Hihara-san, thumped the low table we sat at on the tatami floor. "That's right, that's right. I was an unthinking young man with a beautiful wife and daughter when I contracted leprosy. Society disowned me, ostracized me from my wife and daughter and banished me to a leper colony guarded by a moat. I despaired and attempted suicide. Yet here was Nagai, who had lost everything, was dying and was at peace with himself and the world. The matron kept reading us Nagai, and he began writing to us. He led me to Christ and the Faith that discovers everything in life is a gift and a grace. It's now fifty years since I became a leper, and I can say: Thank God for my leprosy, and thank God for Nagai."

On December 23, 1949, the committee investigating Nagai reported back to Tokyo, and the National Diet voted to honor Nagai as a national hero. The minister of state came to make the presentation and was joined in Nyokodo by the governor of Nagasaki Prefecture and the mayor of the city. The Emperor sent Nagai three silver sake cups on the occasion, a gesture he had made only once before.

Another honor came in December of 1949 when Nagai was declared Nagasaki's first honorary citizen. His friend Professor Kataoka writes that when Nagai was told of this, he said without

[1] A Japanese poem, usually a tanka (short poem).

any trace of affectation: "The moon that lights the night sky is nothing but a cold lump of matter reflecting the sun's light! This honorary citizenship is merely a reflection of light from God. I have no illusions about myself, you know. Without God, I would fill the shoes of that useless servant spoken of in the Gospels."

Less than five minutes from Nagai's hut is Yamazato Primary School. Nine hundred of its 1,100 pupils perished in the A-bomb explosion. When the school was rebuilt, a white granite monument was erected in the playground, where many of them had died. Embossed in bronze on the granite is the figure of a small girl engulfed in flames. Her face is serene, and her hands are joined in prayer. Nagai was asked to compose an inscription. It took the form of a poem seeking to capture the sentiments of their mothers:

Their scribbling remains on the walls at home,
just names penciled by childish hands.
If only we could go and call them just once more
and hear them answer!
Ah! Those children! If only they were with us still.

Remember the athletic carnivals! The loudspeaker marching
them out of classrooms, sending them running pell-mell
for the tape. They looked so smart in their sports uniforms!
Ah! Those children! If only they were with us still.

Even though we know we will never see these faces again,
we still go and look out the front gate at sunset.
But all that's there is red and purple amaranth!
Ah! Those children, if only they were with us still.

The poem was put to a haunting melody and is sung each year when the school assembles somberly to commemorate the tragedy each August 9. A number of Nagai's poems were put to music by top Japanese composers, the most famous of whom was Kosaku Yamada, known and loved through Japan (and overseas) for the extraordinarily moving composition *Aka Tomba* (Red dragonfly).

Two sketches by Nagai—one of Mary assumed into heaven, and one of his wife taken to heaven on the atomic cloud.

28

The Bluebird Who Visited the Bear

Over the last four years of his life, Nagai averaged five letters a day in reply to people who wrote to him. People were coming to see him in Nyokodo from Osaka, Tokyo and all over Japan. When he was first bedridden in 1946, lonely old folk from Urakami began dropping in. "Sensei [Doctor], you must be lonely, so I've come for a chat." The chat would go on several hours! His friends say he never showed impatience, but he confesses in one book how trying it could be when he was in the middle of writing an article or book. Visitors increased so much that he eventually accepted them as a major part of each day. The national express train from the north arrived in Nagasaki at 7:20 A.M. daily, and the station loudspeakers were now greeting alighting passengers with strains of *The Bells of Nagasaki*, fast becoming the unofficial city song. By 7:40 A.M. people from that 7:20 A.M. express train would begin to appear at Nagai's hut. It became so regular a pattern that he arranged to have breakfast and toilet finished daily before 7:40 A.M. The only exception was on Thursdays, when a priest from the cathedral came with the Eucharist, led by Nagai's old friend Yamada-san ringing a small bell. The visitors became so many that often he had no daylight hours left for writing, and he had to find other time for it. You find entries like this in his journal: "Woke at 1 A.M. Coffee and then wrote until 7 A.M." Again: "I grew weary about 4 A.M., stopped writing and went back to sleep until breakfast time." Ever an optimist and an opportunist, Nagai saw the sleeplessness that accompanied acute leukemia as God's way of allowing him to catch up on writing.

Nyokodo was built right beside what was becoming a busy street. The hut was just yards away from the present Nyokodo Mae bus stop, and the increasing stream of passersby was almost on top of him. He could obtain privacy only by sliding the frail *shoji* shut. Nagai loved the subdued glow of sunlight through *shoji*, which someone has described as being like the gentle places in a Beethoven piano concerto. The beauty of *shoji*, however, does little to keep out noise! At nighttime, or during cold weather and storms, protective shutters of glass and wood were slid into place. However, on most days, Nagai lived with the noise of the busy street in front of Nyokodo. Nagai's friend Kataoka writes of one occasion when a large group of students on a school excursion were brought right up to Nyokodo and their teacher proceeded to deliver a lecture on the extraordinary man who lived there. The flimsy *shoji* did little to mute the stentorian voice. The teacher might as well have been speaking inside Nyokodo! "Good grief", thought Nagai. "I've become a bear in a zoo! Someone should teach that teacher some manners. But no, wait. I'm wrong. If it makes the children happy, I should be prepared to be a bear on display."

Like attracts like. October 18, 1948, was a bland autumn day. The foothills behind the cathedral were embroidered with plumes of *susuki*—Chinese miscanthus, the frailer Eastern cousin of pampas grass. Cosmos were flowering in profusion, and Nagasaki Bay sparkled under a high blue sky. Nagai, however, was in great distress, uncharacteristically lying on one side as he pressed his paining stomach with both hands. He was gazing disinterestedly through the open *shoji* when a score of people came into view. His attention was abruptly riveted on a sixty-eight-year-old woman whom he recognized immediately. She held the hand of her secretary and guide, Polly

Thomson, because she was blind and deaf. But she walked resolutely with a high-stepping gait, "like someone in calisthenics class", as little Kayano said later. Nagai recognized Helen Keller from photos in recent newspaper articles.

Nyokodo's tiny garden was scattered with large rocks in Japanese style, and Nagai called out a warning: "Feet, stone! Feet, stone!" But by then Helen Keller was at the threshold, smiling, her hand stretched out to take his. He rolled off his mattress and slithered across the tatami on his back, trying to reach her waving hand. But he was too low, and two right hands did pathetic flights in the air without meeting as he struggled like a helpless beetle. "The bluebird had flown into Nyokodo to see me," he wrote, "but I could not reach her fluttering wing." Polly Thomson took Helen Keller's hand and gently joined it with Nagai's. Nagai continued: "Her hand seemed to release a flow of warmth through my diseased body."

Helen Keller, as a baby of eighteen months, was struck by an illness that left her totally blind and deaf. After a heroic struggle shared by faithful Anne Sullivan, her teacher, she learned to communicate. Anne was a child of adversity too—her migrant parents died when she was a tiny child, leaving her to sink or swim in the swift currents of backstreet Boston. Anne Sullivan taught Helen Keller a hand-touch alphabet. With Anne translating the lectures onto her hand, Helen eventually did four years at Radcliffe College and graduated cum laude. She was then twenty-four and decided to spend the rest of her life helping disadvantaged people lead satisfactory lives. *Collier's Encyclopedia* called her "one of the most remarkable women in history". Feeling great compassion for war-torn, demoralized Japan, she came on a two-month tour in 1948. The Japanese were very impressed by Keller, and her visit bore lasting fruit. Nagasaki was her last stop, and she was leaving for the United States early the next morning. When she completed the public lecture in Nagasaki that afternoon, she made two requests—to pray at the epicenter of the A-bomb explosion and to meet Dr. Nagai at Nyokodo. Now she held his hand.

Nagai was deeply moved and said to her: "I feel ours are two hands of the Mystical Body of Christ." Miss Thomson translated, and Helen smiled warmly as she replied: "That is so, that is so. My heart is simply overflowing, and I wish I could pour out everything I possess right here." At the conclusion of the visit, she said: "We shall never have an opportunity to meet like this again, but our meeting here surely has an eternal meaning." Nagai responded: "I shall treasure what I gained from meeting you today until we meet again in heaven." Helen's face lit with what Nagai described as a smile of exquisite beauty. She was given Grandma's hand and then Makoto's. When they put Kayano's hand into hers and she felt how small it was, tears came to her eyes.

Another blind visitor who came to see Nagai was koto musician Michio Miyagi. The koto, or Oriental floor harp, is the most traditional musical instrument in Japan. It has thirteen strings on a six-and-a-half-foot frame that is laid on the tatami floor when played. The harpist kneels beside it in formal *seiza* posture to pluck the strings. Over twelve hundred years ago its ancestor, the six-stringed koto, was played in the Chinese court. The greatest koto player and composer of modern times is Michio Miyagi. His own musical sense and, to a degree, the receptivity of his audience were sharpened by his total blindness. He died tragically and prematurely when he lost his footing and fell from a train, but by that time he had composed some of the finest koto concertos in existence. From the moment Miyagi was led into Nyokodo, there was the rapport of two who had graduated from the same school of hard knocks, and they engaged in a lively exchange of humor that onlookers found touching. Nagai had once been troubled by the age-old problem: How can there be a loving omnipotent God when there is so much evil and pain in the world? He had resolved that problem to his own satisfaction, and meeting people like Helen Keller and Miyagi confirmed him in his convictions. Suffering, gracefully accepted, refines the human heart, and the experience of darkness sharpens the vision of the spirit. After meeting Keller and Miyagi, he wrote: "Unless you have suffered and wept, you really don't understand what compassion is, nor can you give comfort to someone who is suffering. If you haven't cried, you can't dry another's eyes. Unless you've walked in darkness, you can't help wanderers find the way. Unless you've looked into the eyes of menacing death and felt its hot breath, you can't help another rise from the dead and taste anew the joy of being alive."

In the small museum beside Nyokodo, there are three letters from Helen Keller—two to the doctor and one to little Kayano—typed by Miss Thomson and signed in Keller's pathetically heroic handwriting. Part of one letter to Nagai reads: "I have kept a tender memory of the day we shook hands in Nagasaki and I heard how you believed in God's sustaining Power to work good out of disaster and were bravely using every opportunity to record your daily impressions of a tragic experience for scientific research. Now your books are here—a witness to the triumph of your spirit over physical suffering, and I am filled with reverent admiration."

A ten-minute walk from the Matsuyama Peace Park—the epicenter of the A-bomb explosion—is a prosperous camera shop called Nagasaki Photo. The proprietor is sixty-seven-year-old Itaru Takahara, lifelong resident of Nagasaki and also a *hibakusha*, that is, someone who suffered a significant dose of radiation from the A-bomb. A long and intimate associate of Dr. Nagai, he was a newspaper reporter and covered the Emperor's visit to Nagasaki in May 1949. The Emperor wished to meet Nagai, so they had the failing doctor carried to the university hospital, which was on the imperial itinerary. Takahara had covered several of the Emperor's tradition-shattering trips when he left his age-old seclusion to mix with the people. These sorties, at one time unthinkable, were designed to bolster the morale of a demoralized nation and were also the Emperor's personal contribution to the democratization of Japan. The militarists had once promoted him as semidivine, so exalted "above the clouds" that mere citizens must never look on his face. Now he was going out of his way to let them see him as one of themselves, suffering from the defeat and under strain as they were. He was small, round-shouldered, near-sighted, intensely shy with strangers and awkward. On display, he would often clench his hat in his hand as if it were a baseball mitt, but the people admired him all the more for coming among them in his human weaknesses. Nagai regarded the Emperor's role as vital in Japan's transition from a militaristic state to a democratic one.

Takahara was close by Nagai's bed when the Emperor came to see him. In contrast to his behavior on other trips Takahara had covered, the Emperor was very relaxed with Nagai. He smiled warmly as he spoke to Nagai of his writings, asked about his sickness with real concern and requested Dr. Kagiura to do everything medically possible for Nagai. Then, bringing his face close to the doctor's awestricken children, he said with a twinkle in his eye: "Now don't you forget to do your homework well and make sure you grow up to be fine Japanese!" They each answered yes in pip-squeak voices, and their sovereign responded with a big smile and nods of approval.

Nagai was deeply moved by the Emperor's warmth and concern, and Takahara saw tears in the poet-scientist's eyes as the poet-Emperor said good-bye. Nagai held deep convictions about the importance of the Emperor for the people of tradition-steeped Japan. "The Emperor came to Nagasaki on a pilgrimage", he wrote. "He came to mourn the dead and to encourage the wounded and said to us: 'Citizens of Nagasaki, you have suffered so much, and my heart goes out to you. Your sacrifice, however, can become the rock on which peace is built.' " Nagai found those words all the more convincing because the Emperor's clothing looked cheaper than what his companions wore, and his face possessed the "strength and compassion of one who has shed hot tears".

August 15, 1949, was the four hundredth anniversary of the arrival of the first Christian preacher in Japan, Francis Xavier. The main celebrations were in Nagasaki, and Australia's Cardinal Gilroy came as the legate of Pope Pius XII. The cardinal told Archbishop Yamaguchi of Nagasaki that he wanted to meet an A-bomb victim "and talk to him as one brother to another." The archbishop suggested Nagai, and so the first cardinal born Down Under ducked his head and entered tiny Nyokodo. Nagai tells the story in twelve pages of his three-hundred-page book *Itshigo Yo* (Dear child), written especially with his children in mind. "My little ones, a cardinal is special. He chooses the Pope and can become Pope. And yet here he was, as the archbishop told me before he arrived, talking 'man to man, brother to brother', and you know what? That's how he made me feel. He acted as if he were an old friend from next door, without a dew drop's weight of pomp, self-importance or condescension. He followed the Japanese custom of bringing gifts and presented me with a freshly caught fat eel and a branch loaded with ripe loquats. My hands are skin and bone now—and the way he took my right hand, so gently and warmly! His English pronunciation was straight from Oxford, making it easy to follow.

"He spoke of the worldwide struggle going on between good and evil and of the two camps that are forming, believers and materialists. Prayer is a must, he said, and if the sick can offer their pain and sickness with faith, this becomes a 'sacrifice' and a prayer. I was moved more than I can tell.

"A written record, my little ones, can appear cold and soul-less. Alas, I cannot capture with my poor pencil the emotions he drew from me. I felt like a young brother talking to his wise and unpretentious older brother. I will give an example to explain how I felt. You know what it's like in March when the first warm breeze assures us that the harshness of winter is behind. That's how he made me feel. I even felt like rushing out and inviting every sick person in the whole nation to come and meet this elder brother who spoke so convincingly about the meaning of our sickness and pain.

"Toward the end, I asked him to bless me. Ah, the change! Then I saw the weight of real dignity, then I saw a holy Roman cardinal as he traced the sign of the cross and prayed for God's blessing on me and my little ones. I'm sure you remember the stories I told you about Ryosei the lute player. He was half-blind, crippled and stunted, physically an ugly man, living a hand-to-mouth existence going from house to house playing his lute. Then he heard Francis Xavier preach the Gospel in Yamaguchi. He became a wonderful Christian, a catechist and Brother Lorenso the Jesuit. He wrote the first Christian book in Japanese, the twenty-five-chapter *Dochirina*, and often met the *taiko*, the military ruler of our land then, to explain matters concerning Christians. He died here in Nagasaki before Hideyoshi began the anti-Christian persecutions. Remember that time when Xavier was leaving Japan and blessed Ryosei for the last time? Somehow, when Cardinal Gilroy blessed me, I felt I was Brother Lorenso Ryosei being blessed by Xavier."

The north wind had come like a sickle to cut down the green remnants of summer, and the mountainsides were ablaze with flames of red, yellow and ocher. Nagai loved autumn as the time for deep reflection. Japanese poems are tinged with sadness in autumn because this season brings home the poignant impermanence of life. The ideograph for *ureru*, the

Japanese word for "lament", is a composite of the ideographs for "heart" and "autumn". Nagai thought this insight both true and precious. In several places, he wrote of the need for tears. Tears opened the eyes and the heart to the pain of others. Basho, a seventeenth-century itinerant monk and one of Nagai's favorite poets, expressed it well in a haiku: Aki bukaki tonari wa nani wo suru hito zo. (The depths of autumn. I wonder what that man next door is doing?)

Autumn was a perfect setting for the visit to Nyokodo of violinist Alexandre Moghilevsky on October 21, 1949. On a concert tour of Japan, he had only just been granted political asylum when he sent word saying he wanted to visit Nyokodo and play for Nagai. The latter was delighted but asked: "May I invite the A-bomb children from neighboring Yamazato Primary School and the children attending Nagasaki's School for the Blind?" The violinist gave a hearty assent and arrived to find Nagai lying in Nyokodo, surrounded by a rather ragged crowd of children sitting on the ground. He fixed his violin under his chin to tune it, and the small children were startled by the powerful notes struck from the frail-looking instrument. A violin was a rare luxury in devastated Urakami, and many young children had never seen one.

The violinist was ready and gave a deep bow to Nagai and one to the children. They were now sitting in formal *seiza* fashion and responded with equally deep bows. Suddenly the magic of Schubert's *Ave Maria* flooded the alfresco auditorium, and the children listened, spellbound. For a brief moment they forgot their sightlessness or horrible keloid scars as the music lifted them to a sphere of beauty, goodness and peace. Though only small children, they sat there perfectly still.

Moghilevsky finished, but no one moved and he just stood there, eyes filled with tears. Nagai lay staring at the ceiling, enjoying an extraordinary consciousness of liberation from the strictures of time and space. With reluctance he broke the spell:

"Moghilevsky-sama, arigato gozaima-shita. Thank you very much." The violinist spoke through an interpreter, Takeo Aoyama: "I have given many recitals in magnificent concert halls but have never been so moved by an audience as I have been today."

Sketches by Nagai of his daughter Kayano.

29

The Navel of the World

In Nagai's correspondence with the lepers of Tokyo's Zen-shoen, he makes a point of identifying with them. "My body too is breaking up", he begins one letter. "Yes, it is almost done for. But physical suffering is an opportunity to gather treasure for heaven. Just a few years of honest endeavor carrying our burdens (and burdens are part of everyone's life), and then we will rise renewed and enter unspoiled joy." Another letter runs: "I was deeply moved to know you are praying for me. What a great happiness it is to know this love of God that has inspired our letters and our mutual support." Nagai composed a number of tanka poems for these leper friends he had never met. "The flesh weeps from your bones, but your spirits are bright, strong, immortal! Here is human greatness." Another goes: "On the desolate, wind-swept isle of Molokai, Father Damien's body broke up, and they buried what remained. But he lives in Light." Nagai writes in another letter: "Though our bodies are done for, how much better off are we than if it were our hearts that were corrupting!"

Nagai had his limitations and writes of them freely and with good humor. He could become upset if children fooled around in the library he had built for them beside Nyokodo. Because study had been almost impossible in the first huts built in Urakami and books were rare, he used money from his writing to set up a little library where children could study. When it was completed, he made some stern rules about silence.

Children who broke them would be startled by a roar from Nyokodo: "Be quiet or go home!" There were occasions when he became caustic too, but he would soon repent of taking himself too seriously!

Professor Kataoka, a friend from 1934 who shared his grief in losing home and family members on "that day", joined Nagai in trying to resurrect Christian Urakami. Kataoka wrote the preface for a number of new editions of Nagai's books and put out a 366-page biography of Nagai in 1962. (My copy of the latter is the tenth printing.) Kataoka writes that Nagai combined warm tenderness with tough-as-steel commitment: "I can't remember anyone who met him who was not struck by the love that flowed out of every pore of the man.... He possessed a strong sense of responsibility toward those who have gone before, bequeathing us our culture and civilization, and toward those who will follow us, to whom we must hand on what we have both received and worked to improve. This sense of duty sprang from a real love for and loyalty toward the human race."

Being bedridden can make a person self-centered, capricious and demanding. Kataoka lived close by Nagai the invalid for six years and noted Nagai's freedom from that understandable but irritating weakness. Nagai's books and letters became more other-centered, outgoing and grateful the longer his illness lasted. His leper friends, for instance, say they looked forward to his letters because they were "happy" letters. In a book he finished a month before he died, he wrote: "Sometimes I feel that if I write another page, I'll collapse with exhaustion. But I finish it, and I feel ready for more! Actually, I can write far more swiftly now than years ago when I was writing the thesis for my doctorate. Then I wrote because I had to. I had to keep talking myself into continuing, like the bike team behind a long-distance runner. Now I write, well, like a boy doing what he likes doing. You know, if a boy wakes up and it's a sunny day, he says: 'Wow, a great day for baseball.' If he wakes

up and it's raining, he says: 'Wow, a great day for catching eels.'
Even though I cannot move a foot away from bed, there's a
song deep within, 'Let's go to it', set to the kind of music boys
hear in their hearts.

"There are some people who write haiku poetry to make a
living. You know what I think? We should make our living
become haiku poetry. You might toil in a clattering factory or
on a tossing fishing boat or be battling to make a living in a
dingy shop. There are people who have written inspiring haiku
poems in such unpoetic situations. And we, if we really want
to, can make any occupation, and twenty-four hours of each
day, into a poem. Of course, first we have to create a heart
that is both serious and light! We have to gaze below the surface of things, search out the hidden beauty that is everywhere and discover the glorious things all around us. Then
each day becomes a haiku poem.

"There are some people who do their job because they have
to. They get the job done, but they pay a high price in terms
of freedom and joy. Children, on the other hand, play all out
in their games because they know freedom and joy. And didn't
someone tell us we have to become like children?"

In a number of places, Nagai wrote that the Sermon on the
Mount is very "practical" and applicable to every dimension
of our lives. He left the university, he wrote, believing that a
doctor held the patients' lives in his hands; but actual medical
experiences taught him that all life is in God's hands. He continues: "Those words in the Sermon on the Mount 'blessed
are those who weep' should be taken literally by doctors. A
real doctor suffers with each patient. If the patient is frightened of dying, so is the doctor. When the patient at long last
gets well and says, 'Thank you', the doctor responds, 'Thank
you.' If your patient is an old man, you treat him as your own
father; if the patient is a child, as your own child.... Each
patient becomes your brother, your sister, your mother, for

whom you drop everything else. You anxiously reexamine those tests and x-rays, you pore over the medical chart, leaving no stone unturned.... How mistaken I was as a young doctor when I thought medical practice was a matter of medical technique. That would make a doctor a body mechanic! No, a doctor must be a person who feels in his own body and spirit all that the patient suffers in body and spirit.... I've come to understand that medicine is a vocation, a personal call from God—which means that examining a patient, taking an x-ray or giving an injection is part of the kingdom of God. When I realized that, I found myself praying for each patient I treated."

Like Francis of Assisi, whom he loved deeply, Nagai was just as much at home with the learned rich as with the ignorant poor, and they with him. A veritable cross section of mankind came to talk with this poor man of Nyokodo: scholars, farmers, believers, atheists, Communists. One unusual admirer was Eva Peron, ex-actress and wife of the dictator of Argentina who rode to power on the backs of "the shirtless ones". She sent Nagai a large statue of the patroness of Argentina, our Lady of Luhan, entrusting it to a Japanese ship's captain. Japanese migrants in Brazil were impressed by this and asked the captain to carry a second statue of Mary for the people of Nagasaki. The boat went only as far as Kobe, so ship's captain Watanabe brought the statues by train to Nagasaki. Prefectural and municipal officials gave him a civic welcome at the station, where the flags of both nations snapped proudly in the breeze blowing in off the sea. The two statues, placed in an open car festooned with flowers, were escorted by a lively procession to Nagai's hut. A crowd there greeted the procession with lit candles, singing Marian hymns led by thirty Junshin nuns. Captain Watanabe stepped inside Nyokodo with the statue sent by Eva Peron and saluted. Nagai asked him to bring the base close so that he could kiss Mary's feet. They said good-bye to Nagai, and the whole party continued on to the cathedral in a torchlight procession. Nagai and his faith were now so much part of the Nagasaki scene that Buddhist and Shinto civic officials found nothing odd in participating in this public act of Catholic devotion.

There was something in Nagai of southern European cheerfulness, of that joie de vivre of Mediterranean saints like Francis of Assisi, Philip Neri and Don Bosco. You see it in some of his Chinese ink drawings, for instance the one of Urakami boys in a catechism class. They are about ten years old and in various states of inattention and long-suffering. One is blowing bubble gum, another surreptitiously slipping a lemon drop into a pal's hand; others are studying the ceiling. A not untypical boys' Scripture class! The drawing is accompanied by a poem written in the humorous local dialect, a cockney-like patois that Nagasaki boys use among themselves. In Australian slang, the poem would go: "Left Saint Augustine scratchin' 'is 'ead, it did; scratchin' 'is bloody 'ead. But 'e knew it was fair dinkum.[1] Three Persons, an' only one God." The lighthearted medium carried a hard-won message that was central in Nagai's thought, as in Pascal's: The mystery that is God cannot be grasped like mathematics and science.

Nagai wrote: "The nonbeliever who stands outside and draws harsh conclusions about the Mass is like an old-timer I knew who lived up in the mountains. He had never seen a movie but used to growl about modern youth wasting all that money in cinemas! The Mass, like so much else in life, is experienced rather than explained. It is experienced in the spirit rather than merely comprehended in the head. I know in my spirit that I have experienced Calvary in the Mass. You know what I miss more than anything else as I lie immobile here in Nyokodo? Attending Sunday Mass with Midori and my children. At times I am filled with nostalgia for the days when I

[1] Authentic, genuine.

could drop into the cathedral for a talk with Christ really present in the tabernacle."

Nagai applauded the French poet who said the hole dug for the Cross on Mount Calvary became "the navel of the world". Like many Japanese, Nagai had special affection for this humble part of our anatomy and made it subject matter for a number of sketches and poems—like the haiku for Nobel Prize winner Hideki Yukawa the physicist, who came to visit him in Nyokodo. It read: "One truth, one world, one navel in our belly's center." For Nagai and Buddhists, the navel is not a symbol of self-preoccupation, despite the English expression "navel gazing". It is precisely the opposite. The navel is the reminder that our body and our life are gifts from another. Nature has placed this sign in the very center of our bodies, where we cannot fail to see it. It is a symbol of the love, goodness and heroic sacrifices of our mothers. Nagai saw mothers as images of God and grace.

Nagai thought the navel brought us down to earth and back to basics, counteracting our tendency to swell up with self-importance when things are going well. He writes of one salutary lesson he received when he was taking himself too seriously. He was in the bathroom. Like the poor around him, he had neither a septic tank nor proper toilet paper. He reached into the box of cut-up newspapers and was about to use a piece when he saw his own photo staring up at him!

He did a drawing of a pig and its curly tail that is now the logo of a confectionery line in his native Shimane Prefecture. This drawing, on a postcard, was in response to a letter written by an A-bomb victim who was feeling sorry for himself because he was bedridden and "useless". Underneath his drawing of the curly-tailed pig, Nagai wrote: "Though we are both sick with radiation sickness, let's not retire from life, even if we are behind in everything, like the pig's tail! Even the tail has its part to play." Some time later, the man wrote back:

"With the help of two dogs and a cart I am now getting about, endeavoring to play my pig's-tail part in life, thanks to your letter."

On special nights his two small children were allowed to sleep in Nyokodo beside their father. On one such night, when he awoke in the small hours and heard their peaceful breathing, he was suddenly overwhelmed with joy. Taking a pencil, he wrote: "We're alive, we're alive! And a whole new day is waiting for us!" Sensing his time was running out, he wrote more and more for his two children. He reminisces about the time Makoto was a little boy and resolutely stood in for his soldier father at Grandfather's funeral. Snow swirled around the sad little procession climbing the hill behind the old home with the *kaya* thatch roof. Makoto was only four, but Midori had written telling Nagai how the tiny boy had blinked the snowflakes out of his eyes and quickened his small steps so as not to fall behind. "Climbing that hill in the snow, Makoto," wrote Nagai, "is a symbol of our present lives in defeated Japan."

In a book he wrote especially for them when Makoto was fourteen and Kayano eight, he says: "Soon you will be orphans and, willy-nilly, must climb a steep, rugged and lonely path. Your Christian faith will be no drug that anesthetizes pain. But I can assure you of this: your lonely path is precisely what God in his Providence has chosen, especially for you! Accept it as such and often ask him: How can I use this for your glory? This is no popular psychology, no clever method for shaking off the blues. No, it's the one authentic response to the mystery of life. When you are happy, accept that too as his Providence, and in prayer ask him to guard this happiness for his glory.

"Sickness and trouble are not a sign that we are far from God or that he has rejected us. Look at the lives of great saints of our day—for instance, Thérèse of Lisieux and Bernadette of Lourdes. No, we don't believe in a God of small deeds who lets his favorites win lotteries and capriciously ignores the others. He is too great to act like that. . . . He will always respond to real prayer, though! You'll often see sick people, who know how to pray, getting better. That's not necessarily miraculous. It is often the natural result of living in the milieu of his peace and grace. I could be cured miraculously of leukemia, and that would be good. If I'm not cured, that's good too, and it won't bother me a scrap. All that I am concerned about is what his plans are for me; the only life that interests me is one lived for him . . . one day at a time, supported by prayer.

"God has never said you have to perform great deeds for your country and humanity to have lived well. Where would that leave all the sick people in the world? Look at me, for instance, needing to be assisted all the time. You wouldn't say that we sick and bedridden of the world are 'useful'! But usefulness is not the point. Our lives are of great worth if we accept with good grace the situation Providence places us in and go on living lovingly. A sick person who has grasped this will live so full a life that there will be no room for morbid death wishes.

"Some get themselves into a knot over the 'unfairness' of God's Providence. Why are some people afflicted with low IQs, handicapped bodies, weak physiques, material poverty? I don't know, but I can assure you of this: if all of us accepts ourselves as we are, it is absolutely certain that a day will come when we can see how God's plans have been accomplished, and precisely through our weakness. . . . Our talents and handicaps may differ greatly, but we are all equal in this: each of us is born to manifest God's glory, to know, love and serve him here below and share in his eternal life after death. . . . My little children, you are no geniuses, and you have been called to a tough future. True, but if you make the vital decision to live humbly and lovingly, you will live fruitful lives and be happy.

"All of us will have to render an account of our lives when we die. God will not be interested in who or what we were. No, only in this: how did we live? That will be the sole matter for judgment. A company director won't be able to pull rank on a waiter, and a fisherman's wife will be on a par with a millionaire's wife. Ships' officers will receive no preference over ships' cooks. All will be judged by exactly the same measure: did we use our talents well and for his glory? The poor and largely untalented too will have to answer for it if they chose to ignore the talents they were given. However, if you do your best with what you have, it's no easier or harder for you whether you are cabinet minister or cabinetmaker, ship's captain or cabin boy."

Some young people from Hiroshima sent a gift of lotus blossoms to Nagasaki. The lotus is the emblem of Hiroshima and has long held pride of place in Buddhist hearts. Because it will grow and bloom in stinking swamps, it was chosen as a symbol of the compassionate Buddha, who brings goodness from corrupt human hearts. Nagai was delighted by the Hiroshima gesture and responded with a Christian symbol from his garden at Nyokodo, white roses.

The rose is the Christian symbol of love and is exemplified par excellence in Mary. One of her ancient titles that Nagai loved was "Mystical Rose". He noted that "Rosary" came from *rosarium*, Latin for "rose garden". Prayer to Mary had been one of the essentials in the spirituality of the Hidden Christians of Nagasaki, and it became the same for Nagai. Though his first hut in devastated Urakami was almost bare, he considered it adequately furnished "when it possessed a New Testament, a crucifix and a statue of Mary", objects he kept beside him until the end. Not long before he died, a Protestant fundamentalist appeared in Nyokodo. The visitor was affronted by the statue of Mary and proceeded to reproach Nagai severely for "heathen worship". "Wait there now", replied Nagai, the

smile gone from his lips. He paused so that his words would
hit home. "I think you, through your narrow interpretation,
offend against the Bible's teaching about images. You worship
the images of your own mind, man-made and very prone to
become idols. All the more subtle for appearing spiritual!" He
proceeded to appeal to his own experience and that of centuries of Christianity: praying to Mary leads one to the heart
of the Gospels, which is being a faithful disciple of Christ.
You know a tree by its fruits. Prayer to Mary brings the experience of the fruits of the Holy Spirit.

The Hidden Christians used to sing a folk song, in code so
as to be meaningless to eavesdropping bounty hunters, about
the Church one day returning to Japan, "in ships sent by the
Holy Father with sails carrying the sign of Mary". On May
14, 1949, the Vatican nuncio to Japan, Archbishop Fursten-
burg, came to Nyokodo with a message and a Rosary from
Pope Pius XII. It was almost a literal fulfillment of the song,
and tears coursed down Nagai's cheeks as he took the beads.
That Rosary never left his bed until he died holding it two
years later.

Example of Nagai's calligraphy: Heiwa Wo—Peace!

30

Cherry Blossoms Fall on the Third Day

In February 1950, Nagai's white blood cell count was a staggering 390,000 per cubic millimeter and his doctor said the end must be near. His younger brother Hajime gathered all members of the family around him. Nagai was upset that they looked so gloomy and decided to lift their spirits. He began telling them funny stories about his time in the army and soon had everyone laughing. Biographer Kataoka remarks that this ability to rise above pain and radiate joy was a quality Nagai's friends found very attractive.

Buddhist Japan, as has been said, is proud of a long history of the Nenbutsu, the quiet repetition, often on *juzu* prayer beads, of the prayer "Namu Amida Butsu, I depend on you utterly, Amida Buddha." The accounts of Japanese Christians in the seventeenth century relate the widespread use of a kind of Christian Nenbutsu when torture was used to break the spirit of Christians condemned to death. Some were bound to wooden stakes in Edo (now Tokyo); others were lashed to poles in freezing water in Sendai; others were slowly scalded to death in the Unzen hot springs. They murmured over and over again, like a Nenbutsu, "Jesus, Mary, Joseph. Jesus, Mary, Joseph", in a kind of simple contemplative prayer. We read of the same thing happening in the persecutions of the 1860s and 1870s. This kind of prayer came more and more from Nagai's lips in this last and most painful year of his life. Sometimes his temperature would be 102 degrees for ten hours at a time. Makoto or a family member would tiptoe in to see if Nagai needed anything and would find him turned toward his altar repeating over and over in a scarcely audible murmur: "Jesus, Mary, Joseph."

Nagai's leukemia was now causing pain that came with swelling of the bones, and there was no medicine to ameliorate it. Yet, to the astonishment of his doctor, he was working steadily through a book that many think his best, *Nyokodo Zuihitsu* (Reflections from Nyokodo). He could never sleep beyond 3 or 4 A.M. and on awakening would have a cup of coffee and plunge into his book. His mind dwelled more and more on those old friends, the martyrs of Nagasaki. He had written of them previously, but his style changes dramatically in the lengthy and detailed chapter he accords them in this book. It reads like a personal Way of the Cross. He paints vivid pictures of cruelty and violent deaths, of the terrible silence and apparent failure of God. In assuring his readers that the bloody deaths of the twenty-six are meaningful and beautiful, one senses he is reassuring himself as he ponders his worsening condition and the fate of his two children.

Nagai writes at length and with feeling of the last hour of Paul Miki, one of the twenty-six crucified in Nagasaki. In the *bushido* code of the samurai, the greatest virtue is to live and die faithful to one's *shukun*, or liege lord. The symbol that samurai chose for themselves was the cherry blossom because its petals fall three days after the flower blooms. A samurai must be ready to die young should honor demand it. Nagai saw the dangers inherent in this ideal, but he also saw its magnificent aspects—as did Francis Xavier and his successor, Valignano. Miki gave a "farewell song" before dying, and Nagai, being of samurai descent, thought it time to compose his own. His inspiration was not the cherry blossom but the white rose. English, of course, cannot capture the rhythm of Japanese poetry, but Nagai's poem read: "Good-bye, my flesh.

I must now journey beyond, as the fragrance must leave the rose."

Early in 1951, news came that lifted his spirits and fired his creative powers for a book that would be his last—the Jesuits were building a pilgrim shrine at Otome Tooge, Tsuwano. That was where Jinzaburo Moriyama, father of the priest who baptized Nagai, had suffered the trial of ice and fire and where his brother, fourteen-year-old Yujiro, and thirty-five others died violent deaths for their Christian faith. Nagai had often talked about this "exile in Babylon" with old Jinzaburo and other survivors. He had long intended to write a book about it and had collected much material but suddenly realized he must write it now or never. He began the book on April 1, 1951, and finished it on April 22, three days before a massive hemorrhage paralyzed his right arm. He died less than a week later. Nagai's book is called *Otome Tooge* (The Virgin Pass), the name of the mountain pass on the outskirts of Tsuwano where the Christians were imprisoned and tortured. The spiritual and literary charm of this eighty-one-page book was a big influence in making Tsuwano one of the favorite Christian pilgrim places in modern Japan. The doctors who did the autopsy when Nagai died were amazed that he had managed to write the book when his physical and nervous systems had been literally shutting down. Close friends guessed the strain from the number of mistakes he made in his lifelong love, Chinese ideographs. Nagai accepted that last physical distress as appropriate for one writing about martyrs. The very last line of the book is a quotation from third-century Tertullian: "The blood of martyrs is the seed of Christians." These words were the last that Nagai was to write.

He had told his alma mater, Nagasaki University Hospital, to come and collect him before he died so that the young students could observe the final stages of leukemia. However, there was a matter he wanted to clear up before leaving

Nyokodo. The Association of Catholic Doctors in Italy had written to him saying they had sent him a statue of our Lady of Peace sculpted in white Carrara marble. Before putting it on the boat for Japan, they had taken it to Rome in December of 1950, where Pius XII blessed it. They hoped that this statue, inspired by Nagai's writings, would stand before the Nagasaki cathedral as an invitation to passersby to pray for peace. Nagai was delighted. The administrator of the cathedral came to Nyokodo, and together they decided that the statue should stand at the cathedral's southwestern entrance. Nagai had stonemasons put up a solid base immediately. The ship carrying the statue docked at Kobe in March, but the statue, inexplicably, was missing.

While he waited at Nyokodo for the statue of peace, he spoke with animation to his family, friends and visitors about the necessity of working and praying that war, above all nuclear war, be outlawed. He said: "There is a great need of a peace movement made up of people committed to justice, patience and love, fired by a commitment that includes personal sacrifice and conversion of heart. Without these we cannot rise above the self-centeredness that is the real enemy of peace."

Nagai was in pain almost the whole time now, and his thoughts went back to the Requiem Mass when he invited Urakami Christians to see the A-bomb victims as *hansai*, holocausts to be offered to God in trusting faith. Now he was a kind of living *hansai*, but he retained his peace of heart. He said this was personal confirmation that his *hansai* insight was right.

His mind turned to atheists and agnostics. He never forgot he had been an unbeliever, nor did he lose his sympathy for them. "We have to keep praying for them", he said, but added with a tone of sadness: "A scientist who says we came from the chance mutations of amoeba can't really see rainbows, and that's a great pity!" He did not yet realize the end was only days away. His right arm was now completely paralyzed, and his doctor knew he was in much pain. Nagai's serene face showed no indications of this, however, and he passed the day deep in prayer.

During the night of April 29, he suffered another massive hemorrhage, this time in his right thigh, which swelled to a huge size. He was no longer able to bear the pain silently, and his family, startled by his groaning and fearing the end might be near, knelt around him. They brought his sister from a hospital bed to his side. Shocked to see his state, she begged him to "hold on because so many depend on you." "But it's so painful", he gasped. "If only He would come quickly. . . . Pray for me, please pray for me." The doctor gave him a shot of morphine, and he slipped into sleep for some hours.

Nurse Utako, which means "child of song", stayed beside him all that night. He woke up distressed at 1 A.M. with a raging thirst. "I'll get you a drink", she offered. He replied, "No, I want to receive the Eucharist today, so I will wait until after that." "But Doctor, sick people are not obliged by the fast." "Yes, I know," he replied in a cracked voice, "but I'll wait." He could not get back to sleep and from time to time asked her the hour. When at last she said it was 5 A.M., he said: "Quickly, send my boy Makoto to the cathedral. Father will be up by now. Tell him I would like to receive the Eucharist."

The priest came immediately. Nagai struggled to bow, listened intently to the prayers and with another labored bow received the tiny consecrated Host. He did not move until he had finished fifteen minutes of thanksgiving. The nurse helped him to a drink of crushed strawberries, milk and water. Then his friends from the Society of Saint Vincent de Paul arrived with a wooden stretcher they had made to carry him to the hospital. They lifted him on the stretcher, and Matsuo-san, Nagai's longtime disciple, noticed how each jolt sent waves of pain across his face. Nagai closed his eyes, pretending to be asleep, but outside he opened them and fixed his gaze for the last time on Nyokodo with gratitude and sadness in his eyes— like Saint Francis when he took a last fond look at the town of Assisi and its mountainous backdrop when they carried him inside to die.

The sad little procession went a mile and stopped at the foot of the cathedral hill beside the pedestal of the missing statue, because Nagai said he wanted to pray to our Lady for peace. Nagai gazed at the empty base waiting for the lost statue with pain in his face. He spoke hoarsely of the war raging in Korea, just across the Tsushima Straits, and asked them to join him in a prayer for its cessation.

Nagai bowed to the cathedral and signaled he was ready to continue. Four friends took the handles of his stretcher and started off again. Was it the strong sunlight or the rush of emotions too strong for his weakened nervous system? Matsuo-san could see there was something wrong, signaled the carriers to stop and asked Nagai how he was. "I've gone blind", he replied. One of them dashed off and returned with all he could find, a bottle of whiskey! Nagai smiled, agreed the drink might help and took a nip. His sight returned, and they set off again. As they entered the hospital with its smell of carbolic disinfectant, Nagai sniffed and said with mock seriousness: "This joint stinks like a hospital." Matsuo and his friends, more from relief at his apparent improvement than anything else, put the stretcher down and roared with laughter.

His old friend Matron Hisamatsu appeared and led them to his room. Matron Maeda came in and began to speak cheerily but choked with emotion when she saw how bad he looked. Confused, she tried to cover her face with a handkerchief. Nagai smiled and said: "Yes, this is our Matron Maeda, still as genteel as the empress!" The matrons laughed despite themselves. "Would you like us to sponge you?" Hisamatsu said. "Yes, my whole body, please." They understood—he was asking them to prepare his body for death. It is a Japanese ideal to bathe before dying.

After that, professors and doctors dropped in, and his family arrived and were delighted to see that he looked fresher and stronger. Night fell, and they said evening prayers around the bed. The doctors assured them there was no immediate danger, so they took their leave, telling him to rest well. A shadow of disappointment crossed his face, but he said nothing. His son Makoto and Nurse Utako decided to remain with him. At 9:40 P.M. a sudden dizzy spell caused him vertigo and he gazed about looking lost, asking where the rest of the family was. Convulsions began to shake his whole body, and he whispered hoarsely: "Quick, call Shinpu-sama." Utako told young Makoto to have someone telephone the cathedral and asked Nagai if he would like some Lourdes water. He nodded and quickly drank it. Almost immediately, he lapsed into unconsciousness, and a doctor who had just come into the room injected a stimulant. Nagai's eyes opened and roamed about in a vain effort to focus. "Jesus, Mary, Joseph", he began strongly, but his voice went hoarse and they could barely hear the end of his prayer: "Into your hands I commend my spirit." The startled Utako, pushing the big family crucifix at Makoto, gesticulated toward his father, and the sobbing boy took it to the side of the bed. Nagai's right hand now looked like the shattered wing of a dying bird. His left arm, up to now barely able to hold Pius XII's Rosary, suddenly soared upward and seized the crucifix from his son's hands. In a voice that was startling in its strength, he cried out: "Inotte kudasai. Pray, please pray." Suddenly, it was all over. Matron Hisamatsu thought she had never seen a death throe quite like it—intense and dramatic, yet swift and peaceful.

The priest from the cathedral burst in, shocked and feeling guilty that Nagai had died without the last rites, but the doctor reassured him: "We were all taken unawares. There was no way of telling he would die so quickly." The matron added: "I know Dr. Nagai had one worry. The death of patients with his disease is usually accompanied by bleeding from everywhere, which would distress his family. It was a blessing he went so quickly and peacefully." The priest, accepting this comfort, added: "Today is the first of May, the month of Mary. I don't think it is just accidental. I think she came in person to take him home to the Lord."

Calligraphy by Nagai: Nyko-aijin *(Love others as you love yourself).*

31

For All That Has Been, Thanks;
for All That Will Be, Yes[1]

From 1:30 until 5:30 P.M. on May 2, a group of doctor-professors, department heads from the university hospital, and physician-officials from ABCC, the Atomic Bomb Casualty Commission, performed an exhaustive autopsy. They discovered that Nagai died from heart failure due to leukemia. His spleen weighed a startling 7.52 pounds, whereas a normal one is about 3.3 ounces. His liver was swollen four and a half times its natural size. They were dumbfounded that he had survived so long and had managed to write his last two books.

Friends carried him back in an unvarnished pine coffin to Nyokodo, and a large crowd formed a half circle around the hut, many of them weeping. Makoto, erect and composed like the strong and independent boy his father had trained him to be, suddenly crumpled onto the open coffin, crying: "See, Daddy, see. See how everyone loved you!" Nagai's younger brother Hajime stood by the coffin with Makoto and Kayano and had a photo taken—which was a solemn promise that he would take over Nagai's role as father. He and his wife Takako were to fulfill that promise faithfully.

The funeral was held on May 3 in the Urakami Cathedral with twenty thousand mourners packed in and around it. At

[1] Dag Hammarksjöld.

9 A.M. Archbishop Yamaguchi entered in procession to begin the ancient Latin Requiem that Nagai had loved so much. Nagai's Christian odyssey began in Urakami Cathedral with Mass on Christmas Eve 1932. It was fitting that it should end here with Mass. When the archbishop concluded with the absolution, the mayor of Nagasaki stepped forward and bowed low before the coffin. Straightening slowly, he bowed again to the archbishop and then to the congregation. Solemnly he read out three hundred messages of condolence, beginning with Prime Minister Yoshida's and finishing the last ninety minutes later. The archbishop sprinkled holy water on the coffin of his old friend and invited Nagai's family and the mayor to do so. The mayor had just returned the holy water sprinkler to the altar server when, by that miracle of Japanese timing, the clock hands moved to 12 noon. The Angelus boomed out, rung by Yamada-san, the friend who had gone with Nagai to dig up the very same bell on Christmas Eve 1945. On that night it had been a lonely bell, but today a symphony of bells in church steeples and Buddhist temples answered in a citywide chorus. Factory whistles and the horns and sirens on every boat in Nagasaki Bay were sounded. The city stopped for a minute of silence in honor of its foremost citizen, the poor man of Nyokodo. In nearby Yamazato Primary School, where dying children and teachers had cried for water on "that day", the classrooms fell silent. As the Angelus notes died away, children broke into sobbing and teachers' eyes watered. A great friend had passed from them.

The coffin was carried from the cathedral to the gentle strains of *In Paradisum*: "May angels lead thee into paradise and the martyrs receive thee into Jerusalem, the Holy City. May choirs of angels receive thee into eternal peace with Lazarus, the one who once was poor." The front of the procession moved off on foot to the cemetery, one mile south, and reached it before the chief mourners began moving. The archbishop looked down with emotion at the flowing river of severe black kimonos, softened by the white veils of the Catholic women. One onlooker thought the heavens might almost open and one of Nagai's heroes, Beethoven, appear to conduct the funeral march from the *Eroica* Symphony!

Dr. Nagai's ashes were buried beside Midori's in a garden plot built and maintained by the city. Just a few minutes' walk from the tram stop in front of the Urakami railway station, it is immediately in front of the western entrance to Gaijin Bochi, the "foreigners' cemetery". The epitaphs on the gravestone were chosen by Dr. Nagai from the Gospel of Luke the physician. Midori's is Mary's reply to the angel Gabriel: "I am the handmaid of the Lord. Let it be done unto me according to thy word." His own is Luke 17:10: "We are unworthy servants; we have only done what was our duty."

Thirty-four years later, I was gazing at these graves with a man I had met the day before and who had proved very willing to share his extensive knowledge. He said Nagai had been his *onshi*, his revered teacher, even though the two had never met. He explained: "I was a very angry young man after the surrender and the American occupation. I felt deceived and betrayed by all our leaders, including schoolteachers, who had told us that Nippon, land of the gods, could never be defeated. Japan's future looked very bleak, and so did mine. I chanced on one of Nagai's books in a public library and became interested in him. Here was a man in far worse straits than most of us, and yet he radiated hope. I searched out more of his books, and they took me to a crossroads: either life, human effort and personal values were ultimately meaningless, or there was the all-encompassing plan of Nagai's God, who is always good, even though it may not appear so in the short term. Something in Nagai's books convinced me it was worth my while to engage in a serious study of Christianity. I came to share his faith and was baptized." He was now a high school science teacher and often came on pilgrimage to Nagasaki, visiting Nyokodo and the graves of Takashi and Midori Nagai.

The strong Nagasaki sunlight streamed through the branches above us, etching filigree patterns at our feet. A cool gust of wind swept up from the harbor, touching the trees and setting the patterns of light and shade dancing like partners in a quadrille. Surely there is nothing else in nature more marvelous than sunlight. It has no color and yet contains all the colors; it is colorless and yet makes us see color. A few days before, I had attended a seminar on the dangers of nuclear war. One speaker noted that the photosynthesis that sunlight causes in plants keeps them, and therefore us, alive. He added a comment I found mysterious: "The very process that produces sunlight is used in exploding the H-bomb." I asked my scientific friend if this was a mere hypothesis or if it was a fact.

"It is a scientific fact", he replied and proceeded to explain it to me simply. At the core of the sun there is a gigantic mass of hydrogen, compressed and at a temperature of fifteen million degrees centigrade. Under this heat and pressure, hydrogen atoms fly in fantastic motion, colliding into one another. The collision produces new helium atoms, and stupendous energy is given off in the form of sunlight and as radio waves, microwaves, infrared and ultraviolet rays, gamma and x-rays, and so forth. This solar process consumes one hundred billion tons of hydrogen a day, but there is enough hydrogen to keep it going for millions of years yet. Sunlight would destroy us but for the sun's distance and the earth's atmosphere and the ozone layer. Because the sun's hydrogen atoms fuse to become helium atoms, the process is called "atomic fusion" or "nuclear fusion". In the case of the H-bomb, the pressure and heat needed for the fusion are caused by an initial splitting (fission) of uranium or plutonium atoms. The Hiroshima and Nagasaki bombs were based on nuclear fission and were nowhere near as lethal as the atomic fusion of the H-bomb.

I had nothing to contribute scientifically but added: "Nagai spoke and wrote a great deal about Francis of Assisi. I once visited Assisi, and a Franciscan stationed there made a wonderful observation about the saint that applies also to Dr. Nagai. Francis had composed the first version of *The Canticle of the Sun*, where he calls the sun and wind his brothers and the moon and water his sisters. Then he began to go blind, and the Pope told Rome's best doctors to try to cure him. They adopted current drastic measures—applying red-hot iron plates to his temples! It was after that that he added to his canticle the line about fire: 'Praised be Thou, my Lord, for Brother Fire, by whom Thou lightest the night. He is beautiful and cheerful, robust and strong.' It is easy enough to see God in pleasant sunshine and gentle rain. Francis, and Nagai, could see him in everything in the universe, in midsummer heat, autumn typhoons, midwinter blizzards, darkness and pain. Maybe if Francis were alive today, he would add another line of praise for Brother Nuclear-Fusion-in-the-Sun", I suggested.

"Yes," my Japanese friend replied, "maybe! Saint Francis and Nagai were men who saw the supernatural dimension of nature. Many modern poets struggle in their verses and songs about life because they see only the natural. Their vision is merely earthly, while the Franciscan vision is cosmic. Nagai had a great love of Japan's old *Manyoshu* poetry, which contains some of the finest poems ever written about romantic love. Nagai came to see, however, that the *Manyoshu* lacks the dimension of supernatural love, without which romantic love easily leads to frustration and worse. Nagai understood the kind of love Francis had for Clare, love that doesn't rely on physical expression. So he did not despair when he found the charred skeleton of Midori.

"That", continued my friend, "is the point of Nagai's parable about the hen that found an egg out in the open. Feeling compassion for the motherless egg, it sat on it through all kinds of weather, putting all its energy and warmth into hatching it. At last, sounds came from the egg, and the shell cracked open. A duckling emerged! Without as much as a thank you, it waddled down to a pond and paddled off in search of its own kind. Nagai saw with crystal clarity that everything within and without is God's gift—life, health, our loved ones, our talents and expertise, our responsibilities. So we must never use others. We must be prepared to serve, and to be happy about it. Like Francis, Nagai loved nature and life passionately and yet could accept their loss peacefully because he looked beyond them to God, the Source of all that is true and beautiful." With that, the schoolteacher lapsed back into silence.

Emboldened by his enthusiasm for anything to do with Nagai, I broke the silence: "Sensei, here we are beside his grave in Nagasaki. Would it be too much to ask you to sing *The Bells of Nagasaki*?" That is the song written by poet Hachiro Sato for the first Nagai movie and put to music by Yuji Koseki. It has become a Japanese perennial and has been compared with *Danny Boy* in mood and appeal. The teacher smiled and said, "Yorokonde. With pleasure", and his strong voice took flight and startled the sparrows and pigeons around us.

1. From a glorious blue sky
   Sorrow came that rent my heart.
   This life of ours is as unstable as the waves,
   As impermanent as wild flowers in the field!

   CHORUS

   Ah yes, but they still ring out,
   Comforting and encouraging,
   The Bells of Nagasaki.

2. She died alone, my wife, called to heaven before me,
   Leaving me as keepsake her Rosary.
   Now it glistens with my tears.

   CHORUS

3. That funeral Mass! Under a sky that wept in
     mourning,
   A moaning wind for our hymns.
   I clutched the cross fashioned for her grave.
   The sparkling sea was gray with grief.

CHORUS

4. There I bared my soul in its sinfulness.
   Night fell, its darkness softened by a clear moon
   And the statue of the holy one, Mary,
   Fixed to a wooden beam in my poor hut.

CHORUS

Nagai has been compared with Dag Hammarksjöld, second secretary-general of the United Nations who died in 1961— both left influential writings on peace and shared a love of the abrupt and frugal evocativeness of haiku poetry. Hammarksjöld might have written that poem about Nagasaki maidens singing while they expired as whole burnt offerings. Nagai might have written the opening verse for 1953 in Hammarksjöld's diary, which became the posthumous book *Markings*: "For all that has been, thanks. For all that will be, yes." The two men were alike also in their painful journeys from unbelief and agnosticism to deep faith in the God of the Bible.

Both lived and died in the maelstrom of modern life. They loved life and wrote wisely about education, science, culture, government and peace movements. However, both insisted on the need to view these things through the supernatural light that comes through personal prayer. Prayer became their prism in reverse that gathers the scattered and lurid colors of human experience into the clarity and simplicity of daylight.

Nagai first learned about prayer from Pascal. I cannot think of a more fitting way to end this Nagai story than with a famous passage from Pascal's *Pensées*. It bewildered and bothered

Nagai when he first read it, but later he came to regard it as "the one thing necessary".

The year of grace 1654.

Monday, November 23. From about half past ten in the evening until half past midnight.

FIRE

God of Abraham, God of Isaac, God of Jacob, not of philosophers or scholars.

Certainty, certainty, heartfelt joy, peace.

God of Jesus Christ, God of Jesus Christ.

Deum meum et Deum vestrum.[2]

The world is forgotten and everything except God.

Greatness of the human soul.

O, righteous Father, the world has not known Thee, but I have known Thee.

Joy, joy, joy, tears of joy.

---

[2] My God and your God.

EPILOGUE

When Nagai addressed the A-bomb mourners at the Nagasaki funeral Mass, he used the startling word *hansai*, telling them to offer their dead to God as a whole burnt sacrifice. Many were shocked and even angered by this. Sensitive Nagai examined his conscience about this in a book he wrote not long before he died. He concluded he was right in urging people to accept the deaths as *hansai*. His proof? The peace of heart this acceptance brought. Nagai had become a Word of God man, discerning major matters according to the words of Scripture. He concluded that the *hansai* insight was authentic because it brought him and many others "the fruits of the Holy Spirit". For Nagai, Galatians 5:22 said it all: "The fruit of the Spirit is love, joy, peace, patience, kindness, goodness, faithfulness, gentleness, self-control; against such there is no law." Jeremiah 6:16 says: "Stand by the roads, and look, and ask for the ancient paths, where the good way is; and walk in it, and find rest for your souls." Nagai, standing at the crossroads of death, averred that *hansai* spirituality had brought great peace.

If you speak Japanese and have attended the A-bomb anniversaries in both Hiroshima and Nagasaki, I think you will have observed a great difference. I had noted this over a number of years, and while attending the two ceremonies on the fortieth anniversary in 1985, I heard some regular participants express it this way: "Hiroshima is bitter, noisy, highly political, leftist and anti-American. Its symbol would be a fist clenched in anger. Nagasaki is sad, quiet, reflective, nonpolitical and prayerful. It does not blame the United States but rather laments the sinfulness of war, especially of nuclear war. Its symbol: hands joined in prayer."

Shigeru Idei is a mathematics professor who has lectured in a number of Tokyo universities, including the famous Waseda University. He has now relinquished mathematics for full-time involvement in a peace movement that was mostly of Shinto inspiration. It was begun by his father in the dark days of the Japanese militarists before World War II, after he had spent several years in jail for opposing Japan's headlong rush toward war. His son, following him in his commitment to peace. His group has erected peace stones in Japan, Europe, Australia and the Americas in ecumenical cooperation with other religions. I asked him about the difference between Hiroshima and Nagasaki. He replied: "The popular jingle expresses it perfectly: Sakebi no Hiroshima, inori no Nagasaki—Shouting Hiroshima, praying Nagasaki." Maybe it is a comment on the media, and on human nature, that shouting Hiroshima gets the lion's share of television footage around the world. It must be pointed out, though, that those shouting in the political demonstrations are not predominantly Hiroshima people. They are, according to the indignant Hiroshima residents, outsiders who come from other cities to "use" what should be a day of deep reflection.

Nagai, more than any other individual, is responsible for the very spiritual atmosphere in Nagasaki's commemoration of the A-bomb. His word *hansai* was at first like a slap in the face to the hysterical survivors. A slap in the face can do wonders to hysterical people because it is an experience of rock-hard reality. It is not just the actual A-bomb victims who have been in need of such stern treatment. We have seen not a few of the post–A-bomb generations become hysterical and turn their back on reality—the dropout generation, for instance. Many of these are people who have been demoralized (literally) and terrified out of their wits by the possibility of nuclear warfare. Such despair of soul is surely even worse fallout than the radiation that killed Nagai's body!

I met a woman close to despair when I went to Japan for the fortiethth anniversary of the A-bomb. She was in early middle age, a well-known lecturer in psychology at an Osaka university and a successful counselor and writer of books for wives and mothers. Her bright, brave world came crashing down on her the day she was told she had terminal cancer. For years she had helped nervous patients who could not sleep. Now she joined their ranks! Two days before her dreaded operation, she went glumly to Sunday Mass. It was near the A-bomb anniversary, and the priest gave a homily on Dr. Nagai—short and simple with but one suggestion: "Each of us must experience pain and tragedy, including the ultimate tragedy, death, and maybe a violent one at that. If we have Nagai's kind of faith in the Father's Providence and in Christ's all-embracing death, we can meet anything with peace." The lecturer had heard the words before, but they suddenly hit her with the force of *satori*, the ancient and revered Japanese word meaning "spiritual awakening". She became herself again, went to the hospital peacefully and composed her most quickly written book ever during convalescence. It was a book about a problem as old as our race, a problem that was the cause of many of the breakdowns she had witnessed in her professional work: the problem of not facing up to suffering. Nagai's *hansai* insight was a central element in her book.

Franklin D. Roosevelt, the man who set the A-bomb project in motion, once said: "We have nothing to fear except fear itself." It was precisely when Nagai thought he had lost everything in the nuclear wilderness that he discovered that he possessed everything! In that modern desert, he experienced a kind of return to the Garden of Eden because he "was able to walk there with God". Like his ancestors, who composed the Nenbutsu, he discovered that the only reality is "the now", the here and now. He discovered that when one looks at and accepts that reality as the one thing "really real", one can walk and converse with God in real prayer. This return to Eden is the beginning of paradise without end, the Beatific Vision.

Our society has sought to solve the problem of suffering by removing pain. That is a negative solution that can never be the whole solution. Our great-grandparents lived without our pain-killers, air conditioners, airplanes or paid holidays, and yet, compared with our generation, they do not appear all that unhappy! Their society does not appear to me anywhere near as fractured and alienated, as unpeaceful and complaining, as ours. I wonder if the physical pain in their lives did not help them be realists and face up to the deeper human issues—the ones Nagai called metaphysical or "beyond the physical".

Cancer is not a new problem, nor is midlife crisis. They suddenly became very new for the Osaka university lecturer. Her pleasant and successful past became strangely meaningless overnight. The pathologist's report stripped her naked and left her shivering with fear. Nagai's strong spirituality helped her look at and accept that primeval nakedness and helplessness and discover that the reality of the here and now is not hostile because God is present in it. With that discovery, ever ancient and ever new, she tasted peace and could say with tranquil simplicity: Give me *today* my daily bread.

Each of us has to meet a midlife crisis or the old-age crisis, or hear the pathologist's or heart specialist's report. We must experience in ourselves or in those near to us alcoholism, drug problems, traffic accidents, mental disorders or divorce. For me, Nagai's strongest appeal is that he came through such tough modern problems, and came through the stronger and more attractive for it. He himself told the mourners, at the first funeral Mass, that the coalescence of events surrounding Urakami, the A-bomb, the shattered cathedral and the Emperor's surrender on August 15 were not chance but providential. I feel the same about the extraordinary life of Nagai—God's Providence led him through the worst experiences of the twentieth century to make him a pathfinder for others. He condensed his advice for travelers in his dying words: "Inotte kudasai. Pray, please pray."

Sketch by Nagai of daughter Kayano and a Junshin nun visiting Midori's grave on the anniversary of the A-bomb.

GLOSSARY OF JAPANESE WORDS

Akogare	Yearning
Arigato	Thanks
Banzai	Japanese cheer of enthusiasm or triumph
Bushi	Samurai
Bushido	"Way", or code of chivalry, of samurai
Cha no yu	Formal tea ceremony
Chokata	Head person (of persecuted Japanese Christians)
Chokkan	Intuition
Chonan	Number One Son
Daikon	Thick Japanese radish
Daimyo	Feudal lord
Dozo	Please
Dozo o-raku ni	Please sit comfortably
Furoshiki	Square piece of cloth for carrying things
Futon	Japanese eiderdown
Genkan	Front porch
Gomen kudasai	Excuse me, may I come in?
Haiku	Seventeen-syllable verse
Hanami	Blossom viewing
Haru-gasumi	Spring haze
Hata-age	Kite-flying festival
Hi no Maru	Japanese flag
Hibakusha	Someone injured in the A-bomb explosion
Ikebana	Flower arrangement

Inotte kudasai	Please pray
Itte irasshai mase	Formal farewell formula
Itte mairimasu	Reply to the above formula, from person departing
Jisei no uta	Farewell song or poem before death
Kaa-chan	Mommy
Kamikaze	Divine wind
Kannushi	Shinto priest
Kanpo yaku	Chinese herb medicine
Kenpeitai	Military thought police
Kokoro	Heart (spiritual)
Kokutai	The Japanese people themselves, as a group
Konnichi wa	Good day or good afternoon
Koto	Japanese floor harp
Kun	Familiar form of *san*, used mostly for males
Manyoshu	First Japanese anthology of poetry (literally, "Collection of myriad leaves")
Miai	Formal meeting of prospective marriage couple
Michi	The path or way
Mi-shinja	Unbeliever
Mizu	Water
Monpe	Wartime regulation baggy trousers for women
Moshi moshi	Hello, hello
Nakodo	Marriage go-between
Nemaki	Bed attire
Nihon-teki	Thoroughly Japanese
O-bento	Lunch
O-cha	Thin green tea
O-den	Japanese stew made from vegetables, potatoes and meat
O-furo	Japanese deep bath
O genki de	Get well, take care

O–hayo gozaimasu	Good morning (literally, "It's early")
O–ka–san	Mother
Onshi	Revered teacher
O–tera	Buddist temple
O–to–san	Father
San	Mr., Mrs., Miss
Sama	Honorific form of *san*
Satori	Spiritual enlightenment
Sayonara	Good-bye
Seiza	Formal squatting position
Sennin	Mountain shaman
Sensei	Teacher or doctor
Shigoto	Work (something that is a service)
Shinpu–sama (*or* san)	Father (Catholic priest)
Shinto	The Shinto religion, "the way of the gods"
Shoji	Paper sliding door or window made of Japanese paper stretched over a wooden frame
Shujin	Lord (what wives call their husbands, sometimes tongue–in–cheek!)
Shukun	Liege lord
Susuki	Japanese pampas grass (*Miscanthus sinensis*)
Tada suware	Just meditate
Tanka	Thirty–one–syllable verse
Tatami	Reed mat floor
Tanabata	Festival of lover stars (July 7)
Tempura	Japanese batter–fried vegetables or seafood
Tenbatsu	Punishment from heaven
Tokonoma	Built–in alcove of the main room of a Japanese house where hanging scrolls and other objects of art are displayed

Toochan	Daddy
Tsukisoi	Assistant beside a patient in the hospital
Tsuyu	Rainy season (mid-June to mid-July)
Uguisu	Bush warbler (sometimes called the Japanese nightingale)
Ukiyo	The floating (impermanent) world
Yama	Mountain
Yamato	Ancient name for Japan
Yamato-damashii	Spirit of Japan
Yaoyorozu	Eight hundred million gods
Yin	Negative (dark) cosmic force
Yorokonde	With pleasure
Yoshi	Groom who takes the surname of his bride
Wa	Peace, harmony, reconciliation, unity, comfort
Waka	Thirty-one-syllable verse
Zen	Strict form of Buddhism in which meditation is the essential practice

ACKNOWLEDGMENTS

Grateful acknowledgments go to the following:
Maslyn Williams, Bowral; Rosaleen McVittie and Yayoi Maloney, Urasenke, Sydney; Urasenke Headquarters, Kyoto; Fr. H. Weisen, S.V.D., and parishioners, Otonashi, Nagasaki; Noel Gallagher, Brisbane; Shigeo Hayashi, Sadao Tsuba, Torahiko Ogawa and members of the Anti-Nuclear Photographers Movement, Tokyo; Sister Kataoka, Junshin, Nagasaki; Nagai Museum and its director, Hajime Nagai, Nagasaki; Twenty-Six Martyrs Museum and its director, Fr. D. Yuki, Nagasaki; Nagasaki Peace Museum and Nagasaki City Office; Yamazato Primary School, Nagasaki; Fr. John Glynn, S.M., Catholic Book Club, Sydney; Dr. Padraic J. Grattan-Smith; Carmel, Tokyo; Mr. Paul Maloney, Japan Information Centre, Sydney.

Books by Takashi Nagai: *We of Nagasaki, Living under the Atomic Cloud, Nagasaki no Kane, Kono Ko wo Nokoshite, Hana Saku Oka, Nyokodo Zuihitsu, Heiwa To, Otome Toge, Itoshigo Yo, Rozario no Kusari, Horobinu Mono wo.*

Hiroshima and Nagasaki, edited by the Committee for Compilation on Damage Caused by A-bombs. *Nagasaki, August 9, 1945*, by the staff of Junshin Girls' Academy, Nagasaki. *Nagai Takashi no Shogai*, by Professor Y. Kataoka. *In the Sky over Nagasaki*, by the Nagasaki Hibakusha Peace Association. *The Rising Sun*, by John Toland. *Japan, Past and Present*, by Edwin Reischauer.

Tsurezure-gusa, translated by Donald Keene. *The Martyrs of Nagasaki*, by Diego Yuki. *Musume yo, Koko ga Nagasaki Desu,* by Kayano Tsutsui (Nagai). *Nagasaki no Kane wa Hohoemu,* by Makoto Nagai. *The Japanese Fairy Book* (Tuttle). *We Japanese* (Fujiya Hoteru, Hakone). *2001 Kanji,* by J. de Roo. *Kotowaza Jiten* (Musashi).